Congress
and the
American
People

Congress and the American People

William J. Keefe
University of Pittsburgh

PRENTICE-HALL, Inc., *Englewood Cliffs, New Jersey 07632*

Library of Congress Cataloging in Publication Data

KEEFE, WILLIAM J
   Congress and the American people.

   Includes bibliographical references and index.
   1. United States. Congress. I. Title.
JK1061.K39   328.73   79-14650
ISBN 0-13-167569-9

Editorial production supervision and interior design by Alison D. Gnerre
Cover design by Frederick Charles, Ltd.; photo by Stan Wakefield
Manufacturing buyer: Harry P. Baisley

(

© 1980 by Prentice-Hall, Inc., Englewood Cliffs, N.J. 07632

Printed in the United States of America

10 9 8 7 6 5 4 3 2 1

PRENTICE-HALL INTERNATIONAL, INC., *London*
PRENTICE-HALL OF AUSTRALIA PTY. LIMITED, *Sydney*
PRENTICE-HALL OF CANADA, LTD., *Toronto*
PRENTICE-HALL OF INDIA PRIVATE LIMITED, *New Delhi*
PRENTICE-HALL OF JAPAN, INC., *Tokyo*
PRENTICE-HALL OF SOUTHEAST ASIA PTE. LTD., *Singapore*
WHITEHALL BOOKS LIMITED, *Wellington, New Zealand*

For my family

Contents

PREFACE   *ix*

1   **THE POLITICS OF CONGRESS**   *1*
The Dispersal of Congressional Power
The Exceptional Tenure of Members
The Tradition of Localism
The Importance of Norms
The Differences between the Chambers
The Tasks of Congress

2   **THE ELECTORAL TERRAIN**   *30*
Congressional Constituencies
Campaigning for Congress
Electoral Processes and Outcomes
The Member of Congress
The Stability of Congress

3   **THE INTERNAL DISTRIBUTION OF POWER**   *61*
The Committee System
The Congressional Parties
Professional Staffs

4   EXTERNAL PRESSURES *101*
President and Congress
Interest Groups and Congress
Constituencies and Congress

5   CHANGE AND CONSTANCY *143*
Congressional Reform
Constancy

INDEX *173*

Preface

Next to writing the first and last lines of a book, writing the preface is hardest. It is a chore. But convention seems to require it. And the editor repeatedly asks, "When's the preface going to be ready?"

Writing a book, like planting a tree or fighting a bull, involves certain rites and incantations. And a notch below rite and two above incantation comes justification. Why write a "little" book on Congress? One reason might be that exposition and analysis of our national legislature have been neglected. But everyone knows that is not so—the literature on Congress is impressive. Royalties cannot be the reason. So other justifications must be sought. Two occur.

First, I find Congress an unusually interesting and congenial subject to think about, teach about, and write about. For me, Congress-watching is not as enjoyable as playing golf or as edifying as raising tomatoes, but it is a close second to each, particularly during the winter. The second reason is almost as simple.

That reason turns on the fact that for decades Congress was viewed as intractable, so attached to inherited and customary patterns as to resist internal changes. Yet in recent years a Congress new in many ways has emerged. Not everyone sees the changes in the same way. Another book that describes them and reflects on their significance is not necessarily redundant.

There is a new Congress. There is also an old one. Congress has acquired the layered look. It may be that there are more illusions in the discovery of the new one than in the rediscovery of the old one. At any rate that is what the conclusion argues: "The more Congress changes, the more it remains the same."

The best feature of the preface is the acknowledgment section. I am much indebted to friends and colleagues (mainly at the University of Pittsburgh) for their help. They "slipped me" information, data, books, journals, chapters, and viewpoints—unobtrusively on occasion, ostentatiously as a rule. They read portions of the manuscript (aloud in many cases), insisted on certain additions and deletions, bootlegged the book's main arguments into their lectures and passed them off as their own, and offered encouragement. Some, of course, assisted more than others. Since it would be awkward to identify them in a clear fashion, I list all names in a sequence that is close to alphabetical: Holbert Carroll, Morris Ogul, Paul Beck, Keith Burris, Edward Cooke, Joseph Cooper, Robert Donaldson, Charles Jones, David Kozak, Thomas Mann, Michael Margolis, Raymond Owen, Bert Rockman, Robert Walters, and Sidney Wise. Anonymous reviewers also made many useful suggestions.

Stan Wakefield and Alison D. Gnerre of Prentice-Hall helped in numerous important ways, none of which, at this moment, comes to mind.

Kathy, Nanci, Jodi, and John—close friends of mine—did nothing whatsoever to help in this enterprise, but requested that their names be mentioned anyway. And finally: steadfastly loyal, glued to the chair, back against the wall, shoulders hunched, forehead furrowed, brows arched, eyes riveted on the page, muscles tensed, nerves jangling, teeth clinched, jaw set, and fingers poised, my wife, Martha, typed the manuscript—uncomfortably. I typed the preface myself.

W.J.K.
Oakmont, Pennsylvania

Congress
and the
American
People

The
Politics
of
Congress

1

Congress is the first branch of government. Its permanent importance is that it is positioned, both by the Constitution and by the expectations of the people, at the center of national policy-making. No leadership guarantees, however, come with its central position. At times its power appears to have withered, and at times to have been snatched away by others— perhaps by the president, or by the bureaucracy, or by the courts. Congress is steadily nudged, pushed, pressured, and sometimes captured because it is a remarkably accessible institution. But if it is sometimes captured, it is not easily held. Those periods in the twentieth century in which it has been dominated by the executive have been followed by periods of relative parity between the branches and occasionally by periods of congressional ascendancy.

The choices of Congress are the choices of the nation. Whatever the origins of legislative ideas and grand national designs, it is Congress that determines which will be examined, shaped, and transformed into public law. All new policy ventures require congressional approval; all prior political settlements require congressional forbearance. Congress can do and undo, as it chooses. Its decisions on appropriations determine the scope of public programs. In an era in which national legislatures everywhere have lost ground to executives, sometimes all but forced out of business, Congress remains independent and powerful, not under the thumb of anyone, not to be taken for granted by anyone.

The first lesson on Congress is that its organization, responsibilities, and decisions are preeminently political. This book focuses on the politics of our national legislature, beginning with an examination of its leading characteristics and responsibilities.

THE DISPERSAL OF CONGRESSIONAL POWER

The structure of power in Congress provides an important key for understanding the nature of the institution. And by far the most important thing to be known about power in the contemporary Congress is that it is dispersed—that is, distributed among a variety of different, often competing, individuals and units. Dispersal begins, of course, with the constitutional provision for bicameralism—the division of the legislative branch into two houses.

The best evidence of this characteristic of Congress, however, is found in the relative independence of committees and subcommittees in both chambers and in the power of individual members of the Senate. Although committees are not free from chamber controls, it is clear that the content of legislation owes far more to the decisions made at committee and subcommittee levels than to decisions made on the floor. Indeed, a multitude of lesser facts about congressional policy-making, and about congressional careers as well, fall into place once it is seen that the center of legislative activity lies in the committee structure.

Diffusion of power is one thing in the House and another in the Senate. In the House it is exhibited in the power of committees and subcommittees, contributing to a decision-making system heavily characterized by decentralization. As Nelson W. Polsby has observed:

> [The committees of the House] have won solid institutionalized independence from party leaders both inside and outside Congress. . . . Committees nowadays have developed an independent sovereignty of their own, subject only to very infrequent reversals and modifications of their powers by House party leaders backed by large and insistent majorities.[1]

The dispersion of power in the Senate is no less evident, but it is less the result of a preference for decentralization than it is a preference for an "individualistic" model of power distribution. Randall Ripley makes this distinction:

> There is substantial feeling [among senators] that committees should retain a high degree of autonomy, but this is not an effort to give power to the committee chairman. Rather it is an attempt to disperse power to individual

[1]Nelson W. Polsby, "The Institutionalization of the U.S. House of Representatives," *American Political Science Review*, 62 (March 1968), 156.

senators through their positions on committees and subcommittees. . . . The distribution of power based on personal skills and institutional positions is predominantly individualistic. Party leaders make few requests of the members; the bargaining position of the individual senators is good, even when weighed against that of the leaders. Senators can use the leaders to help them attain their own individual ends. Committee chairmen have more power than many nonchairmen, and they have a number of sources both to develop and to maintain their power. But they are not strong enough to threaten the basic independence or substantive power of individual members. They are limited in what they can do by the necessities of the accommodating and consensual style of life that dominates the Senate.[2]

Or as Ralph Huitt has observed, "No member of Congress can escape the lonely awareness that he is essentially on his own. This explains a basic fact of life in the Senate; no one finally can make anyone else do anything."[3]

There have been periods in the history of Congress when power was centralized, such as around the turn of the twentieth century and during the early years of the New Deal. During these intervals party leaders held considerable power. The development of party positions on legislation was a common occurrence.[4] A record of loyalty to the party leadership and support for party programs was important for advancement in the congressional system. The periods of centralization, however, have been relatively brief and, in recent years, nonexistent. The truth is that members of Congress are uncomfortable in a decision-making structure characterized by conspicuous control and direction from the center. To borrow the observation of Joseph Cooper, "Congress has a low tolerance for hierarchy, for highly differential distributions of authority in its formal or official role structure."[5]

The prominence of committees in congressional organization results from the need to come to terms with highly complex policy problems and to manage the consideration of an extraordinary volume of bills and resolutions, perhaps a total of 25,000 during a Congress.[6] Through their members' expertise, acquired from years of service and seasoning, committees bring specialization to the examination of public policy questions. Not many proposals in any session are likely to appear brand new to a

[2]Randall B. Ripley, *Power in the Senate* (New York: St. Martin's Press, 1969), pp. 218, 228–29.

[3]Ralph K. Huitt, "The Internal Distribution of Influence: The Senate," in *The Congress and America's Future*, ed. David B. Truman (Englewood Cliffs, N.J.: Prentice-Hall, Inc., 1965), p. 80.

[4]See the evidence on party voting during these periods in Table 3.4, p. 90.

[5]Joseph Cooper, "Congress in Organizational Perspective," in *Congress Reconsidered*, eds. Lawrence C. Dodd and Bruce I. Oppenheimer (New York: Praeger Publishers, 1977), p. 147.

[6]One indicator of the importance of committees is their sheer number. Currently there are 37 standing (or permanent) committees, 22 in the House and 15 in the Senate. In addition, there are some 250 subcommittees. The committee structure is examined in detail in Chapter 3.

member who has served a number of terms on the same committee; nor are they likely to slide through committee because no one understands their implications. Veteran members are also likely to be intimately familiar with the executive agencies whose responsibilities fall within the committee's legislative jurisdiction. In addition, the professional staffs of committees are a rich source of policy guidance. The broad point is that by vesting substantial authority in its committees, Congress strengthens not only its lawmaking capabilities but also its overall position in the political system.

The Personal Equation

It is easy to lose sight of the fact that Congress is more than an institution of government. It is also a collection of individuals, each of whom is actuated by goals, ambitions, and, above all, political needs. Congressional structure, including committee power, bears heavily on their careers. When this is recognized, the members' preference for the decentralization of congressional power is better understood. Decentralization magnifies personal influence and serves all manner of personal interests, as these observations suggest:

> A committee is an institution of Congress; it exists to serve the purposes of congressmen. These are individual purposes as often as they are institutional or partisan. . . . [The committee] affords the member a chance to get *his* job done. He may wish to make himself a national leader, build a reputation as a subject-matter expert, advertise himself to the constituency, do a favor for a supporter, discharge some of his own aggressions—the list could be a long one. What is important is to see that in every aspect of congressional life it is necessary to satisfy both the system needs and the largely personal needs of the member who must keep himself solvent in a free-enterprise politics.[7]

> Whatever else it may be, the quest for specialization in Congress is a quest for credit. Every member can aspire to occupy a part of at least one piece of policy turf small enough so that he can claim personal responsibility for some of the things that happen on it. Better yet, he can aspire to rise in seniority and claim ever more responsibility—perhaps even be christened a "czar" or a "baron" by the press. What the congressional seniority system does as a system is to convert turf into property; it assures a congressman that once he initially occupies a piece of turf, no one can ever push him off it. And the property automatically appreciates in value over time.[8]

Committees and Compromise

The centrality of committees in decision-making is a natural outgrowth of the way in which ideas for public policy are turned into public

[7]Huitt, "The Internal Distribution of Influence: The Senate," p. 92.
[8]David R. Mayhew, *Congress: The Electoral Connection* (New Haven: Yale University Press, 1974), pp. 95–96.

law. No legislature produces a piece of important legislation in one fell swoop. Bills are shaped gradually, with provisions added, dropped, and modified as information accumulates about their implications and probable consequences.

In the real world of Congress the critical test of proposals is less their presumed wisdom than their political feasibility. Can they be adopted? What changes are required to make them acceptable to the successive majorities that will be needed for passage? Far better than the chamber as a whole, committees are able to ferret out agreements on provisions that meet at least the minimal expectations of interested parties and opposing spokesmen. Through compromise and accommodation, buttressed by log-rolling and tradeoffs, committees are able to negotiate political settlements that could rarely be won if left for determination by the much larger parent chamber. Put another way, it is the committee members who have the best sense of the opportunities available for reaching compromise and understanding among divergent interests. Committee power helps to make congressional decision-making tolerable for most participants, since it inflates the influence of individual members and affords disparate interests the opportunity to be heard and to advance their proposals.

The Costs of Dispersion

The fragmentation of power in Congress is not without substantial costs. No one really controls Congress. The powers of the party leaders[9] are largely personal and ad hoc, based more on their political skills than on formal authority. The principal result of this is that the leadership is limited in its capacity to establish legislative priorities and to promote coherent programs; what Congress does is determined, in considerable measure, by its scattered and largely autonomous committees and sub-committees, acting independently of each other. Inevitably, coherent programs addressed to large and complicated questions are difficult, perhaps impossible, to fashion. Committee government diminishes the likelihood that interrelationships among major issues will be perceived and that future policy requirements will be anticipated. Policies that work at cross-purposes are not uncommon. In sum, committee government invites piecemeal solutions to immediate problems on the congressional agenda and provides a virtual guarantee that policy-making will be incremental rather than coherent and comprehensive.

The fragmentation of institutional power not only contributes to an inchoate policy-making process but also diminishes the possibilities for holding Congress responsible for its decisions. Power is steadily

[9]See Chapter 3 for a discussion of party leaders and agencies.

wielded in out-of-the-way places. Even the most attentive observer finds it exasperatingly difficult, and often impossible, to make judgments that fix credit or blame for particular things that Congress has done or failed to do.

The root of the difficulty is often the committee system. How is a committee that refuses to act or that emasculates legislation or that rewards narrow interests excessively to be held accountable? The answer is that there is nothing that the public can do and relatively little that the parent chamber can do. Once their leadership is established (or reaffirmed at the beginning of a Congress), committees are mainly on their own, free to follow such policy courses as suit their members' interests. Protected both by the seniority system and the norm of reciprocity, the risks to committees and committee members for being out of step with a majority of their party or with a majority of Congress or with a majority of the American people are minimal. Disciplinary measures are rare. Because no one can control Congress, no one can do much about a committee that ignores or demeans national priorities while responding to particularistic demands and pressures.

The Representativeness of Committees

The critical influence of committees and subcommittees on policy outcomes raises a question concerning their representativeness. An examination of the composition of certain committees shows clearly that they are much less representative than Congress as a whole. For the most part this occurs because members are assigned to committees whose jurisdictions coincide with their interests—which typically means the interests of their constituencies. One result is that some committees are heavily populated with liberals, other committees heavily populated with conservatives.[10]

More important is the special-interest bias of several committees. The Committee on Agriculture in each house is nothing quite so much as a caucus of members from farm-belt states. In the House, members from coastal areas are disproportionately represented on the Committee on Merchant Marine and Fisheries, while members from western states dominate the Committee on Interior and Insular Affairs. The Armed Services Committee in each chamber invariably contains an impressive number of members whose constituencies hold military installations of one kind or another. House Education and Labor has long been a haven for liberal, urban Democrats whose constituencies are characterized by heavily unionized work forces. And so it goes.

[10]Carol F. Goss, "House Committee Characteristics and Distributive Politics," a paper presented at the Annual Meeting of the American Political Science Association, San Francisco, September 2–5, 1975.

In its worst form, the bias in committee representation produces a politics of boodle under which self-interested members link up with interest groups and segments of the bureaucracy to distribute benefits to narrow segments of society at the expense of the public as a whole. The House or Senate can of course rewrite or defeat committee bills that strain the limits of propriety and credulity, but this is not their usual inclination. Special interest preferments, moreover, are so inextricably scrambled in some legislation that it is difficult even to identify them, let alone to remove them.[11]

Centralization vs. Decentralization

When Congress turns to matters of "reform" and reorganization, the issue of centralization versus decentralization is never much below the surface. Institutional changes can of course cut in either direction. In passing the Legislative Reorganization Act of 1946, for example, Congress sought to bring under control a committee system that was in vast disarray. Nearly fifty standing committees were eliminated by the act—a consolidation that at first glance suggests a move toward greater centralization of power. But at the same time the act did much to strengthen the independence of the surviving committees, since provisions were made for additions to their professional staffs. Moreover, a proposal designed to increase the centralization of power through the creation of party policy committees in each chamber was defeated in the House. Further dispersal of power took place shortly as both houses turned to the creation of numerous new subcommittees. Indeed, the proliferation of subcommittees since 1946 represents a substantial victory for the forces of decentralization.

Congress is not anxious to break away from the familiar pattern of power dispersal. The House of Representatives, for example, became even more decentralized in the 1970s as a result of the adoption of a "Subcommittee Bill of Rights." Under its terms, the powers of committee chairmen over subcommittees and their chairmen were curtailed. Now largely on their own and protected by relatively clear jurisdictional allocations, subcommittees are assured of the right to control their own budgets, staffs, meeting times, and agendas. So great has been the change, in fact, that it is not at all unusual to find subcommittee chairmen, rather than chairmen, managing legislation on the floor. All this comes down to the fact that

---

[11]For further analysis of the representativeness of congressional committees, see two instructive studies by Roger H. Davidson, "Representation and Congressional Committees," *The Annals*, 411 (January 1974), 48–62, and "Breaking Up Those 'Cozy Triangles': An Impossible Dream?" in *Legislative Reform and Public Policy*, eds. Susan Welch and John G. Peters (New York: Praeger Publishers, 1977), pp. 30–53.

opportunities are now more widespread than ever for numerous members to lay claim to a piece of the action. The integration of the House has of course become more difficult. As Representive John Brademas, Democratic whip, has observed: "We've gone as far as we could have gone to disperse and diffuse power. Any more diffusion, and it would make it difficult for the House to function."[12]

Although a preference for the decentralization of power dominates the tone and mood of Congress, not all of the changes of recent years have been on this order. Several changes designed to strengthen party and leadership control—thereby increasing centralization—were introduced in the early and middle 1970s. Party caucuses in both chambers are now empowered to vote (by secret ballot) on the conferral of committee chairmanships. Seniority no longer automatically awards the chairmanship to the member with the longest consecutive service on a committee. Committee chairmen, moreover, can be removed by an adverse vote of their caucus. In a further action to strengthen the party apparatus in the House, a Democratic Steering and Policy Committee was created in 1973 to develop and shape legislative strategy. In 1975, the authority to make committee assignments was transferred from the Democratic members of the Ways and Means Committee to the Steering and Policy Committee. Finally, as a means of bolstering the Speaker's control over legislation, the Democratic caucus gave him the power to nominate the Democratic members of the Rules Committee. None of these changes, however, limits the freedom of party members to vote as they choose or to pursue such policy objectives as suit their aims. They do little, in fact, to dent the autonomy of committees.

When all is said and done, the political skills and personal influence of party leaders remain the most important elements for the centralization of power in Congress. By exploiting every stray fragment of power available to them and using their talents of persuasion,[13] strong leaders can sometimes offset the centrifugal and parochial cast of congressional decisionmaking. Speaker Sam Rayburn (1940-47, 1949-53, 1955-61) and Senate

---

[12]*New York Times*, March 20, 1977.

[13]The ingenuity of party leaders can help to overcome the corrosive effects of power fragmentation. Consider the action in the House on the president's energy package in 1977. His proposals were parcelled out to five different standing committees, which ordinarily would have been an invitation to the design of a patchwork program. Instead, Speaker Thomas O'Neill won House acceptance for the creation of a super committee, an Ad Hoc Committee on Energy, whose function was to reconcile the various provisions adopted by the individual committees. Although this committee was not empowered to alter the recommendations reported by the standing committees, it was authorized to propose amendments for consideration on the floor. Most of its amendments were adopted, and the administration bill was largely intact when it passed the House. The Senate, it should be noted, unraveled major portions of it. See an account of the Ad Hoc Energy Committee and the role of the Speaker in controlling this legislation in the *Congressional Quarterly Weekly Report*, July 16, 1977, pp. 1435–39.

Majority Leader Lyndon Johnson (1953–61) are often cited as the proto-types for leading Congress and harnessing its scattered powers. Because so much depends on the persons who hold these offices, the problem of congressional leadership becomes obvious. Whether it is vigorous and effective or merely an empty promise is determined by chance—the chance that the House and Senate will elevate to their central leadership positions individuals of extraordinary political ability or opt for blandness. Even rewarding talent may not be enough to get the job done, so habituated to freedom from hierarchy are the members of the modern Congress.

THE EXCEPTIONAL TENURE OF MEMBERS

One of the sharpest differences between modern and nineteenth-century Congresses lies in the tenure of the membership. Election to the modern Congress typically turns out to be election to a career. By contrast, tenure during most of the nineteenth century was low.[14] Men moved in and out of Congress as if in a game of musical chairs. Table 1.1 brings these facts into sharper focus. Of the members serving in the Forty-second Congress (1871–72), only about one-half of the representatives and one-third of the

Table 1.1   Veteran Congressmen in Congress

Congress	Date	Representatives Elected to House More than Once	Senators Elected to Senate More than Once
42nd	1871	53%	32%
50th	1887	63	45
64th	1915	74	47
74th	1935	77	54
87th	1961	87	66
95th	1977	85	58

Source: Samuel P. Huntington, "Congressional Responses to the Twentieth Century," in *The Congress and America's Future,* ed. David B. Truman (Englewood Cliffs, N.J.: Prentice-Hall, Inc., 1965), p. 9 (as updated).

[14]For an analysis of membership turnover in nineteenth-century Congresses, see Samuel Kernell, "Toward Understanding 19th Century Congressional Careers: Ambition, Competition, and Rotation," *American Journal of Political Science,* 21 (November 1977), 669–93. Also see Charles S. Bullock III, "House Careerists: Changing Patterns of Longevity and Attrition," *American Political Science Review,* 66 (December 1972), 1295–1300; and Morris P. Fiorina, David W. Rohde, and Peter Wissel, "Historical Change in House Turnover," in *Congress in Change: Evolution & Reform,* ed. Norman J. Ornstein (New York: Praeger Publishers, 1975), pp. 24–57.

senators had been elected more than once. In the Ninety-fifth Congress (1977–78), eighty-five percent of the representatives and fifty-eight percent of the senators had been elected to office two or more times. Long careers have become commonplace. In the Fifty-eighth Congress (1903–4), only 1.8 percent of the members of the House had served ten or more terms,[15] while in the Ninety-fifth Congress 13.6 percent could claim this distinction. The broad base of congressional careerism is shown by the fact that more than forty percent of the members of the Ninety-fifth Congress had served five or more terms.

The presence of so many veteran legislators tends to obscure the recent changes that have taken place in the congressional membership. In the first place, Senate incumbents were somewhat less successful in getting reelected in the 1970s than they were in the previous decade. Nine incumbents, for example, were defeated in 1976. In the off-year election of 1978, three incumbents lost primary battles and seven were defeated in the general election. But a more dramatic change results from the growing number of retirements in both houses. Some members who choose retirement face unusually serious challenges for renomination or reelection. Rather than risk defeat and incur heavy campaign expenses as well, they drop out. Others are confronted by failing health. And an increasing number apparently are just tired of the job, its tensions and demands. Life in Congress has become something of a "hassle," as these comments suggest:

> A common complaint is that it isn't fun here any more. There used to be time for conviviality and companionship. Not any more. The job just grinds you down.

> We can't keep up with the work. All eyes turn to Washington for solutions to all problems. It's an entirely different world.

> Half of the reporters in town are looking on you as a Pulitzer Prize waiting to be won.

> Congress used to be a lifetime career. You died in Congress, or you tried to become Governor or Senator. On a clear day, some guys even saw the White House. Now members are cashing in early. Congressmen are being watched more closely, criticized more and prosecuted more. And the pay is not that munificent. Lobbyists make twice as much.[16]

Whatever the reasons that prompt retirement, attractive pension benefits diminish the pain. A member with thirty-two years of service, for example, can retire with an annual pension of $46,000. The generosity of

---

[15]T. Richard Witmer, "The Aging of the House," *Political Science Quarterly*, 79 (December 1964), 538.

[16]*Time*, January 23, 1978, pp. 10–11. The comments are by Congressman Morris Udall, Congressman George Mahon, Senator Lawton Chiles, and Congressman John Conyers.

retirement allowances doubtlessly has encouraged some veteran members to abandon elective politics.

Elections pose no more than minimal risks for a strong majority of incumbents. Indeed, in most recent House elections about three out of four incumbents have won by wide margins—by at least sixty percent of the two-party vote.[17] The ability of incumbents to retain their seats prevents a major turnover in congressional membership in any one election.

Over several elections, however, the membership of Congress can be markedly changed as incumbents die, retire, run for other offices, or are defeated. The Ninety-fifth Congress (1977–78) illustrates the point. Of the 435 House members serving in that Congress, 210 were first elected in 1972 or later; similarly, 33 of the senators were first elected during this period.

These newcomers to Congress not only are younger but also more independent of party—some fiercely so. The vast majority owe their election to their personal organizations and efforts, leading them to view party claims and congressional leadership with greater skepticism.[18] It seems plain that the decay of the electoral parties and the growing independence of voters have their counterpart in Congress: a bloc of new legislators who can take party or leave it, knowing that the only masters they must serve are their renomination and reelection constituencies.

THE TRADITION OF LOCALISM

One of the major facts to be appreciated about Congress is that its members are local products. The Constitution requires representatives and senators to be inhabitants of the states from which they are elected. Custom and political reality require representatives to be residents of the districts from which they are elected. At bottom, these constitutional and political requirements have a greater impact on the behavior of legislators than anything else in their environment, including party and president. Localism shapes the job of the legislator and the thrust of representation, sensitizing the member to the need to cater to his constituents and to seize every opportunity to advance their interests in legislation.

[17]Viewed in another way, of the 380 incumbent House members on the ballot in the 1976 presidential election, only 13 were defeated. (Three additional incumbents had earlier been defeated in primaries). State delegations in the 95th Congress were identical to those of the 94th in eighteen of the fifty states.

[18]It is interesting to find that the large bloc of *northern* freshman Democrats in the 95th Congress (first session) were more likely to vote in opposition to a majority of their party and in support of the conservative coalition (defined as a majority of voting southern Democrats and a majority of voting Republicans in opposition to a majority of voting northern Democrats) than were their senior party colleagues. *Congressional Quarterly Weekly Report,* January 21, 1978, pp. 116–117.

Virtually all general legislation is vulnerable to skewing in the interest of local, narrow, or regional advantage. Transportation policies can be written to give advantage to highway interests (trucking and automobile industries, among others) at the expense of mass transit development; housing policies to favor the older cities of the East and Midwest or the faster growing cities of the Sun Belt; energy policies to favor producing states at the expense of consuming states, or the oil and automobile industries at the expense of the consumers; water pollution policies to favor industries or environmentalists; international trade policies to favor industries that profit from free trade or those that profit from protectionism; and labor policies to facilitate or to impede union organizing. It is hard to find legislation that carries no opportunities for promoting provincial interests and equally hard to believe that the sum of all provincial interests is somehow the national interest.

Localism generates its own imperatives. James L. Sundquist writes:

> [Whatever] the merits of the local or regional claim, it must be pressed. Representatives of Texas must see the national interest in terms of oil, those of South Dakota in terms of cattle, and those of Detroit in terms of automobiles. Foreign policy seen through the eyes of a constituency may predispose a representative toward the Greek, the Israeli, or the Irish view of particular problems. The budget appears as a "pork barrel" to be distributed among districts as well as a fiscal program for the country. What weapons the military forces should get are liable to be judged by what factories are located in a state or district. And so it goes across the whole range of policy. Political incentives propel the member—especially the House member who represents more specialized constituencies—from the broad to the narrow perspective.[19]

Accounting for the pervasiveness of localism in Congress is not difficult. In addition to the local residence requirement, it owes something to the structure of the institution, something to the inclinations and "decision rules" of members, and something to the attitudes of the public. The dispersal of power among a vast number of committees and subcommittees and the weakness of the parties as centralizing agencies are structural features that encourage members to write legislation in such a way as to take care of local dislocations and to promote local interests. The deference shown specialization helps to defend the bargains and settlements struck in committee from being pulled apart on the floor. The disposition of members to engage in logrolling—sharing perspectives, "backscratching," helping each other out in the mode of quid pro quo, and trading votes—is the cement of localism and of the norm of reciprocity. Members need each other:

---

[19]James L. Sundquist, "Congress and the President: Enemies or Partners?" in *Congress Reconsidered*, eds. Lawrence C. Dodd and Bruce I. Oppenheimer (New York: Praeger Publishers, 1977), p. 230.

A feeling of camaraderie develops in the committees. You tend to go along with your fellow committee members on bills in which they are particularly interested. I find myself going along sometimes even with members on the other side. . . .[20]

We all support anything that's for Pennsylvania no matter where it goes. You have to in this place with its logrolling.[21]

Members are surprised when reciprocity is not forthcoming. When threatened by an amendment (to an omnibus farm bill) that would eliminate tobacco sales from the Food for Peace program, a Kentucky congressman upbraided the amendment's sponsor, a Colorado member representing a district notable for its sugar-beet acreage:

I recall distinctly that last week, when sugar was in trouble . . . about 20 states which produce tobacco marched right down the road with that gentleman. They do not produce any sugar beets . . or sugar cane in Kentucky. But when sugar is in trouble, sugar beets and sugar cane, the people in Kentucky are concerned about it.[22]

Finally, the public expects their representatives to pay close attention to constituency interests and to provide services of all kinds. Many members, so it appears, are not put off by errand-running, by having to manage answers and solutions to thousands of letters and requests, or by the pressure to produce tangible results (a public building, a dam) for their states or districts. Quite the contrary, constituent service is a boon to congressional longevity and, in addition, an attractive explanation to be given voters in search of information about how things are done in Washington:

[The members of Congress have] changed from legislators to ombudsmen. Rightly or wrongly, we have become the link between the frustrated citizen and the very involved Federal Government in the citizens' lives . . . We continually use more and more of our staff time to handle citizens' complaints, constituents' problems. . . . I do not know how you get out of this, since it becomes apparent to most people that if you want to be reelected it is more important how you handle your constituents in their relationships and problems with the Government than it is how you vote. I think it is one of the reasons that at the same time Congress is going down, down, down in the overall opinion of the American public, the rate of incumbents being reelected is going up, up, up. I think that has nothing to do with how we vote, but I think it has a lot to do with the fact that we have a staff which spends an incredible amount of its time handling constituent problems.[23]

[20]Charles L. Clapp, *The Congressman: His Work as He Sees It* (Washington, D.C.: The Brookings Institution, 1963), p. 15.

[21]Barbara Deckard, "State Party Delegations in the United States House of Representatives—An Analysis of Group Action," *Polity*, 5 (Spring 1973), 330.

[22]*Congressional Quarterly Weekly Report*, August 6, 1977, p. 1654.

[23]*Hearings and Meetings* before the Commission on Administrative Review, House of Representatives, 95th Cong., 1st sess., 1977, p. 62. The statement is by Congressman Joel Pritchard (R., Wash.).

Public Works is a sugar committee. I could always go back to the district and say, "Look at that road I got for you. See that beach erosion project over there? And those buildings? I got all those; I'm on Public Works."[24]

I have represented this district for the last twenty years. And I come to you to ask for a two-year renewal of my contract. I'm running because I have a twenty-year investment in my job and because I think you, as my constituents, have an investment in my seniority. In a body as large as the House of Representatives with 435 elected, coequal members, there has to be a structure if we're ever going to get anything done. And it takes a long time to learn that structure, to learn who has the power and to learn where to grease the skids to get something done. I think I know the structure and the people in the House better than any newcomer could. And I believe I can accomplish things for you that no newcomer could.[25]

THE IMPORTANCE OF NORMS

Congress is a human group. Like all groups, it has established ways of going about its business and a set of norms that shape, in greater or lesser fashion, the conduct or behavior of its members. The observance of norms (folkways, rules of the game) contributes a degree of continuity to a membership that itself is changing. Norms limit individual discretion, prescribing acceptable ways for new members to adjust to the group life of Congress.

The norms of each house of Congress focus on the management of interpersonal relations and the member's relationship to his work. In an instructive study of the Senate, published in 1960, Donald R. Matthews identified six major folkways: apprenticeship, legislative work, specialization, courtesy, reciprocity, and institutional patriotism.[26] New senators, he found, were expected to serve an appropriate apprenticeship, listening and learning, before engaging vigorously in the activities of the Senate, including floor debate. Under the pressure of new members, this norm has lost much of its force in recent Congresses. But the other norms are generally intact—in the House as well as in the Senate.[27]

The norm of legislative work prescribes that members not ignore their legislative responsibilities, including committee work, in a personal quest for publicity. The folkway of specialization insists that members concentrate on a limited range of legislative matters—those falling within the

[24]James T. Murphy, "Political Parties and the Porkbarrel: Party Conflict and Cooperation in House Public Works Committee Decision Making," *American Political Science Review*, 68 (March 1974), 171.

[25]Richard F. Fenno, Jr., *Home Style: House Members in Their Districts* (Boston: Little, Brown and Company, 1978), p. 138.

[26]Donald R. Matthews, *U.S. Senators and Their World* (Chapel Hill: University of North Carolina Press, 1960), pp. 92–117.

[27]See an analysis of the norms of the House of Representatives by Herbert B. Asher, "The Learning of Legislative Norms," *American Political Science Review*, 67 (June 1973), 499–513.

jurisdiction of the committees to which they are assigned or those of vital interest to their constituencies. The norm of courtesy serves to keep personal relationships on an even keel, to keep conflict over major issues from spilling over into personal conflict between members. The thrust of reciprocity, as discussed earlier, encourages members to assist others with their political problems; most commonly it appears in the trading of votes. Finally, institutional patriotism calls for members to exhibit a strong emotional attachment to the institution and to his or her colleagues.[28]

Norms are never perfectly observed. Some members have won large public reputations by paying little attention to them. Nor are they immune to change. Apprenticeship gave way because it diminished the new member's opportunities to shape public policies and to make a record on which he could run for reelection. And specialization has never been as important in the Senate as it has in the House, in part because committees are less powerful in the upper chamber. The important points to recognize about legislative norms are that they contribute to problem-solving (hard work and specialization), to reaching decisions (reciprocity), and to moderating conflict (courtesy and institutional patriotism). In the broadest sense, they make the legislative system less volatile, less subject to change. They are one of the many faces of the status quo.

THE DIFFERENCES BETWEEN
THE CHAMBERS

Congress is of course a bicameral institution. In drafting the Constitution the Founding Fathers gave scant attention to the creation of a single house, even though the colonies had experimented with unicameralism and the national legislature under the Articles of Confederation was itself unicameral. Bicameralism carried a special appeal for the delegates because it meshed comfortably with their preferences for balanced and divided government—one house to check the other, the more democratic House to balance the more aristocratic Senate. Each house was awarded equal standing under the Constitution, though their powers were not identical.

---

[28]The norm of institutional patriotism is observed more in Washington than in the constituencies. Members of the House in particular have found that campaign attacks on Congress strike a responsive chord among voters. See Fenno, *Home Style: House Members in Their Districts*, especially pp. 164–68. And consider the observations of David Broder of the *Washington Post*: "The most important communications from Congress to the people are, of course, those that are conducted by the Members of Congress themselves. You cannot cover a campaign in this country without being somewhat distressed at the experience of seeing so many Members of Congress back home in their districts speaking not for Congress and of Congress, but running against and speaking against Congress as an institution." *Hearings* before the Commission on Administrative Review, U.S. House of Representatives, 94th Cong., 2nd sess., November 30 and December 1, 1976, p. 69.

The Senate was empowered to "advise and consent" to major presidential appointments and to consent to the ratification of treaties, while the House was given the authority to originate all revenue bills. By custom, the House also initiates appropriations bills.

Although the House and Senate share certain large characteristics— an organizational mode that disperses power, a tradition of protecting provincial interests, a similar set of norms, among others—the differences between the chambers are pronounced. The House and the Senate are not peas in the same pod. The differences define the character of each house, the way each goes about its legislative tasks, and how each thinks about itself (not to mention how each thinks about the other).

Table 1.2, the work of Lewis A. Froman, captures the important differences between the House and the Senate. In his judgment, the two most important differences are size and constituency: first, the House is over four times as large as the Senate, and second, senators represent sovereign states while House members represent districts. The difference in size of the two chambers is at the root of most of the other differences.[29]

Table 1.2   Major Differences Between House and Senate

House	Senate
Larger (435 members)	Smaller (100 members)
More formal	Less formal
More hierarchically organized	Less hierarchically organized
Acts more quickly	Acts more slowly
Rules more rigid	Rules more flexible
Power less evenly distributed	Power more evenly distributed
Longer apprentice period	Shorter apprentice period
More impersonal	More personal
Less "important" constituencies	More "important" constituencies
Less prestige	More prestige
More "conservative"	More "liberal"

Source: Lewis A. Froman, Jr., *The Congressional Process: Strategies, Rules, and Procedures* (Boston: Little, Brown and Company, 1967), p. 7.

The organization of the House, the distribution of power within it, its procedures, and the careers of its members are all affected by the factor of size. Sheer numbers dictate the need for a formal and hierarchical organization as well as for a relatively rigid set of rules under which business is conducted. From one perspective, the large size of the House is a residual source of power for the leadership, since it is forced to make many

---

[29]This analysis of House-Senate differences is based mainly on Lewis A. Froman, Jr., *The Congressional Process: Strategies, Rules and Procedures* (Boston: Little, Brown and Company, 1967), pp. 5–15.

decisions affecting the disposition of legislation, such as scheduling it for floor consideration, without the extensive consultation of members. By contrast, the Senate leadership takes great pains to schedule legislation and debate to suit the preferences of as many members as possible, at times even for the convenience of a single member. The Senate is as informal in its procedures as the House is formal.

The opportunities for the individual House member to make his mark are largely limited to his committee work. On the floor he is lost in the crowd. But in committee his expertise can be demonstrated and brought to bear in the shaping of legislative provisions. Subject-matter specialization and technical knowledge are honed far more sharply among representatives than among senators. Moreover, senators are not content to limit their legislative interests to matters that come before their committees; indeed, the claims registered by their heterogeneous constituencies propel them to an active involvement in a wide sweep of legislative issues. A senator who has served in both chambers makes this observation:

> The House is a body of 435 struggling individuals whose only chance to have an impact is through their committees. The office of Senator is such, the prestige of office is such that a Senator can dabble in two or three areas that aren't necessarily in his committees. A House member can't do this.[30]

Another important difference between the chambers is that power is distributed more widely in the Senate than in the House. In the Ninety-fifth Congress, (1977–78) for example, ninety percent of the Senate Democrats— the majority party—held either a committee or subcommittee chairman-ship, while in the House the percentage for Democratic members was forty-seven. Similarly, while the typical senator serves on three or four committees, the typical representative serves on only one or two. The individual senator is thus in a better position to influence legislation in a larger number of policy fields.

The House and the Senate are quite unlike in their treatment of legislation on the floor. The large size of the House has made it necessary to develop rules and procedures that facilitate decision-making and permit it to act with dispatch. Major legislation is brought to the floor under a special order of the Rules Committee that specifies the amount of time to be given the measure; ordinarily these special rules limit general debate to one or two hours. It is comparatively rare for any bill to be debated in the House for more than a day. By contrast, the much smaller Senate may debate a single bill, on and off, for weeks or even months. The tradition of "unlimited debate" is one of the central characteristics of the Senate.

---

[30]Quoted in Richard F. Fenno, Jr., *Congressmen in Committees* (Boston: Little, Brown and Company, 1973), p. 147.

At times, of course, it results in filibustering designed to prevent action from being taken on legislation.[31]

Differences in the decision-making process and in the general thrust of the House and the Senate are aptly described by Nelson W. Polsby:

> The essence of the Senate is that it is a great forum, an echo chamber, a publicity machine. Thus "passing bills," which is central to the life of the House, is peripheral to the Senate. In the Senate the three central activities are cultivating national constituencies; formulating questions for debate and discussion on a national scale (especially in opposition to the President); and incubating new policy proposals that may at some future time find their way into legislation.[32]

Finally, the offices of congressman and senator differ in their visibility and prestige. House members represent artificial units of about half a million people, while senators represent states. Apart from the leadership, few members of the House ever gain national attention, except of course when they are brushed by scandal of one sort or another. No one outside their districts—save a few professors, newspaper reporters, bureaucrats, and lobbyists—even knows their names. It is unusual for a member of the House to meet the tests of presidential "availability," to be widely considered as an appropriate or logical candidate for the presidency. The Senate, by contrast, is a breeding ground for presidential candidates. And the Senate itself, individualistic to the core, is structured in such a way as to give its members maximum opportunity to advertise their wares before a national audience.

THE TASKS OF CONGRESS

The tasks of Congress are mixed. Viewed broadly, Congress helps to lend legitimacy to government by being responsive and accountable to the American people. In the process of representing the people, it helps to illuminate and resolve conflict and to build consensus. It listens to grievances, addresses public problems (sometimes converting local or private problems into national or public problems),[33] explores alternatives, protects or alters past decisions and policies, considers the nation's future

---

[31]Under the revised cloture rule adopted in 1975, debate can be terminated by a three-fifths vote of the entire membership—60 votes out of 100. Previously, rule 22 provided for a two-thirds vote of senators present and voting to cut off debate. There were more *successful* cloture votes in the 1970s than at any time since the Senate adopted its first cloture rule in 1917.

[32]Nelson W. Polsby, "Strengthening Congress in National Policy-Making," *Yale Review*, 59 (June 1970), 487.

[33]Among the best books ever written about how private problems become public problems is E. E. Schattschneider, *The Semisovereign People* (New York: Holt, Rinehart & Winston, Inc., 1961).

requirements, and does what the people are not organized to do for themselves. Not surprisingly, it also thinks about itself and, commonly, about its relations with other branches of government. It takes itself seriously, knowing that it is the most independent national legislature in the world. There is no "authorized version" of its functions. Congress is what Congress does. And most of the important things that it does are captured in these four activities: lawmaking, representation, oversight of administration, and public education.

Lawmaking

The Constitution of the United States places Congress at the core of the American political system by vesting all legislative power in its two houses. Although all constitutions are ambiguous at points, the powers given Congress in Article I, Section 8 are set forth with sharp clarity. For example, Congress is specifically empowered to levy taxes, borrow and coin money, regulate commerce, declare war, create an army and navy, regulate standards of weights and measures, create courts, establish post offices, and to adopt laws relating to bankruptcy, naturalization, patents, and copyrights. The concluding clause in this section authorizes Congress to make such other laws as "shall be necessary and proper" to carry out its powers. In addition, Article VI, Section 2 declares that the laws of Congress "made in pursuance" of the Constitution "shall be the supreme law of the land." Plainly, the Founding Fathers intended that the broad mission of the new government was to be charted by the national legislature.

It is one thing to say that the lawmaking power is securely vested in Congress and quite another to say that Congress originates most of the ideas that ultimately wind up as public law. Congress is first and foremost a representative institution, open and accessible to others who want things from it. What they want are sympathetic attention, favorable decisions, and public policies (or exemptions from the applications of public policies). The president, executive agencies, private interest groups, citizens at large, other governments (state, local, foreign), even regions (e.g., sunbelt, industrial northeast)—all look to Congress for solutions to problems that confront or are likely to confront them. In seeking relief, a better deal, a new settlement, a way of meeting contingencies, these outsiders often bring their own ideas to Congress. And it is a strange request, an unusual bill or amendment, that finds no members of Congress willing to sponsor it.

Chief among the outsiders in making claims on both Congress's attention and on its lawmaking authority is the president. Though his programs often encounter opposition in Congress—to the point of being drastically reshaped or lost altogether—it is nonetheless true that the major proposals on the congressional agenda usually are those of the chief executive. Important elements in the president's program, or what passes as *his* program, may of course have been "kicking around" Congress for years. Aggressive presidents have a way of claiming credit for policy departures that members of Congress can never match.

Lawmaking involves choices. Clues to the volume of choices made in Congress appear in Table 1.3, which shows a range of legislative activities in the House of Representatives from the Eightieth through the Ninety-fourth Congress—from the days of President Truman to those of President Ford. The outstanding fact shown by the data is simply the growing volume of legislative work. More than twice as many bills and nearly three times as many resolutions were introduced in the Ninety-fourth Congress as in the Eightieth Congress. Vastly more committee meetings and votes take place now than formerly. With the sharp increase in the number of votes, the member is put on the record more times, increasing the opportunities for challengers to criticize his performance. Committees compete with one another and with the floor for the time and attention of members. Hours spent in session have increased sharply. The only items to show a decline are the number of bills reported by committees and the number passed by the floor.[34]

Buffeted by constituent and interest group claims,[35] reelection politics, frequent trips home, and an enormous volume of legislative work, no member can elude massive pressures on his time and schedule, not to mention on his psyche. "There's no time to think ahead on important issues," one new member remarks. "It's even impossible to think out just the political effects of a decision."[36] Congress now wears down its members as never before, which helps explain why in increasing numbers they voluntarily abandon Washington.

Representation

The concept of representation is basic to any democratic political system. The public itself cannot govern. But it can choose representatives to

---

[34]The decline in legislative output probably says little about the role or effectiveness of Congress. Writing on the Senate, Allen Schick points out that some legislative matters that used to be handled by individual measures are now covered by general or omnibus legislation. The average length of bills enacted is now much longer than in the past. Routine and special legislation captures much less of the attention of Congress than formerly. See his explanation for the decline in legislative enactments in "Complex Policymaking in the United States Senate," a paper prepared for the Commission on the Operation of the Senate, *Policy Analysis on Major Issues*, 94th Cong., 2d sess., 1977, pp. 4–7.

[35]One way a member can diminish interest group pressures is to make an early decision on legislation. As observed by two House members: "You need to stake out a position early to avoid group pressures"; "I get committed early. That's why, though I've heard of pressure politics, I've never felt it." As quoted by David C. Kozak, *The Conditional Nature of Congressional Decision-Making (Ph.D. Dissertation, University of Pittsburgh, 1979), p. 175.*

[36]*Time*, January 23, 1978, p. 10.

Table 1.3 U.S. House of Representatives Legislative Activity, 80th—94th Congresses

Congress	Time in Session Days	Hours	Number of Bills Introduced	Reported	Passed†	Number of Resolutions Introduced	Reported	Passed†	Number of Committee Meetings	Number of Quorum Calls	Number of Yea and Nay Votes	Number of Recorded Votes‡
80	254	1,224	7,611	1,840	1,739	950	340	481	NA	122	159	0
81	345	1,501	10,502	2,523	2,482	1,193	401	586	NA	268	275	0
82	274	1,163	9,065	2,018	2,008	990	279	432	NA	183	181	0
83	240	1,033	10,875	2,093	2,129	989	349	519	NA	124	147	0
84	230	937	13,169	2,334	2,360	935	364	473	3,210	132	147	0
85	276	1,147	14,580	2,094	2,064	1,080	356	482	3,750	222	193	0
86	265	1,039	14,112	1,676	1,636	1,394	318	481	3,059	202	180	0
87	304	1,227	14,328	1,941	1,927	1,381	368	497	3,402	284	240	0
88	334	1,251	14,022	1,375	1,267	1,277	367	467	3,596	296	232	0
89	336	1,547	19,874	1,613	1,565	2,125	436	583	4,367	388	394	0
90	328	1,595	22,060	1,369	1,213	2,167	376	446	4,386	397	478	0
91	350	1,613	21,436	1,137	1,130	2,139	405	512	5,066	369	443	0
92	298	1,429	18,561	1,010	970	1,897	391	499	5,114	285	456	193
93	318	1,487	18,872	906	923	2,223	457	601	5,888	375	632	446
94	311	1,789	16,982	985	968	2,389	510	656	6,975	419	810	463

Source: Commission on Administrative Review, U.S. House of Representatives, *Scheduling the Work of the House*, 94th Cong., 2d sess., 1976, p. 24.

†Occasionally measures are taken up on the floor without having been referred to or reported from committee.

‡The Legislative Reorganization Act of 1970 provided for recording of teller votes.

govern on its behalf. All theories of democratic representation ultimately turn on the idea that those who are entrusted with office are accountable to those who elect them. Representative government and responsible government are currents in the same stream of democratic politics. Responsibility, of course, is imperfectly enforced. The people never do everything that theories specify they should. Voters are often uncertain of the positions and intentions of candidates and, at the next election, unaware of what their representatives have done—presumably on their behalf. But the differences between the theory and reality of representation should not obscure the fact that legislatures owe both their origin and their continuing justification to the need to take steady account of popular preferences. Legislators understand this as well as anyone.

Representation may be examined along dimensions of style and of focus. In terms of style, a representative may see his role as that of *delegate* (the legislator who is disposed to consult his constituents on pending matters and to accept their instructions), as that of *trustee* (the legislator who is disposed to decide on legislative matters in a Burkean manner, acting on the basis of his conscience and his own best judgment), or as that of *politico* (the legislator who finds merit in both orientations and alternates between them). In terms of focus, a representative may be oriented primarily to his local constituency, to the nation, or to some combination of local and national interests.

Taken from a study by Roger H. Davidson, Table 1.4 shows the distribution of representational styles and foci among a sample of House members. What emerges most clearly from the data is that members of the House do not see their role as representative in the same light. The concept of representation is as complex for them as it is for others, including those who write about it. About one-quarter perceive themselves as pure trustees, about one-quarter as pure delegates, and about one-half as both trustees and delegates. The foci of representation are more revealing. Only about one-quarter of the members see their role as one of representing national

Table 1.4   Distribution of Representational Style and Focus Among Members of the U.S. House of Representatives

Style		Focus	
Trustee	28%	Nation dominant	28%
Politico	46	Nation and district equal	23
Delegate	23	District dominant	42
Undetermined	3	Nongeographic	5
		Undetermined	3
	100%		101%

Source: Adapted from Roger H. Davidson, *The Role of the Congressman* (New York: Pegasus, 1969), pp. 117, 122. Reprinted with permission of The Bobbs-Merrill Co., Inc.

rather than local interests, while nearly one-half (forty-two percent) are primarily oriented to their districts. Other evidence shows that a strong majority of trustees have a national focus in their conception of representation, while nearly all delegates have a district focus.[37] Style and focus, though not identical, are obviously closely associated.

The parochial cast in congressional policy-making is shown in these observations by a rural, Republican member:

> I am a purist. I feel that a House member's job is to represent the people back home. For example, the only four wet-corn growers in the country are in my district, and I am their sole voice. Likewise, the date growers should be represented only by *their* Congressman; the salmon industry should be able to count on Pacific Northwest Congressmen, and so forth. I might concur with Representative X from Anywhere for the good of the country, but my primary responsibility must always be [my] district. A Representative is interested primarily with his own little piece of land. A combination of the actions of all Congressmen creates, in effect, House policy.[38]

Constituency service, or errand-running, is another form of representation. Except for the electoral support it induces and the satisfaction it may give those who confer it or who benefit from it, constituency service has no more lasting impact than a stone dropped in water. For every constituent problem solved, another emerges. Handling problems is a credit-earning opportunity for all members, a rationalization and a pretext for some, and an incubus for others. The volume of requests is so great as to virtually outstrip Congress's capacity to respond:

> A congressman's primary job is to legislate. Yet our society and government are so complex that we spend less than a third of our time on legislative matters. A congressman is not only a legislator: he is also an employment agent, passport finder, constituent greeter, tourist agent, getter-outer-of the armed services, veterans' affairs adjuster, public buildings dedicator, industrial development specialist, party leader, bill finder, newsletter writer, etc. His typical day will be far more concerned with these problems than with national defense, foreign aid, or appropriations for public works.[39]

Oversight of Administration

Another traditional activity of Congress involves oversight of the national bureaucracy.[40] The responsibility of Congress does not end

---

[37]Roger H. Davidson, *The Role of the Congressman* (New York: Pegasus, 1969), p. 126.
[38]*Ibid.*, p. 123.
[39]Robert L. Peabody, ed., *Education of a Congressman: The Newsletters of Morris K. Udall* (Indianapolis: The Bobbs-Merrill Company, Inc., 1972), p. 248.
[40]See an instructive study of legislative oversight by Morris S. Ogul, *Congress Oversees the Bureaucracy: Studies in Legislative Supervision* (Pittsburgh: University of Pittsburgh Press, 1976). This book is the source of the main arguments of these paragraphs.

with the passage of laws. Laws are language, often unclear and never self-executing. Moreover, decisions must be made concerning their implementation. As the representative assembly of the nation, Congress is charged both by law and custom (and to some extent by popular expectations) with reviewing, supervising, and controlling administrative conduct. In the broadest sense, legislative oversight seeks to insure that administrative agencies will execute the laws in a manner consistent with the intent of Congress. Bureaucrats are not to be left to their own lights, free to interpret and administer laws in any fashion that suits their values.[41]

By engaging in oversight activities Congress helps to legitimize the decisions of government. It fosters the belief that government can be held in check. When effective, congressional surveillance helps to clarify the application of laws, equalizes or softens their impact, provides for redress of citizen grievances, leads to new and improved procedures, curbs administrative excesses, and promotes greater fidelity to the laws themselves. Not surprisingly, oversight often falls short of achieving these goals.

Most of the interactions between the executive and legislative branches present opportunities for oversight or in fact turn on some form of it. Hearings and investigations give Congress, particularly its committees and subcommittees, a chance to secure information about programs, to ask administrators difficult and embarrassing questions, to make demands, and to offer suggestions for changing administrative practices. The appropriations process is replete with openings for interested members to inquire into agency operations as a way of learning how government is being conducted. Administrators who fail to satisfy Congress—in particular the members of its appropriations committees—may find their budget requests cut back and their programs altered. Oversight is also facilitated to some extent by requiring agencies to report to Congress on their activities. Much oversight occurs simply in the informal contacts of members and staffs with executive personnel. When informal means succeed, the need for formal oversight, such as hearings or investigations, diminishes. Finally, in handling constituent problems with government (casework), members may engage in a form of oversight, helping to make bureaucracy more responsive to the citizenry it is designed to serve.

The adequacy of oversight is another matter. In the view of both scholars and members of Congress, it is neither systematic nor comprehensive. Why this is the case is not hard to discover. For one thing, the job of

---

[41]Contrary to conventional interpretations, a recent study finds that bureaucrats and members of Congress are *not* notably different in their values and outlooks. In fact, they are surprisingly alike along many important dimensions, including their ideology and the way they think about public problems. See Joel D. Aberbach and Bert A. Rockman, "The Overlapping Worlds of American Federal Executives and Congressmen," *British Journal of Political Science*, 7 (January 1977), 23–47.

keeping track of a farflung bureaucracy is simply too big and too complex for a legislature pressed hard by other responsibilities. For another, most members of Congress attach relatively low significance to oversight activities. The "payoff" for engaging in it ordinarily appears too thin. And related to this, members are simply more interested in legislating and in tending to constituency problems and interests than in monitoring the faithfulness of executive agencies. All this comes down to the fact that oversight is more likely to occur intermittently rather than steadily, in bits and pieces rather than by broad and conscious design, and indirectly rather than directly.

Oversight thus tends to be incidental—occurring as members, staffs, and committees go about their other business. But it does occur. Moreover, the fact that all elements of the bureaucracy *know* that Congress can inquire into their conduct at any time probably induces them to act more responsibly than they would otherwise. That itself is no mean contribution.

⌁ Educating the Public

An idea deeply imbedded in democratic theory insists that office-holders have an obligation to instruct the public on the issues that come before government. The effectiveness of popular control over government depends ultimately on the public's acquisition of information about the choices made, or to be made, by their representatives. In the absence of information, the reasoning goes, the public is not only unable to discern its interests in legislation but impaired in its capacity to choose wisely among competing candidates. A poorly educated public is easily bamboozled by artful politicians. In his classic study of Congress, Woodrow Wilson wrote: "[Even] more important than legislation is the instruction and guidance in political affairs which the people might receive from a body which kept all national concerns suffused in a broad daylight of discussion."[42]

There is some evidence that the contemporary Congress takes its function of providing instruction for the public more seriously than earlier ones did. Various changes in the 1970s, for example, sharply diminished congressional secrecy. "Sunshine" rules in both houses require committee sessions to be open to the public—unless committee members vote publicly to close them. Even most party caucuses are now open to the public. And following the lead of other countries and numerous state legislatures, Congress is now exploring the use of television coverage of its floor proceedings. The opportunities for the public to learn more about Congress, its processes and policies, are now better than ever.

[42]Woodrow Wilson, *Congressional Government* (New York: Meridian Books, 1956), p. 195. Wilson's study was first published in 1885.

The significance of congressional teaching is nonetheless not large, except for the most attentive of constituents. In part it is minimized by the general institutional design of Congress, under which the less visible committee structure plays a much larger role in shaping public policies than the parent chambers. In part the subordination of teaching results from the preoccupations of members. Despite their routine preachments on the importance of this function, most members are trapped in the reality of attending numerous committee meetings, handling voluminous casework, entertaining visiting constituents, managing their offices, meeting with staff, getting home and back, and building support for their reelection. Public instruction sometimes results from these activities, as in the case of committee hearings and investigations, but it is more incidental than direct. Finally, the function of educating the public suffers because much of the public cares little about receiving that which is offered. All in all, it would be difficult to exaggerate the indifference and inattentiveness of the American public toward political business and political analysis. Even that half of the population that votes is not distinguished for its awareness and understanding of political issues and positions or for its tolerance of what it sees as the tedium of politics. This electoral reality fully matches the reality that faces the member of Congress, pressed and buffeted on all sides by claims and responsibilities too numerous to accommodate in any normal working environment.

Perceptions of the Role
of the Legislator

Table 1.5 concludes this analysis of legislative tasks. It shows how members of the House and a cross-section of the American people view the activities of congressmen. In particular, it depicts how congressmen actually spend their time and how they would prefer to spend it and how voters think congressmen spend their time and how they would prefer that they spend it.

Several conclusions are suggested by the data. First, it is apparent that House members do not have sufficient time to do all the things they would like to do and that, more importantly, there are notable differences between what members actually do and what they would prefer to do.

Second, members generally believe that the lawmaking role (such as studying and developing legislation, engaging in floor activities, working in committees and subcommittees) should hold higher priority than certain constituency and representative activities (such as meeting with constituents in Washington, helping constituents with personal problems involving government, interacting with local government officials, explaining to citizens what their government is doing, making sure their districts secure government projects, or giving speeches).

Table 1.5 The Activities of House Members as Viewed by Members and Voters

Activity	Proportion of Congressmen Who Report Spending a Great Deal of Time on Activity	Proportion of Congressmen Who Believe They *Should* Spend a Great Deal of Time on Activity	Proportion of Voters Who Believe Congressmen Spend a Great Deal of Time on Activity	Proportion of Voters Who Believe Congressmen *Should* Spend a Great Deal of Time on Activity
Meeting personally with constituents when they come to Washington	13%	34%	23%	48%
Getting back to your District to stay in touch with your constituents	67	74	29	68
Studying and doing basic research on proposed legislation	25	73	31	71
Helping people in your District who have personal problems with the government	35	57	24	62
Working in subcommittees to develop legislation	60	82	—	—
Staying in touch with local government officials in your District	16	26	34	63
Debating and voting on legislation on the floor of the House	30	64	41	76
Keeping track of the way government agencies are administering laws passed by the Congress	10	53	31	64

Table 1.5 *(continued)*

Activity	Proportion of Congressmen Who Report Spending a Great Deal of Time on Activity	Proportion of Congressmen Who Believe They *Should* Spend a Great Deal of Time on Activity	Proportion of Voters Who Believe Congressmen Spend a Great Deal of Time on Activity	Proportion of Voters Who Believe Congressmen *Should* Spend a Great Deal of Time on Activity
Taking the time to gain a first-hand knowledge of foreign affairs	17	44	19	50
Working in full committees to develop legislation	46	72	30	62
Taking the time to explain to citizens what their government is doing to solve important problems and why	33	54	26	67
Working in committee or subcommittee on oversight activities	16	56	—	—
Managing and administering your office	15	28	—	—
Sending newsletter about the activities of Congress to people in your District	10	34	28	49
Making sure your District gets its fair share of government money and projects	23	44	43	77
Working informally with other members to build support for legislation about which you are personally concerned	21	54	—	—
Giving speeches and personal appearances to talk to interested groups about legislative matters before the Congress	26	31	—	—

Source: Adapted from member and voter survey data supplied by House Commission on Administrative Review, House of Representatives, 95th Cong., 1st sess., 1977.

Third, the general public attaches more importance than members to constituency service and to the representation of local interests. The public is especially concerned to have its representatives "bring home the bacon"— to secure government money and projects for the district. Moreover, two of the largest gaps between practice and preference, from the perspective of the general public, involve the constituency service role: voters want congressmen to return to their districts more frequently than they think they do and to spend more time helping people who have personal problems with government than they think they do. Doubtlessly some of the tension in the lives of representatives derives from the conflicting perspectives of members and citizens as to the job of the legislator.[43]

Another source of tension is the electoral process. Members not only must deal with nagging problems of public policy but also with a range of political problems involving reelection and the safeguarding of their careers. The following chapter on election politics examines these matters.

---

[43]In addition to using such generic terms as "legislator," representative," and "House member" to refer to the men and women of Congress, I have referred to them in the masculine gender—"he," "his," "him." This is simply a matter of style. These pronouns, like the term "congressman," are employed generically.

The
Electoral
Terrain

2

An important element in understanding Congress is the electoral environment of the members. Voters choose who will represent them. In determining which candidates win seats in Congress, voters help to establish the boundaries within which legislative decisions will later be made. Election outcomes can facilitate basic policy changes by the new Congress or make them all but impossible.

This chapter on the electoral environment of Congress begins with an analysis of constituencies, continues with an examination of campaigns and elections, and concludes with an analysis of the backgrounds of members. Its major premises are two: first, that the electoral terrain affects Congress in fundamental ways, and second, that members work steadily and imaginatively to soften and manipulate this environment, seeking to cut the risks that elections pose for them.

CONGRESSIONAL
CONSTITUENCIES

Each congressional district shows a profile of its own. There are congressional districts in which as much as eighty percent of the population is white collar and others in which the proportion is as low as thirty percent. The median family income varies between a low of less than $5,000 to a high of more than $17,000. There are about a dozen congressional districts in which over one-quarter of the population are Mexican-Americans (Chicanos exceed fifty percent of the population in several Texas, New Mexico, and California districts) and a number of other inner-city districts that are composed predominantly of blacks.[1] German-, Polish-, Italian-, and Irish-Americans are especially numerous in certain big-city districts, such as those of Milwaukee and Chicago, while voters of Scandinavian extraction are common in certain Minnesota districts.

Home ownership is high in some districts and low in others. At times unemployment is twice as high in some districts as it is in others. There are districts that are based flatly on agricultural interests, or on mining interests, or on manufacturing interests, or on defense industries. There are others whose characteristics are nothing quite so much as hybrid. There are districts whose voters have an ingrained conviction for the conservation of traditional values and those whose voters press steadily for change. The range of differences is so great as to make it impossible to depict a "typical" congressional district.

Representation and Apportionment

In the midst of this diversity is a factor congressional districts now have in common: size of population. As recently as the early 1960s, however, there were a number of states in which the most populous congressional district contained three or four times as many people as the least populous district. Disparities of over two-to-one within states were common throughout the country. The effect of this was to inflate the vote (or *overrepresent* the interests) of residents of smaller districts and to deflate the vote (or *underrepresent* the interests) of residents of larger districts. The principal beneficiaries of these inequitable apportionment acts fashioned by state legislatures were the rural and agricultural interests of the nation. More broadly, this structure of misrepresentation served conservative interests more fully than liberal ones.

After years of caution and timidity on cases involving malapportionment, the nation's courts finally took action on the problem. A few decisions in the 1950s suggested that the courts might be ready to abandon the idea that apportionment was a "political question"[2]—hence one that should not be addressed by the judiciary. In 1958, for example, a federal district court accepted jurisdiction of a case involving the Minnesota state legislature, which had not been reapportioned since 1913. Instead of ruling

---

[1] Congressional district data are available in Michael Barone, Grant Ujifusa, and Douglas Matthews, *The Almanac of American Politics* (New York: E. P. Dutton, 1978).

[2] The holding that apportionment was a "political question" was enunciated in 1946 in *Colegrove v. Green.* "Courts ought not to enter this political thicket," the majority opinion declared. "The remedy for unfairness in districting is to secure state legislatures that will apportion properly, or to invoke the ample powers of Congress." 328 U.S. 549, at 556 (1946).

on the case immediately, the court advised the legislature that it would postpone its decision until the legislature had time to write a new apportionment act.[3] Under this nudging, the legislature responded by passing an act that brought district representation largely into line with district population.

A quickening of interest in congressional reapportionment occurred in 1962 when the Supreme Court ruled in *Baker v. Carr,* a case involving unfair representation in the Tennessee state legislature, that reapportionment was not a "political question."[4] Judicial remedies could thus be sought as a means of gaining equitable representation. The landmark case in the struggle for fairly apportioned congressional districts was decided in 1964. In *Wesberry v. Sanders,* the Supreme Court ruled that the congressional district lines of Georgia must be redrawn in order that "as nearly as is practicable one man's vote . . . is to be worth as much as another's."[5] The Georgia legislature promptly passed its first congressional reapportionment act since 1931. Other states followed suit, and in a relatively short time all were in substantial compliance with the "one man-one vote" ruling. All congressmen now represent about the same number of people (roughly half a million), and malapportionment is no longer a device for the containment of popular majorities.

The arrival of equitable apportionment has not taken the politics out of redistricting. It still matters who draws the district lines and where they are drawn. When district lines are laid out in a way that gives special advantage to the candidates of one party, the scheme is called a gerrymander. The majority party (or dominant coalition) in state legislatures gerrymanders districts by two techniques: concentration and dispersion. Neither one calls for unusual imagination among those who draw the lines. All that is required is a set of accurate statistics on the past voting records of the state's political subdivisions and reasonable hunches about their future behavior.

Using the concentration technique, the majority party compresses the minority party's area of electoral strength into the smallest feasible number of districts. It concedes these districts to the minority's candidates, giving them votes beyond their needs, and helping them to win future elections by lopsided margins. Surrounding districts can thus be made more secure for their own candidates. Using the second method, the majority party draws district lines to disperse the voting strength of the minority party, parcelling out its traditional supporters among several districts and thus reducing their influence on election outcomes.

All reapportionment acts contain an element of gerrymandering, and some appear to be dominated by it. District lines are never neutral. The

[3]*Magraw v. Donovan,* 163 F. Supp. 184 (1958).
[4]369 U.S. 186 (1962).
[5]376 U.S. 1 (1964).

location of a party's (or an incumbent's) "friendly" and "hostile" areas is no secret. The manner in which areas are combined to form districts is of great importance to incumbents, challengers, parties, regions, counties, and other subdivisions. Redistricting can cut the risk for some incumbent congressmen, prompt others to retire, discourage or activate potential challengers, and distort popular preferences. Redistricting legislation is not ordinary business. Its transactions are peculiarly political and redistributive. Someone always wins, someone always loses.[6]

For well over a century, congressmen have been elected from single-member districts.[7] This arrangement not only facilitates campaigning—the district is small enough to be manageable for candidates—but also voter awareness of the candidates, since ordinarily there are only two. Another feature of this system is not so well understood. It is that single-member districts often distort the popular vote within a state. From one perspective, single-member districts are highly effective structures for wasting votes. Only one candidate can win in each district, and the votes cast for the losing candidate are lost.

The extent to which this system scrambles congressional representation, giving the majority party an "unearned" increment of seats while shortchanging the minority party, is apparent in Table 2.1. Consider the

Table 2.1 The Iron Law of Single Member Districts: Exaggerated Representation for the Winning Party

	Democratic		*Republican*	
State	Percent of Statewide Congressional Vote	Percent of Seats Won	Percent of Statewide Congressional Vote	Percent of Seats Won
Washington	58%	86%	42%	14%
Missouri	57	80	43	20
Wisconsin	57	78	43	22
New Jersey	56	73	44	27
Massachusetts	65	82	35	18
Colorado	46	60	54	40

Source: The data are for the 1976 election, drawn from the *Congressional Quarterly Weekly Report,* November 6, 1976, pp. 3147-54.

[6]It should be remembered that even if the districts of all incumbents are made more secure—which sometimes happens and which scarcely troubles either party's incumbents—someone loses. The losers are those potential candidates in the "out" party who decline to run and the congressional challengers who merely go through the motions of campaigning, knowing that they cannot win. The public also loses in "doomed" districts, since elections are "settled" before the first vote is even cast. It is reasonable to suppose, moreover, that a party long accustomed to defeat in its efforts to capture a congressional seat may find its capacity to attract outstanding talent diminished. Political structures create more losers than meet the eye.

[7]In the five least populous states (Alaska, Delaware, Nevada, Vermont, and Wyoming), each entitled to only one representative, candidates for the lower house run at large—that is, the boundaries of their "district" are the boundaries of the state.

vote in the state of Washington in 1976. Although the Republican congressional candidates received forty-two percent of the statewide vote, their party won only one of seven House seats, or fourteen percent. The party won one district by a margin of almost three-to-one, narrowly lost another, and lost five others by varying margins. This skewed outcome resulted from the way in which the district lines had been drawn. Devices for wasting votes are about as old as American political experience.

Representation in the U.S. Senate is a legacy of the Constitutional Convention of 1787. Based on the principle of federalism, the Senate was designed to represent states while the House of Representatives was designed to represent people. Each state was awarded two senators, to be chosen by the state legislatures rather than by the voters, and to serve terms of six years.

The Senate that emerged from the drawing boards of the Founding Fathers was to be the stable and enlightened branch of the new legislature, a check upon the capriciousness and excesses of the popularly-elected lower house. With the passage of the Seventeenth Amendment in 1913, providing for the direct election of senators, this distinction lost whatever meaning it may have had. As enforced through elections, senators became as responsible as House members to "the people." The formula for Senate representation, of course, continues unchanged. The 300,000 citizens of Alaska are entitled to the same representation in the Senate as the 20 million citizens of California—in all but name a classic example of malapportionment.

The House Member's
Perceptions of the Constituency

Constituency is a vague concept in common discourse, but it can be brought into sharper focus by employing certain distinctions. Richard F. Fenno, Jr., identifies four congressional constituencies, one lodged within another, ranging from the most inclusive to the most exclusive. The most inclusive constituency is the member's *geographical constituency,* his legal district that includes the total population within its boundaries. Nestled within his geographical constituency is the congressman's *reelection constituency,* composed of those people who he believes vote for him:

> My supporters are Democrats, farmers, labor—a DFL operation—with some academic types. . . . My opposition tends to be the main street hardware dealer. I look at that kind of guy in a stable town, where the newspaper runs the community—the typical school board member in the rural part of the

district—that's the kind of guy I'll never get. At the opposite end of the scale is the country club set. I'll sure as hell never get them, either.[8]

A still smaller constituency is the *primary constituency*—the member's most intense, rain-or-shine supporters. They help to finance his campaigns, work for him, and guard him against defeat, particularly in primary elections.

> Everybody needs some group which is strongly for him—especially in a primary. You can win a primary with 25,000 zealots. . . . The most exquisite case I can give you was in the very early war years. I had very strong support from the anti-war people. They were my strongest supporters and they made up about 5% of the district.[9]

The congressman's most exclusive constituency is his *personal constituency*—his closest friends, advisers, and confidants. The member feels "at home" with them. They help him to keep "in touch." Doubtlessly they help to shape his perspectives on politics and policies.

A congressman stays in office by knowing and monitoring his constituencies and by choosing how to respond to them. He develops a distinctive and complex "home style" that helps him to cultivate his constituencies and to deal with electoral conditions. How he perceives his constituencies will influence how he interprets himself to them, how he stays in touch with those who reelect him, how many trips home he will make, how much of his total staff allowance will be allocated to staff salaries in his district, how he will "present" himself to voters (for example, emphasizing person-to-person contacts, on the one hand, or issue-orientations, on the other), how much time and attention he will give to each of his supporting segments, how he will deal with electoral difficulties, and how he will explain his activities (e.g., voting) in Washington to those constituents who want to know about them.

The crucial matter is the member's reelection. A district never appears as secure to the incumbent as it does to an outsider. How a member carries his district may be as much a matter of the "home style" he develops as it is one of congruence between his constituents' policy preferences and his voting behavior in Washington. What works in one district may not work in another. The successful member is the one who puts first things first: the development and maintenance of political support among those constituents who can keep him in office.

---

[8]Richard F. Fenno, Jr., *Home Style: House Members in Their Districts* (Boston: Little, Brown and Company, 1978), pp. 9–10.
[9]*Ibid.*, pp. 18–19.

CAMPAIGNING FOR CONGRESS

Getting elected to Congress is a complicated undertaking—especially, of course, for challengers. Analysis of congressional campaigns is also complicated because of the differences from state to state and from district to district. One way to discuss the nature of these campaigns is to examine the conditions that face most congressional candidates.

Characteristics of Congressional Campaigns

Most candidates for Congress confront a basic fact of political life: a large share of the voters do not know their names. This is more the case for House candidates than for Senate candidates, more the case for challengers than for incumbents. Even the name of the incumbent is not exactly a household word—except perhaps in his own household. Consistent with earlier findings, a national survey in the late 1970s found that only fifty percent of the people knew the name of the House member who represented them; an even smaller number, forty-two percent, knew the party to which he belonged.[10]

The absence of voter information about candidates helps to explain why the party label under which they run is important: it provides voters with a point of reference. A substantial proportion of all votes cast for candidates for Congress are cast on the basis of the voters' party identifications. Dominant in the electorate, the Democratic party profits in this environment.

A second characteristic of campaigns for Congress is that candidates find it necessary to develop their own personal campaign organizations. The importance of party identification in influencing voters' decisions in congressional elections is not the result of vigorous, purposeful activity by the party organizations. Throughout most of the country, in fact, party

[10]*Final Report of the Commission on Administrative Review*, U.S. House of Representatives, 95th Cong., 1st sess., 1977, vol. 2 of 2, p. 814. Although all scholars agree that the public's information about congressional candidates is limited, the case has almost surely been overdrawn. The public knows more than is revealed by a question that asks them to recall a candidate's name. One study has shown that many voters who are unable to recall the name of a candidate can recognize it when they hear it or see it (as in a voting booth) and most will be able to offer a positive or negative evaluation of the individual. Moreover, there are substantial differences among congressional districts in the extent to which voters recognize the names of candidates, thus indicating that some individual candidates are able to enhance the saliency of their names. In general, incumbents have a strong advantage in name recognition—an advantage of about twenty percent. See Thomas E. Mann, *Unsafe at Any Margin: Interpreting Congressional Elections* (Washington, D.C.: American Enterprise Institute, 1978), especially Chapter 3.

organizations are enfeebled and in disrepair, scarcely capable of putting together a comprehensive campaign. The result is that the burden falls on the candidate, his friends and advisers, the contributors and workers who are enlisted, and the groups which have a stake in the election. The malaise that plagues the party system has made the American political system peculiarly candidate-centered. Most incumbents probably prefer it this way. Being largely on their own in campaigns frees them from party controls in the legislature.

Third, campaigns in competitive districts are laced with uncertainties concerning the strategies most appropriate to winning. It would be impossible to snare all the stray ideas that have been used in winning, or in losing, congressional elections. No one knows for certain what works, or what does not work, as this account by a candidate for the House makes clear:

> A candidate cannot experiment. He must act promptly on limited information, as though he were an officer in battle, taking his troops over a hill when he does not know what is on the other side. Because no one knows what works in a campaign, money is spent beyond the point of diminishing returns. To meet similar efforts by the opposition, all advertising and propaganda devices are used—billboards, radio, TV, sound trucks, newspaper ads, letter writing or telephone committee programs, handbills, bus cards. No one dares to omit any approach. Every cartridge must be fired because among the multitude of blanks one may be a bullet.[11]

Fourth, congressional campaigns are a promiscuous blend of policy, ideological, constituency, and personal issues. Policy issues involve specific questions of public policy, such as taxation, inflation, unemployment, and energy conservation. Ideological issues often turn on verbal imagery, symbol-rattling, and sloganeering. "Liberal," "conservative," "ultra-liberal," "right-winger,"—all such labels are designed to evoke an emotional response among voters. Constituency issues involve, from the perspective of the incumbent, his accomplishments for the district and, from the perspective of the challenger, his failures. Personal issues are concerned with the attributes, qualifications, beliefs, and associations of the candidate; they emerge in questions concerning a candidate's age, experience, marital status, morality, or occupation, among other things.[12]

The discussion of campaign issues is a major intellectual exercise in all congressional campaigns. But more important is the matter of their significance for election outcomes. How much do issues influence voting

---

[11]Stimson Bullitt, *To Be A Politician* (New Haven and London: Yale University Press, 1977), p. 110.
[12]See Robert J. Huckshorn and Robert C. Spencer, *The Politics of Defeat: Campaigning for Congress* (Amherst, Mass.: The University of Massachusetts Press, 1971), especially pp. 193–226.

behavior? The answer is that neither candidates nor voters believe that issues *ordinarily* win or lose congressional elections.[13] They are not thought to be as critical as personality and image, party affiliation, incumbency, organization, or financial resources. Consider the observations of members of Congress:

> The people back home don't know what's going on. Issues are not most important so far as the average voter is concerned. The image of the candidate plays a much greater role. If voters feel the candidate is conscientious and is trying hard to serve them, then that man has a good chance of coming back. Some people in marginal districts are able to hang on just because the public has this view of them.

> Personality is so important that it outweighs the issues in people's minds, and they tend to vote for candidates who have attractive personalities . . .

> Too many politicians, whether they are in state legislatures or in Congress, run away from a vote because they are afraid of the consequences when they get back to the hustings. I don't think votes mean a thing. It is the image the politician creates in his district. In my district they think I am a fighter. I can do anything I want down here and they will say, "He is the greatest fighter we ever had down there." No one pays attention to the votes.

> In my campaign last year I had ten or twelve joint appearances with my opponent and in not a one of them did he criticize a vote I cast. Most of the time he talked about state issues. And the people didn't seem to know which was the state issue and which was the federal issue.

> I don't think issues mean a great deal about whether you win or lose. I think issues give you a chance to [demonstrate] your intellectual capacity. Issues are a vehicle by which voters determine your honesty and candor. I don't think a right or wrong answer on an issue makes up anyone's mind but the ideologues . . .[14]

With its emphasis on rational discussion of political ideas, the exploration of alternative courses of action, and the accountability of office-holders for their policy positions, the theory of representative democracy imposes a heavy burden on both candidates and voters. The obligations of issue politics, ordinarily, are larger than either can meet. In the real world

[13]For evidence on the significance of issues in congressional campaigns, see Huckshorn and Spencer, *The Politics of Defeat*, p. 195; David A. Leuthold, *Electioneering in a Democracy: Campaigns for Congress* (New York: John Wiley & Sons, Inc., 1968), pp. 48–60; Charles O. Jones, "The Role of the Campaign in Congressional Politics," in *The Electoral Process*, eds. M. Kent Jennings and L. Harmon Zeigler (Englewood Cliffs, N.J.: Prentice-Hall, Inc., 1966), pp. 21–41; and Alan L. Clem, *The Making of Congressmen: Seven Campaigns of 1974* (North Scituate, Mass.: Duxbury Press, 1976), pp. 10–11.
[14]The first four statements were made by members of the House of Representatives, drawn from Charles L. Clapp, *The Congressman: His Work as He Sees It* (Washington, D.C.: The Brookings Institution, 1963), pp. 373–74; the last was made by a member of the Senate, taken from the *Congressional Quarterly Weekly Report*, May 4, 1974, p. 1105.

of congressional candidate strategy and voter decisions, issue salience is largely a myth—one that we can easily afford to perpetuate, but nevertheless still a myth.

Fifth, congressional campaigns ordinarily have minimal repercussions for the stability of Congress. The factor of incumbency puts a lid on abrupt institutional change: collectively, congressional challengers have about one in five chances of winning.[15] Put baldly, "the campaign-election period is a time when the incumbent is re-elected—returned to office to represent as he has in the past."[16] A primary reason for this is that incumbents campaign all the time. Each election victory signals the opening of the next campaign, to be carried on in Washington and at home. Indeed, many congressmen believe that elections are won in the off-year, as these candid statements show:

> You can slip up on the blind side of people during an off-year and get in much more effective campaigning than you can when you are in the actual campaign.

> I have the feeling that the most effective campaigning is done when no election is near. During the interval between elections you have to establish every personal contact you can, and you accomplish this through your mail as much as you do it by means of anything else. At the end of each session I take all the letters which have been received on legislative matters and write each person telling him how the legislative proposal in which he was interested stands. Personally, I will speak on any subject. I am not nonpartisan, but I talk on everything whether it deals with politics or not. Generally I speak at nonpolitical meetings. I read 48 weekly newspapers and clip every one of them myself. Whenever there is a particularly interesting item about anyone, that person gets a note from me . . . [You] cannot let the matter of election go until the last minute.

> There is nothing like going home after the session and making personal reports to the people. Last time I made 173 personal appearances. I go before anybody who will listen to me, before groups of one hundred to seven hundred, to a candy pulling or a county fair. I have been doing that for ten years and in that time have made over 1,200 reports to the people. It is by far the most effective thing I do.[17]

Finally, all candidates for Congress are met by three overarching problems of *organization, strategy,* and *finances.* The weakness of party organizations in most jurisdictions has led to the development of candidate-centered campaign organizations. Increasingly these personal organizations are directed by professional campaign management firms that offer a

---

[15]Jeff Fishel, *Party and Opposition: Congressional Challengers in American Politics* (New York: David McKay Company, Inc., 1973), p. 3.

[16]Jones, "The Role of the Campaign in Congressional Politics," p. 38.

[17]The quotations are taken from Clapp, *The Congressman: His Work as He Sees It,* pp. 331, 332, and 382.

wide variety of services to the candidate. For a fee, candidates can hire firms that have experts on public opinion polling, voter behavior, fund raising, advertising, speech writing, issue development, precinct organization, media selection, television coaching, strategy formulation, film making, and voter canvassing. The planning and execution of a congressional campaign can, in a word, be turned over to professional managers. So firmly institutionalized is this activity today that there are some campaign management firms that cater only to Democratic candidates and others that contract only with Republican candidates. And there are still others that work both sides of the street.[18]

Congressional campaign strategies are of such variety as to elude any systematic form of description. Variance in strategies results from such factors as the qualities of the candidate himself, the distribution of party identification in the district (or state), the level of inter-party competitiveness, the character of the electorate, the vitality and unity of the party organization, the nature of group support (or opposition), the ideological stance and visibility of the opponent, the availability of campaign resources (particularly money and manpower), the election timetable (for example, presidential or off-year election), the state of the economy,[19] and, most important of all, the presence or absence of an incumbent.

The important point about these conditions is that, for the most part, they are beyond the control of the individual candidate. Thus no candidate, however imaginative, is ever able to invoke a full range of strategies. Rather, what he does is sharply circumscribed by political, social, and economic constraints that give his district (or state) its distinctiveness.

The lesser facts about campaign strategy may be fused into three broad propositions. The candidate first seeks to *reinforce party supporters*—that is, to induce those voters who regularly support candidates of his party to turn out at the polls. This is by all odds the most important requirement. The second strategy is to *activate latent support* among those voters who participate erratically but belong to groups and social categories that are generally disposed to support the candidate's party. The third is to *change the opposition,* to lure away partisans of the other party. The prospects for gaining the support of these three categories of voters fall in the same order as shown, dictating in most campaigns that the candidate concentrate his resources on mobilizing supporters and latent supporters instead of ap-

[18]See a comprehensive analysis of professional campaign management firms in Robert Agranoff, *The New Style in Election Campaigns* (Boston: Holbrook Press, Inc., 1972).

[19]Whether the national economy is sluggish or buoyant in the pre-election period has a clear effect on congressional election outcomes. Congressional incumbents of the party controlling the administration have good reason to be apprehensive if the economy is doing poorly as the election approaches. Some members representing marginal districts will be swept out of office. See Edward R. Tufte, *Political Control of the Economy* (Princeton, N.J.: Princeton University Press, 1978), especially Chapter 5.

pealing to outward and probable opponents. For candidates of the minority party in the electorate, obviously the conversion of opponents holds a greater urgency in the design of campaigns.[20]

This analysis may be summarized as follows: The constraints that shape and define campaigns make strategy development a study in political feasibility rather than a blueprint for winning office. There are only proximate solutions to the problems of mounting an effective campaign for Congress. Those candidates who are most likely to discover them, and who are best poised to use them, are the incumbents. Congressional challengers cannot bank on a large and attentive public audience. No matter how tirelessly they transmit their messages, much of what they say is lost on a public preoccupied with other things. Taking congressional campaigns as a whole, relatively few surprises occur on election day. Candidates win where they are expected to win and lose where they are expected to lose. As one writer has put it, "The behavior of the candidates during the campaign is one of the least influential factors in determining electoral outcomes."[21]

Financing Congressional Campaigns

No problem involving the machinery of American politics has been harder to solve than the financing of elections. Money is the "mother's milk" of politics, and no participant can get very far without it. Candidates rarely feel their campaign coffers are adequate. They wonder where they can acquire more funds, and they worry over how much they should accept and from whom they should accept them. For its part, the public wonders whether those individuals, groups, and families who contribute heavily to political campaigns are gaining unusual preferments from government, and it worries over the corruptive influence of money in politics. The wonder and worry are well-placed. The sleazy affair of Watergate that toppled the Nixon presidency has made the subject of campaign money a major concern in contemporary American politics.

Nothing about political money is simple and direct. Nor is the passage of legislation to regulate it. Following the disclosures of illegal contributions in the 1972 campaign—a central theme of Watergate—Congress finally passed the Federal Election Campaign Act of 1974.[22] Its

---

[20]Lewis A. Froman, Jr., "A Realistic Approach to Campaign Strategies and Tactics," in *The Electoral Process*, eds. M. Kent Jennings and L. Harmon Zeigler (Englewood Cliffs, N.J.: Prentice-Hall, Inc., 1966), especially pp. 5–11.

[21]*Ibid.*, p. 4.

[22]See accounts of illegal contributions, the "laundering" of funds, and the money hustle of 1972 in Herbert E. Alexander, *Financing Politics: Money, Elections and Political Reform* (Washington, D.C.: Congressional Quarterly Press, 1976), pp. 112–26; and William J. Crotty, *Political Reform & the American Experiment* (New York: Thomas Y. Crowell Company, 1977), pp. 139–67.

most notable features were its provisions for partial public funding of the presidential nominating process (through the allocation of matching federal funds) and for full funding of the presidential election campaigns of the major parties.

Among its many provisions regulating campaign contributions, expenditures, and reporting were several of major importance concerning Congress. First, the law placed limits on the *personal expenditures* of candidates for Congress: $35,000 for Senate candidates and $25,000 for House candidates. Second, it placed limits on the *total expenditures* of Senate and House candidates in both primaries and general elections. Senate candidates were limited to $100,000, or 8 cents per eligible voter (whichever is greater), in primaries and $150,000, or 12 cents per eligible voter (whichever is greater), in general elections—except that certain fundraising costs (up to twenty percent of the spending limit) could be added to these amounts. Candidates for the House were limited to $70,000 in primaries and $70,000 in general elections. Including allowance for fundraising outlays, the effective expenditure total for House candidates was $84,000 for each election. Third, the law provided that the national party organizations could spend $10,000 on behalf of each candidate for the House and $20,000, or 2 cents per eligible voter, on behalf of each Senate candidate. No provision was made for public financing of congressional campaigns.

To no one's surprise, the constitutionality of the law was challenged on the ground that it violated the rights of free speech and free association as protected by the First Amendment. In *Buckley v. Valeo*, decided in early 1976, the Supreme Court ruled that limits on individual expenditures constituted a substantial impairment of political speech and were therefore unconstitutional.[23] Hence, neither limitations on the personal expenditures nor on the total expenditures of candidates were in effect for the 1976 congressional elections. The result was an explosion in spending in congressional races. In large part this occurred because the presidential election was financed primarily by public funds. Individual donors and special interest groups, shut out of the presidential campaign and looking for places to put their money, contributed heavily to congressional campaigns.

The evidence of growing interest group involvement in financing congressional campaigns is impressive. In 1972 interest groups contributed less than $7 million to congressional campaigns; in 1974 their contributions totaled $12.5 million; and in 1976 they rose to $22.5 million, almost double that of 1974. The leading group contributors in 1976 were the American Medical Association and its political committees ($1.8 million), agriculture and dairy groups ($1.4 million), the AFL-CIO Committee on Political Education ($1 million), and maritime-related unions (nearly

$1 million). Altogether, business, health, and agricultural interests contributed over $11 million to congressional campaigns, while various labor unions contributed about $8 million.[24]

There are four main things to be known about interest group contributions to congressional campaigns. First, candidates of both parties profit from it. Second, in making contributions to congressional candidates, interest groups do not invoke strict standards of ideological purity. Political committees representing business interest groups frequently make contributions to Democratic incumbents, and the contributions may be sizable. Less commonly, political committees of labor unions make contributions to some Republicans. Contributions are targeted. Groups are most likely to give to members who sit on committees whose jurisdictions affect their interests. Third, incumbents receive vastly more in contributions from organized groups than do challengers, probably on the order of twice as much.[25] And fourth, incumbents who occupy key positions, such as a committee chairmanship or membership on a major committee, are the leading beneficiaries of interest group largesse. In 1976 the members of the Senate Finance and House Ways and Means Committees averaged $42,000 in campaign contributions from interest groups representing business, labor, and professional associations—a sum about sixty-five percent more than contributed by these groups to the average Senate and House candidate. Several senators received between $100,000 and $200,000 in special interest group contributions.[26]

A number of factors influence how much money is spent in a congressional campaign, including the geography and size of the district (rural or urban), the competitive position of the parties, the strength of the overall ticket (of particular importance in presidential election years), the strength of the opponent, the utility of television and the disposition of candidates to rely on it, the availability of volunteers and interest group supporters, the attitudes of the candidates toward campaign spending, the presence of an open seat (which typically stimulates heavy spending), and of course the availability of campaign funds. Candidates spend as much as they do

---

[24]See Common Cause's *Frontline*, November–December, 1976, p. 3, and *Congressional Quarterly Weekly Report*, April 16, 1977, pp. 707–713.

[25]Crotty, *Political Reform & the American Experiment*, p. 114; and Alexander, *Financing Politics*, pp. 224–25. Also consult a study which finds that money spent by congressional challengers has a much larger effect on election outcomes than money spent by incumbents. What campaign money buys for nonincumbents is voter recognition. Gary C. Jacobson, "The Effects of Campaign Spending in Congressional Elections," *American Political Science Review*, 72 (June 1978), 469–91.

[26]*New York Times*, March 7, 1977. For data concerning interest group contributions to Senate committee chairmen, see the *New York Times*, January 16, 1977. Fourteen major committee chairmen in the Senate received about $900,000 in campaign contributions from interest groups in 1976; this was about twenty percent of the funds which they spent to win reelection.

because they are never certain of the best strategies for winning votes. Conflicts between spending priorities can be resolved, if the treasury is sufficiently large, by spending on virtually everything.

Campaign spending is difficult to bring into focus. It seeps into the political process at every opening in every jurisdiction. A general idea of its magnitude and variability is available in the spending reports of candidates for Congress in 1976. On an average, major party candidates for the House of Representatives spent about $80,000 on their campaigns, including primaries. The members of the Senate Finance Committee spent an average of about $450,000 on their primary and general election campaigns. Some campaigns were much more expensive. According to the Federal Election Commission, fifteen candidates for the House spent in excess of $250,000 in their campaigns; in one California district the combined expenditures of the two major party candidates exceeded $1 million. In Pennsylvania the Senate candidates together spent over $4 million, while in New York and California the total Senate campaign expenditures surpassed $3 million. The loophole created by the Supreme Court decision permitted wealthy candidates to spend unlimited sums in their campaigns. H. John Heinz III spent over $2 million of personal funds in his successful race for the Senate in Pennsylvania. Senator William Proxmire of Wisconsin won reelection with campaign expenditures of only $1,800.[27]

For reasons numerous and complex, popular confidence in American political institutions is at a low point.[28] Although there is no way of knowing whether the public's disenchantment is to be a continuing condition or is merely a phase, it seems plain that the seamy side of campaign finance is an important explanation for the widespread uneasiness over politics and politicians. The problem is one to which public policy can be addressed. Some of the mystery can be removed from campaign finance. Some unsavory private dealings can be eliminated. One approach would be to apply the principle of public financing to congressional elections.

Inside Electioneering

Congress is exceptionally hospitable to the individual member's quest for reelection. It may be extravagant to argue that Congress is under the thumb of the individual member, but it is not awkward to argue that the member steadily uses (or exploits) the institution to serve his reelection goal. Nothing surprising appears in this. Successful politicians have always

---

[27]The data on campaign spending are drawn from the *Congressional Quarterly Weekly Report*, October 29, 1977, pp. 2299–2311; and the *New York Times*, March 7, 1977.

[28]See, for example, Arthur H. Miller, "Political Issues and Trust in Government: 1964–1970," *American Political Science Review*, 68 (September 1974), 951–72; and Jack Dennis, "Trends in Support for the American Party System," *British Journal of Political Science*, 5 (April 1975), 187–230.

shown a keen sense of where the best opportunities lie for gaining advantage in the political system.

The key to understanding the behavior of members of Congress lies in their preoccupation with remaining in office. Congress is a career, not an interlude. To increase the chances of their reelection, members seize upon institutional circumstances and opportunities to gain recognition and approval among their constituents. Three kinds of activities, David R. Mayhew contends, strengthen their "electoral connection."[29]

The first is *advertising*. Countless ways are open to the member for advertising his name and position without resort to the "yellow pages." In advertising, the overall objective is to picture oneself as sincere, concerned, independent, experienced, and responsive. A favorable image among voters can be created in messages, transactions, or encounters that carry no hint of issue content. Name recognition is important. Accordingly, members visit home frequently, prepare newsletters for their constituents, make radio and television appearances, solicit constituent opinions in questionnaires, write columns for newspapers, conduct field hearings in their localities, and give "nonpolitical" speeches to civic associations. Much advertising can be done at public expense.

Credit claiming is the second activity. By its nature, government provides a lot of credit to pass around. The task of the member is to "try to peel off pieces of governmental accomplishment for which he can believably generate a sense of responsibility."[30] Credit is gained by doing "casework" or "running errands" for constituents. Because constituents encounter problems with the federal government, casework has become a central task of members of Congress. There are constituents who want to get out of the armed services, those who are worried about their Social Security benefits, those who want to enter one of the service academies, those who want information, those who want to obtain a federal contract, and so on. They contact their representatives, their requests generating opportunities for members to settle problems and to earn credit.

Similarly, credit can be earned by members who can "bring home the bacon"—in the form, for example, of construction projects (post offices, dams, river improvements, highways) and defense contracts. Claiming credit for the pleasing things that government does is a way of life for most members.

The third activity is *position taking*. Roll call votes are one form of position taking. Ordinarily more important are the judgmental statements that members make:

---

[29]The analysis in this section is based on David R. Mayhew, *Congress: The Electoral Connection* (New Haven: Yale University Press, 1974), particularly pp. 49–77.
[30]*Ibid.*, p. 53.

As a newly elected U.S. Representative from Allegheny County, I want to let the people know how I am dealing with [the] proposed congressional pay raise of $12,875 a year. I oppose the pay raise for a number of reasons: It is too big. The average citizen's yearly earnings are less than the amount of the raise . . . The sacrifices needed to hold down costs and stop inflation must start with public officials if others are to be asked to join in. If we are to have government by the people, salaries of our representatives must not be way out of line with those of the people.[31]

I do not believe that President Carter's decision to grant full, complete and unconditional pardons for tens of thousands of Vietnam-era draft evaders will bring the Nation together. Rather, I fear it will have a divisive effect among our citizenry. I have been and continue to be opposed to amnesty. In my opinion, the granting of amnesty to draft evaders and deserters cannot be justified when thousands of other Americans have served in military duty, in many cases at great sacrifice, great suffering, and all too often with the loss of life. I believe the President's action to be ill-timed and unjustified.[32]

"The congressman as a position taker is a speaker rather than a doer," Mayhew observes. "The electoral requirement is not that he make pleasing things happen but that he make pleasing judgmental statements. The position itself is the political commodity."[33]

The broad point of these paragraphs is that members, supported by their staffs, search steadily for ways to win the next election. Congress is there to help them. They use public business to distribute private and local side benefits. And they do it with exceptional skill. By imaginatively exploiting their institutional position, the vast majority of members have insulated themselves from the risks and vicissitudes of elections.

ELECTORAL PROCESSES AND OUTCOMES

Congressional Nominations

The congressional nominating process is not distinguished for turbulence. Taking the country as a whole, the chances that a congressional challenger can defeat an incumbent in a primary election are slight. Of those House members who seek reelection, typically less than two percent lose at the primary stage. The risks for senators are greater, but still are not high—only about seven percent have lost primary elections in recent years.[34] Among those senators who lose, a disproportionate number are

[31]*Pittsburgh Press*, January 30, 1977.
[32]*Congressional Record*, 95th Cong., 1st sess., January 25, 1977, p. S 1347. (Daily edition.)
[33]Mayhew, *Congress: The Electoral Connection*, p. 62.
[34]For additional data, see William J. Keefe, *Parties, Politics, and Public Policy in America* (Hinsdale, Ill.: The Dryden Press, 1976), p. 39.

southern Democrats. It continues to be true that the only rigorous competition for Senate seats in some southern states occurs in the Democratic primary; whoever wins here usually wins the general election. As the Republican party gains strength in the South, the importance of the region's Democratic primaries should diminish.

Of the many things that might be said about the congressional nominating process, three are especially important. First, one rarely sees queues of voters waiting to case their ballots in primary elections. Many voters simply ignore them. Only about one-fourth of the eligible electorate will turn out to vote in a typical congressional primary. Second, many nominations are won by default. In the case of the majority party, prospective challengers choose not to file because their prospects of defeating an incumbent appear so slim; in the case of the minority party, prospective candidates stay out because their prospects appear so slim in the general election. And third, about the only evidence that primary candidates are members of a *national* political party is that found on stray bumper stickers and the party row on the ballot.

Almost everything about congressional nominations is peculiarly local and idiosyncratic. The candidates who run, the issues they discuss, the campaign styles they adopt, the ideologies they profess—all bear personal and local imprints. Enforced in primaries, congressional localism is worth knowing about because it is a major explanation for party disunity in Congress. The candidate who wins the primary is the party's nominee. National party leaders, including the president, know better than to interfere in congressional primaries by supporting one candidate over another. No matter how much a candidate's political philosophy may depart from that of his party's, no one can do anything about it except the people. They rarely do. American voters have long had a warm spot for the party maverick.

Popular Turnout
in Congressional Elections

There are substantial differences between states in the extent to which voters cast ballots for congressional candidates. In northern states it is common to find districts in which more than 200,000 votes are cast in presidential years for the two major party candidates for the House of Representatives; in certain southern states the total vote may not reach much above 125,000. Similarly, there are great variations between states in the number of votes received by the winning candidate. As a rule, winning northern candidates amass far more votes than winning southern candidates. These regional differences in participation, shown in Table 2.2, are due mainly to the greater degree of inter-party competitiveness in northern

Table 2.2   Average Vote Cast for Both Major Party Candidates and Average Winning
Vote, All Contested House Elections, Selected States, 1976

State	Average Vote Cast for Both Major Party Candidates	Average Vote of Winning Candidate
Minnesota	222,716	149,923
Wisconsin	221,567	143,814
Iowa	205,586	123,952
Colorado	196,594	111,143
Massachusetts	183,445	112,610
Kansas	177,263	109,819
Pennsylvania	176,431	112,350
Alabama	158,973	103,092
Mississippi	134,115	101,188
Georgia	136,990	92,283
South Carolina	130,673	80,183

Source: The election data on which this table is based were drawn from the *Congressional Quarterly Weekly Report*, November 6, 1976, pp. 3147-54.

districts, to the demographic character of their populations, and to the existence of election laws (such as election-day voter registration) that facilitate voting.

Turnout in off-year congressional elections is unusually poor. The most important fact to be known about these elections is that large numbers of citizens do not take part in them. In a typical off-year congressional election well under one-half of the *eligible* voters will cast ballots. In 1974 and 1978, turnout fell below forty percent. The importance of Congress to their lives is thus missed by considerably more than half of the American people in nonpresidential years. As everyone knows, participation statistics are not a great deal more impressive even when a president is to be elected.

Congressional Elections:
Who Wins? Why?

When both houses of Congress are captured by the Democrats, the results are insouciantly described as normal. This is not a law of nature, but it is a law of contemporary politics. Since 1932 the Democratic party has controlled Congress for all but a handful of years in the late 1940s and early 1950s and continuously since 1955.

The Democrats regularly win control of Congress because they are the majority party in the electorate. At times in recent years the proportion of individuals identifying themselves as Democrats has been *twice* as large as the proportion identifying themselves as Republicans. The Democratic edge is reduced, however, by the lower rate of turnout among Democratic identifiers. Even so, the normal vote expectation in congressional elections, based on party identification in the nation, favors the Democrats by a comfortable margin of about fifty-four to forty-six percent. The actual popular vote, moreover, has deviated as much as five percent from the expected normal vote in only one election since 1952,[35] that of 1974 when Republican support declined sharply in the wake of the Watergate scandal. The nationwide vote for congressional candidates is a good measure of the relative strength of the parties among the voters.

The stability of the congressional vote has suffered some decline. In the off-year election of 1958, only eight percent of party identifiers defected from their party to vote for a Senate candidate of the other party and only ten percent defected in House elections. In 1970, the defectors numbered eighteen percent in Senate elections and fifteen percent in House elections; in 1974, the percentages were sixteen and eighteen, respectively. The rate of defections in the mid-1970s was thus about twice as great as it was in the late 1950s.[36] This trend in congressional voting is of course consistent with the general erosion of party in the electorate. It remains an impressive fact, however, that eighty percent or more of partisans vote for congressional candidates of their own party in off-year elections and usually in presidential years as well.

Ticket-splitting by the American electorate has nevertheless increased dramatically in recent years as the linkage between the parties and their supporters has weakened. One measure of the decline of partisanship appears in Table 2.3. It shows the proportion of congressional districts in which one party wins the presidential vote while the other wins the congressional vote. Split election outcomes, the result of substantial ticket-splitting, are far more numerous today than they were a generation ago. In 1972, in the midst of the overwhelming rejection of the Democratic presidential candidate, George McGovern, split results occurred in forty-four percent of the nation's congressional districts. Increasingly, the party-oriented voter is being replaced by the candidate-oriented voter—especially at the presidential level.

The Competitiveness of
Congressional Elections

The caprices of popular choice are nowhere less evident than in congressional elections. It is an illusion that either major party can win any

[35]Warren E. Miller and Teresa E. Levitin, *Leadership & Change: The New Politics and the American Electorate* (Cambridge, Mass.: Winthrop Publishers, Inc., 1976), p. 40.

[36]Norman H. Nie, Sidney Verba, and John R. Petrocik, *The Changing American Voter* (Cambridge, Mass.: Harvard University Press, 1976), pp. 50–51. Also consult David Knoke, *Change and Continuity in American Politics* (Baltimore: The Johns Hopkins University Press, 1976), pp. 141–45.

given election for the House or the Senate. Quite the contrary, the outcome of the typical election can be predicted before the first campaign speech is made or before the candidates are nominated. With some allowance for hyperbole, the only surprise most congressional candidates encounter on election day is the weather.

Table 2.3   Congressional Districts with Split Election Results: Districts Carried by a Presidential Nominee of One Party and by a House Nominee of Another Party, 1920-1976

Year and Party of the Winning Presidential Candidate	Number of Districts	Number of Districts with Split Results	Percent
1920R	344	11	3.2
1924R	356	42	11.8
1928R	359	68	18.9
1932D	355	50	14.1
1936D	361	51	14.1
1940D	362	53	14.6
1944D	367	41	11.2
1948D	422	90	21.3
1952R	435	84	19.3
1956R	435	130	29.9
1960D	437	114	26.1
1964D	435	145	33.3
1968R	435	141	32.4
1972R	435	193	44.4
1976D	435	124	28.5
Total	5973	1337	22.4

Source: Milton C. Cummings, Jr., *Congressmen and the Electorate* (New York: Macmillan Publishing Co., Inc., 1966), p. 32, as updated. Presidential returns for some congressional districts were not available between 1920 and 1948. See also an analysis that expands the Cummings study: Charles M. Tidmarch and Douglas Carpenter, "Congressmen and the Electorate, 1968 and 1972," *Journal of Politics*, 40 (May 1978), 479-87.

A clear majority of congressional seats are comfortably safe—if not for the party at least for the incumbent. It is a rare election in which as much as one-fifth of the 435 House seats are won by relatively close margins—that is, by less than fifty-five percent of the vote. Marginal congressional districts thus number well under 100—sometimes as few as 65, as in 1976. As Table 2.4 shows, there is a remarkably large bloc of relatively, even overwhelmingly, safe districts. "Super-safe" districts vastly outnumber "super-close" districts. Uncontested elections, the epitome of safety, are by no means uncommon. Senate elections are somewhat, but not markedly, more competitive.

Table 2.4   The Competitiveness of Congressional Elections

	Super-Close	Marginal	Safe	Super-Safe	Uncontested
House	6%	9%	28%	50%	7%
Senate	7	19	58	9	7

Source: The data are for the 1976 election, drawn from the *Congressional Quarterly Weekly Report*, November 6, 1976, pp. 3147-54. Elections are defined as follows: super-close, won by less than 52 percent of the vote; marginal, won by 52-54.9 percent of the vote; safe, won by 55-64.9 percent of the vote; super-safe, won by 65 percent or more of the vote.

The success rate of incumbents is striking.[37] (See Table 2.5). It is quite common for ninety percent or more of the incumbent House members seeking reelection to win. Senators running for reelection fare almost as well. The reason that most members of Congress worry about their re-election is that they can remember a close call, probably early in their congressional career and perhaps in a primary. Reelection to Congress for most members is like removing olives from a bottle—after the first, the rest come easy. In all truth, close elections for most incumbents are more psychological than objective threat.

Members of Congress begin each reelection campaign with advantages so great as to reach the edge of embarrassment. All have gained at least the beginnings of reputation. Their names are recognized by many constituents who have seen them on television, heard them on the radio, read about them in the newspapers, and perhaps even met them at civic meetings. Some constituents have been the beneficiaries of "casework"—all those activities in which members serve as friendly brokers for citizens in their dealings with the federal bureaucracy.[38]

---

[37]There are various ways of defining the safeness of House and Senate seats, but the net conclusion is the same: they have become increasingly safe for incumbents. Between 1956 and 1974, Albert D. Cover and David R. Mayhew have shown, the proportion of House incumbents winning *at least 60 percent* of the major party vote was never less than 58.5 percent (1964). In 1970, 77.3 percent of the incumbents won by 60 percent or more; in 1972, 77.8 percent; and in 1974, 66.4 percent. Between 1970 and 1974, 44 percent of all Senate incumbents won reelection by at least 60 percent of the major party vote; this overall percentage has not changed much over the last three decades. But significant internal changes have occurred. Fewer southern incumbents now win by lopsided margins, but many more northern incumbents do. "Congressional Dynamics and the Decline of Competitive Congressional Elections," in *Congress Reconsidered*, eds. Lawrence C. Dodd and Bruce I. Oppenheimer (New York: Praeger Publishers, 1977), pp. 55–56.

[38]A nationwide survey by Louis Harris and Associates in 1977 disclosed that fifteen percent of American families had requested some kind of assistance from a member of Congress or his staff. Of equal interest, more than two-thirds of those who had sought assistance were satisfied with the way their requests were handled. *Final Report of the Commission on Administrative Review*, U.S. House of Representatives, 95th Cong., 1st sess., 1977, vol. 2 of 2, pp. 830–31.

Table 2.5   The Advantage of Incumbency in House and Senate Elections, 1956-76

Year	Defeated in Primary	Running in General Election	Elected in General Election	Defeated in General Election	Percentage of Incumbents Running in General Election Elected
		Total Number of Incumbents			*Percentage of Incumbents Running in General Election Elected*
1956					
House	6	404	389	51	96.29
Senate	0	28	25	3	89.29
1958					
House	3	393	355	38	90.33
Senate	0	31	20	11	64.52
1960					
House	6	400	374	26	93.50
Senate	0	29	28	1	96.55
1962					
House	12	396	381	22	94.34
Senate	1	34	29	5	85.29
1964					
House	5	389	344	45	88.43
Senate	1	32	28	4	87.50
1966					
House	11	402	362	40	90.05
Senate	3	29	28	1	96.55
1968					
House	3	401	396	5	98.75
Senate	4	24	20	4	83.33
1970					
House	7	391	379	12	96.93
Senate	1	29	23	6	79.31
1972					
House	13	380	367	13	96.58
Senate	2	25	20	5	80.00
1974					
House	8	383	343	40	89.56
Senate	2	25	23	2	92.00
1976					
House	3	381	368	13	96.59
Senate	0	25	16	9	64.00

Source: Congressional Quarterly Weekly Report, March 25, 1978, p. 755.

Members exploit their position to the hilt. To report on their accomplishments, they use the franking privilege to send mail to constituents, including questionnaires that elicit their views on public problems. A large allowance permits members to hire a staff that, among other things, tends steadily and imaginatively to reelection business.

Even the most ingenuous members know what it takes to get elected, how to assemble political talent, where to locate campaign money and workers, how to orchestrate the media, how to activate interest-group support, how to establish indebtedness, how to create a winning image—in short, how to win. As many members have noted in candid moments, there is really no excuse for losing. The congressional system was designed by winners for the benefit of winners.

Rigorous inter-party competition for congressional seats is now at about its lowest point in the twentieth century.[39] It is not easy to weigh all the diverse factors that account for this, but reasonable hypotheses can be adduced. One explanation is that Democratic and Republican state legislators increasingly cooperate to insure the longevity of incumbents: they draw congressional district lines (along with their own) in such a way as to create as many safe seats as possible.[40] Incumbent congressmen of both parties obviously prefer this solution when confronted by redistricting. David Mayhew suggests that incumbents may have become more adept in "advertising" their names, in "claiming credit" for federal governmental programs that have a favorable impact on their districts, and in "position taking" on salient issues among their constituents. Finally, it may be that competition has declined because voters now attach more importance to incumbency than to party affiliation in casting their ballots.[41] Whatever the explanation, members of Congress now are almost as secure in their positions as tenured professors—a fact that may at least give students some pause.

Southern Republicanism

Until recently Republicans found it futile to challenge Democrats for southern House and Senate seats. From the late nineteenth century until midway through the twentieth, the South voted solidly Democratic—in both congressional and presidential elections. The "real" election in the

[39]See Charles O. Jones, "Inter-Party Competition for Congressional Seats," *Western Political Quarterly*, 17 (September 1964), 461–76; and Charles Bullock III, "Redistricting and Congressional Stability, 1962–72," *Journal of Politics*, 37 (May 1975), 575.

[40]Edward R. Tufte, "The Relationship Between Seats and Votes in Two-Party Systems," *American Political Science Review*, 67 (June 1973), 551; and "Determinants of the Outcomes of Midterm Congressional Elections," *American Political Science Review*, 69 (September 1975), 812–26.

[41]David R. Mayhew, "Congressional Elections: The Case of the Vanishing Marginals," *Polity*, 6 (Spring 1974), 295–317. Agreement on the explanations for the decline in marginal seats is lacking. See also analyses by John A. Ferejohn, "On the Decline in Competition in Congressional Elections," *American Political Science Review*, 71 (March 1977), 166–76; Morris P. Fiorina, "The Case of the Vanishing Marginals: The Bureaucracy Did It," *American Political Science Review*, 71 (March 1977), 177–81; Albert D. Cover, "One Good Term Deserves Another: The Advantage of Incumbency in Congressional Elections," *American Journal of Political Science*, 21 (August 1977), 523–41; and Warren Lee Kostrowski, "Party and Incumbency in Postwar Senate Elections," *American Political Science Review*, 67 (December 1973), 1213–234.

South took place in Democratic primaries—whoever won the Democratic nomination was largely assured of victory in November. Often Democratic congressional candidates won without Republican opposition.

All this has changed. The appeal of Republican presidential candidates, beginning with Dwight D. Eisenhower, has helped to make the party respectable throughout the confederacy. Although the Republican party fielded candidates in only about one-fourth of the southern congressional districts in the 1950s, it now offers candidates in about three-fourths of them. And it wins with growing frequency. In recent Congresses, about twenty-five percent of the southern contingent have been Republicans. Winning a congressional seat in states such as Georgia and Texas is still difficult for the Republican party, but in certain states of the upper South, such as Virginia, it has become commonplace.

A leading obstacle to Republican victories in the South is incumbency. Few Democratic officeholders are turned out of office in general elections. But when a "sitting" Democrat dies or retires, it is another matter. With no Democratic incumbent in the race, Republican chances improve dramatically. The party now wins about four out of ten such elections.[42] The long-run prospects for Republican congressional candidates in the South would appear to be excellent.

Presidential Influence on Congressional Elections

Every four years all members of the House and one-third of the Senate are confronted by an event that will benefit some and cost others: the presidential election. For some members of Congress, ordinarily not a large number,[43] control over their destinies comes to rest momentarily in the hands of their party's presidential candidate. A popular presidential candidate will gain votes for congressional candidates they ordinarily would not receive while a less popular presidential candidate will cost them votes they ordinarily would receive. This intrusion on normality occurs most often in those states whose ballots facilitate straight-ticket voting.

[42]Richard G. Hutcheson III, "The Inertial Effect of Incumbency and Two-Party Politics: Elections to the House of Representatives from the South, 1952–1974," *American Political Science Review*, 69 (December 1975), 1399–1401.

[43]In the 1976 presidential election, for example, only 22 of the 292 Democrats elected to the House ran behind Jimmy Carter in their district. Only one of the 21 Democrats who won Senate seats trailed Carter in his state. By contrast, in 1972 Richard Nixon ran stronger than winning Republican House candidates in 104 out of 192 districts. *Congressional Quarterly Weekly Report,* April 22, 1978, p. 971.

Safe-seat members are not greatly affected by the popularity of the presidential candidates. Their vote may slide up or down, reflecting in some measure the presidential vote, but their reelection is not often threatened. Members from closely competitive districts or states, on the other hand, are especially vulnerable to the spillover produced by straight-ticket voting. These are the members who worry the most about the response to their presidential ticket. They are the Republicans from northern marginal districts with Barry Goldwater as their presidential nominee in 1964 and the Democrats from marginal districts everywhere with George McGovern as their presidential nominee in 1972. Members who anticipate their party's presidential candidate is likely to fare poorly in their areas try to stake out their independence, edging or scrambling away from his campaign. When "dealignment" fails, some are sure to lose.

The president's cold hands are present even in midterm elections. Again it is the marginals who feel them. A loss of congressional seats by the president's party at midterm is virtually certain. Only once in the twentieth century has the party in control of the administration gained seats in an off-year election; this occurred in 1934 when the Democratic party's New Deal was gaining momentum. As often as not, the losses are severe, though it is rare to have a shift of party majorities in either house. Of recent interest, the Republican party lost forty-seven House seats and thirteen Senate seats in 1958, the Democratic party forty-seven House seats and three Senate seats in 1966, and the Republican party forty-three House seats and four Senate seats in 1974. In 1978, by contrast, the Democrats lost only twelve seats in the House and three in the Senate.

Midterm losses are not produced by chance. They occur as the electorate, no longer tilted by the presidential contest, returns to its normal partisan equilibrium. The most interesting question concerns the extent of the administration party's losses. Why are losses great in some cases and minimal in others? The answer is that it depends—it depends on the popularity of the president at the time of the election and the performance of the economy in the year of the election. If the public awards high marks on one or both counts, the losses are apt to be minimal. If the president's prestige is sagging or if the economy is floundering, or both, the losses are apt to be severe.[44]

The individual member of Congress cannot do much about these conditions.[45] He lives with them, more a hostage than anything else. If he is a newcomer to Congress or if he represents a marginal district—worse yet, both—his chances of being returned to Washington are diminished.

---

[44]Tufte, "Determinants of the Outcomes of Midterm Elections," 812–26.
[45]See Mayhew, *Congress: The Electoral Connection*, especially pp. 28–31.

THE MEMBERS OF CONGRESS

Social Background Characteristics

In certain ways Congress is not especially representative. Little resembling a cross-section of the population, its membership is distinctly middle and upper class in origin. Indeed, the reflections of elevated social class appear in all the background characteristics that describe the members.

Consider the formal education of the members. While only about one-fourth of the adult population of the nation has received some college education, almost all members of Congress have attended college, and a heavy majority are college graduates. Among the latter are a great many who have advanced degrees. Plainly, formal educational attainment ranks very high among the criteria that govern the recruitment, nomination, and election of members of Congress.

The occupations of members (prior to their election) reveal a similar distinctiveness, as shown in Table 2.6. About two-thirds of the members in each house are lawyers. Next most common is business or banking, followed by "public service/politics" and education. Farmers trail a distant fifth.

Table 2.6 The Occupations of Members of Congress (95th Congress)

| | House | | Senate | | |
Occupation	Dem.	Rep.	Dem.	Rep.	Total
Law	155	68	46	22	291
Business or Banking	69	49	14	10	142
Public Service/Politics	34	26	12	14	86
Education	57	15	8	4	84
Agriculture	6	10	3	6	25
Journalism	10	4	3	1	18
Law Enforcement	7	0	0	0	7
Clergyman	4	2	0	1	7
Labor Leader	6	0	0	0	6
Medicine	1	1	1	0	3
Scientist	2	0	0	1	3
Engineering	0	2	0	0	2

Source: Congressional Quarterly Weekly Report, January 1, 1977, p. 20. (As adapted.) The totals exceed the membership of Congress because some members list more than one occupation.

The predominance of lawyers in Congress is understandable. Law and politics are inextricably mixed in American society. With its emphasis on the mastery of complex and technical information, the study of law is particularly appropriate training for the role of policy-maker. Moreover, lawyers are steadily engaged in the representation of individual and organized interests in society, leading them to frequent interactions with governmental agencies. Finally, few careers provide comparable flexibility; unlike most other occupations, a lawyer can take time to run for public office without abandoning his practice.

The unrepresentativeness of Congress is shown in another important respect. Women and blacks have never held representation in Congress in proportion to their numbers in the population. Only seventeen women and sixteen blacks, for example, served in the Ninety-sixth Congress (1979–80). Winning a seat in the Senate has been especially difficult for both groups.

Congress is not an assembly of average people. It is composed of successful politicians who are drawn disproportionately from the elite sectors of the social structure. Nonetheless, it is far from obvious that their backgrounds shape their outlook on public policy questions, leading them to use their positions to confer unusual benefits on the upper-class interests in society. To put it another way, whatever the real or imagined deficiencies of Congress, no systematic evidence exists that links them to the social-class characteristics of members.

Changes in Congressional Membership

The force of incumbency and the strength of the partisan congressional vote in elections serve to brake the rate of turnover in congressional membership. But membership changes do take place, as some incumbents die, retire, or are defeated. Over a number of Congresses the cumulative impact of membership changes can be sizable.[46]

The partisan division in both houses has changed sharply since the 1950s. During the early and middle years of the Eisenhower presidency (1952–60), the parties competed fairly evenly in both houses, though especially in the Senate. Since the landslide congressional vote of 1958, however, the Democrats have held majorities ranging from comfortable to massive in both chambers. In several Congresses during this period the Democrats held well over sixty percent of the seats in Congress, confining the Republicans to a role more like that of spectator than of participant.

A second line of membership changes involves the sectional basis of the congressional parties. During the 1950s the South and the West were the main areas of strength for the Democratic party, while the Midwest and East produced numerous Republican lawmakers. Today all regions of the

---

[46]See the analysis of Norman J. Ornstein, Robert L. Peabody, and David W. Rohde, "The Changing Senate: From the 1950s to the 1970s," in *Congress Reconsidered,* eds. Lawrence C. Dodd & Bruce I. Oppenheimer (New York: Praeger Publishers, 1977), pp. 4–6; and Dodd and Oppenheimer, "The House in Transition," *ibid.,* pp. 23–26.

country produce Democratic majorities. Within this structure of Democratic dominance, however, lies a major change: the declining importance of southern members in the Democratic congressional party. In 1956, for example, southerners constituted forty-nine percent of the Democratic membership of the Senate and forty-seven percent in the House.[47] In 1978, southern members made up only thirty-one percent of the Democratic membership in each house. In part this change results from the growth in southern Republicanism and in part to the heightened successes of Democratic candidates in all sections of the country outside the South. The overall effect of this shift has been to make the Democratic congressional party less conservative.

A third change involves the average age of members. While it is true that committee chairmen are usually in their sixties or seventies, the average age of members of both the Senate and the House has declined steadily in recent years. In the Ninety-fifth Congress (1977–78), the average age of House members was only 46.8—the lowest average age since World War II. Somewhat higher, the average age of senators was 54.6. For Congress as a whole, the average age was only 48.1.[48] The growing successes of younger candidates represent not only an electoral threat to aging members but also a threat to hoary institutional traditions and practices. The restiveness that has characterized Congress in recent years and the continuing drive to reform the institution are clearly associated with the infusion of new and younger members.

The Compensation of Members

The salary of a member of Congress is $57,500—a sum established in 1977. Prior to this raise, members were paid $44,600 a year.

The issue of congressional pay is a baneful matter for members. Each time an effort is made to increase salaries, controversy erupts in the press— at least in the provincial press. In the usual newspaper account, the "pay hikes" are excessive, the members are greedy, and the average citizen is both baffled and outraged by the action. A salary increase is not a "no win" issue for those members who oppose it; quite the contrary, the more vocal their opposition, the more visible their position taking, the more accolades they receive from the media.[49]

---

[47]As defined here, the South includes Alabama, Arkansas, Florida, Georgia, Kentucky, Louisiana, Mississippi, North Carolina, Oklahoma, South Carolina, Tennessee, Texas, and Virginia.
[48]*Congressional Quarterly Weekly Report*, January 1, 1977, p. 19.
[49]Legislators pay careful attention to fashioning strategies for taking unpopular actions. In the matter of pay raises, the best strategy for muting public criticism is to link the raise with some type of legislative reform. Shortly after the 1977 salary increase went into effect, both

Seen in perspective, not in the light of prevailing exaggeration, the salary of members of Congress is not excessive. The costs of congressional office are high. Members ordinarily maintain two residences—one in Washington, one at home. Entertainment expenses, including those for constituents, are heavy. Travel expenses in excess of the congressional travel allowance are common. In addition, most members of Congress are burdened with a wide-ranging assortment of political expenses. They are expected to contribute to the campaigns of their friends and colleagues at all levels of government, to numerous party organizations, and to charities of great variety. The costs of congressional office, nevertheless, have never made much of an impression on critics. The belief that legislators are overpaid has lived long and dies hard.

A catalogue of fringe benefits accompanies membership in Congress. The standard items include life and health insurance, an excellent pension system, and a range of services from a full-time staff of physicians and nurses. The medical benefits include such things as physicals, lab services, physiotherapy, inoculations, and free drugs. In addition, there are literally dozens of other perquisites of congressional office, including subsidized rates in Walter Reed or Bethesda Naval Hospital, bargain prices in the Senate and House restaurants and barber shops, free picture framings, gymnasiums for each house, and the like. As one senator has been quoted on Congress's "election-to-grave" welfare system, "It's an incredible hypocrisy. It's socialism for us and fiscal restraint for the rest of the country."[50]

THE STABILITY OF CONGRESS

Congress is a relatively stable institution. The proportion of new members produced in any one election is ordinarily not large. Even so, there is more turnover today than in the 1950s or 1960s. Interestingly, voluntary retirements account for a growing proportion of the departures from Congress.

Once established in Congress, a member bent on reelection is remarkably hard to dislodge. If he keeps his political fences in repair, he often finds no serious candidates lining up to challenge him. If he is seriously challenged, the odds are stacked in his favor.

Incumbency is the major key to congressional stability. In the case of House members, the districts from which they run may have been shaped

---

houses adopted stricter codes of ethics, placing limits on member's outside income, tightening financial disclosure requirements, and banning the conversion of campaign funds to personal use, among other things. This action eased some of the heat on Congress.

[50]See a four-part series by Robert Shrum, "The Imperial Congress," *Pittsburgh Post Gazette*, May 10–13, 1977. (Quotation from issue of May 11, 1977).

deliberately to keep them in office. For the member of either house, there are the usual advantages: a public record, a greater degree of visibility than that of almost any challenger, a surfeit of opportunities for publicity gathering, a greater name recognition among voters, a record of problem solving for constituents and constituencies, a network of influential elites, an established campaign apparatus, a staff and offices, and the omnipresent franking privilege. With these advantages the wonder is that incumbents ever lose.

The fact that a strong majority of voters cast congressional ballots on the basis of their partisan affiliation gives an advantage to those incumbents whose party holds a majority in the electorate. Interestingly, the erosion of electoral partisanship—the lessening significance of party labels as cues for voting—also works to the benefit of incumbents. Voter defections from their party in congressional elections may of course hurt incumbents as well as help them. But a study of House races between 1958 and 1974 shows that the proportion of defections from the challenger's party (thus favoring the incumbent) has been larger in each instance. The number of pro-incumbent defections has grown over the years. During the 1970s roughly three-fourths of all voter defections occurred in the challenger's party.[51]

The effect of membership stability on Congress as an institution is hard to judge. Undoubtedly there are advantages to having many experienced legislators. But there may be disadvantages as well. Abrupt changes in the thrust of public policy are unlikely. Established members tend to examine public problems within established frameworks. The status quo is difficult to abandon. New ventures are hard to launch. One reason for the lack of public confidence in Congress may be that the public finds the institution slow to respond to new problems and to the intensification of old ones.

---

[51]Cover and Mayhew, "Congressional Dynamics and the Decline of Competitive Congressional Elections," pp. 62–68.

The
Internal
Distribution
of Power

3

Congress is not an easy institution to understand. Great complexity marks its structure, its written and unwritten rules, and its procedures. Its power, moreover, is nowhere assembled. Numerous individuals and units hold keys to congressional power, a fact that makes decisions not only more difficult to reach but also more unpredictable. Because it is an institution with limited hierarchy, all major policies are the product of compromise and accommodation.

This chapter examines the internal distribution of power in Congress, focusing on the committee system, the legislative party organization, and the professional staffs. The decentralization of power owes much to the strength and independence of committees. The congressional party system, in contrast, is the principal force for the centralization of power.

THE COMMITTEE SYSTEM

In the early years of the republic the congressional committee system was of limited significance. "Randomly structured and unsophisticated,"[1] the committee system was distinctly secondary in influence to the chamber as a whole. In the early House, for example, proposals were debated initially in the chamber to reach agreement upon general principles before they were assigned elsewhere, perhaps to an officer of the executive branch instead of

[1]William L. Morrow, *Congressional Committees* (New York: Charles Scribner's Sons, 1969), p. 14.

to a committee, for detailed consideration.[2] Committees functioned more to refine policy proposals than to shape them. During the nineteenth century the committee system often performed as an instrument of the party leadership or of the president. Not until the twentieth century did it become a force in its own right.

Today the main paths along which Congress moves all lead through the committee system. The power that committees have come to wield is not accidental. The legislature needs, first, a relatively efficient way to sift the thousands of proposals that are introduced during each session and, second, a structure designed to satisfy the claims of individual members to a "piece of the action"—a substantial opportunity to influence legislation that bears on their interests, districts, and states. From these perspectives, a powerful committee system serves both institutional and member interests alike.

The volume and complexity of legislation is so great in contemporary Congresses as to make it impossible for the chambers as a whole to deal with it intelligently. What the chambers can do is to respond to committee decisions on legislation—questioning, clarifying, modifying, or rejecting them. Because the earliest decisions taken on legislative proposals are those of the committees, their power to frame alternatives, to work out political as well as technical settlements, is enormous. To some extent, the House and Senate chambers assume the role of a "court of appeal"[3] for committee decisions. Or, put more starkly, "Congress is a collection of committees that come together in a chamber periodically to approve one another's actions."[4]

Committee decisions do not necessarily constitute the last word on legislation, but they do represent the last specialized word. It is the expertise of committee members and the specialization of committees—even more, the specialization of their subcommittees—that make it difficult for the chambers to control them. The years of experience in handling certain kinds of legislation and in dealing with the interest groups that are affected by it give committee members an important advantage in information over non-committee members.[5] This advantage is supported by a widespread inclination among members to defer to the judgments of specialists. Moreover, members do not want to be faced on the floor with numerous

---

[2]Nelson W. Polsby, "The Institutionalization of the U.S. House of Representatives," *American Political Science Review*, 67 (March 1968), 156.

[3]Donald G. Tacheron and Morris K. Udall, *The Job of the Congressman* (Indianapolis: The Bobbs-Merrill Company, Inc., 1966), p. 145.

[4]Clem Miller, *Member of the House* (New York: Charles Scribners Sons, 1962), p. 110.

[5]The expertise of committee members can easily be exaggerated. The "efficient" members of any committee—those who take the leadership in shaping legislation and steering it through to passage—probably number less than a majority of members. See Holbert N. Carroll, *The House of Representatives and Foreign Affairs* (Boston: Little, Brown and Company, 1966), pp. 27–29.

conflicts that the committees have been unable to settle. Hence the committees steadily feel pressure to fashion legislation that draws the greatest range of support from among the contesting interests—in a word, to write legislation that can pass the chamber.

A source of congressional malaise is sometimes said to be the committee system, with its capacity to set its own course and to resist the initiatives of party leaders, the president, or the wishes of the chamber majority. At times, clearly, certain committees are out of step with other major elements of Congress. When a committee decides to "bottle up" legislation—refusing to clear it for floor consideration—it often wins. But it is an exaggeration to contend that committees are free to do anything they choose or that there are no effective controls over their actions.

Richard F. Fenno, Jr., has shown that the behavior of the prestigious money committees of the House—Appropriations and Ways and Means—is steadily influenced by the expectations of House members. In general, House members expect these committees to be *influential* and *responsive*. To meet the first prescription the committees must exercise independent policy judgments, especially in relation to the executive branch, and to reach settlements that will be accepted by the House. In the exercise of its judgment the House Appropriations Committee, for example, operates on the strategic premise of reducing executive budget requests. As described by a former chairman:

> It has long been an unwritten rule of the Committee on Appropriations that the budget estimate is to be taken as the maximum and the efficiency of the subcommittee has been judged—and the chairman of each subcommittee has prided himself on—the amount he was able to cut below the budget.[6]

The display of independent policy judgments by its money committees enhances the strength and autonomy of the House vis-a-vis the rest of government. But the committees are also expected to be responsive to the interests of their House colleagues. Excessive budget-cutting by the Appropriations Committee, for example, will imperil programs that House members, no less perhaps than the executive, desire to see developed or maintained. Hence the second strategic premise of committee members is to provide for adequate funding for executive programs—and as Fenno wryly observes, "the stronger the House member participation in a given policy coalition, the more 'adequate' the funding."[7] In sum, responding to the expectations of House members, the Appropriations Committee seeks to strike a balance between reducing and funding executive budget requests,

---

[6]As quoted by Richard F. Fenno, Jr., *Congressmen in Committees* (Boston: Little, Brown and Company, 1973), p. 48.

[7]*Ibid.*, p. 49. For elaboration of the themes of these paragraphs, see especially Chapters 2 and 3 of *Congressmen in Committees*.

the former to demonstrate its independent influence in money matters, the latter to acknowledge its obligation to interested House members. Its success in divining this balance is reflected by the high "batting average" of its recommendations on the floor.

An effective chamber control—more precisely,. a party caucus control—is found in the process of making committee assignments. In the case of certain prestigious committees, such as Appropriations and Ways and Means in the House, great pains are taken to select "responsible" legislators. These are members who have earned the respect of fellow legislators by their abilities, their understanding of the legislative process, their willingness to cooperate with other members, and their loyalty to the institution. Past performance is the key. In filling vacancies on these committees, the committee-makers show no enthusiasm for members who are uncompromising and who demean the institution and its processes. Their objective is to choose responsible and responsive members as a way of fostering a cooperative relationship between these powerful committees and the chamber.[8]

The ultimate control over committees lies in the chamber's power to amend or defeat their legislation. The committees fare unevenly in this respect. The House Committee on Education and Labor, for example, typically encounters stiff opposition to its proposals on the House floor. Over the period 1955–1966, only fifty-nine percent of its major bills passed the House as compared with ninety-four percent of those recommended by the Ways and Means Committee. One explanation for this is the inherent controversiality of the policy jurisdiction of Education and Labor; it regularly confronts such ideologically-laden subjects as labor-management questions and minimum wage legislation. A second explanation lies in the intensely partisan and ideological makeup of the members. The committee tends to be a jousting ground for liberal Democrats and conservative Republicans. Finally, the committee is a highly permeable committee—that is, its members are sharply and sympathetically oriented to their external coalition allies, liberal forces (e.g., labor) in the case of Democratic members, conservative ones (e.g., business) in the case of Republican members. The net result is that intra-committee compromise holds relatively low priority among members, and the conflicts that occur in committee are repeated and enlarged on the floor, leading often to the alteration or defeat of the committee's recommendations.[9]

[8]See Nicholas A. Masters, "Committee Assignments in the House of Representatives," *American Political Science Review*, 55 (June 1961), 345–57, and Fenno, *Congressmen in Committees*, pp. 18–21.

[9]Fenno, *Congressmen in Committees*, pp. 226–42. For additional evidence on how committees fare on the floor, see Anne L. Lewis, "Floor Success as a Measure of Committee Performance in the House," *Journal of Politics*, 40 (May 1978), 460–67.

The importance of committees varies by chamber. The small size of the Senate is an invitation to members to pursue their individual interests aggressively, whether or not they are related to their committee assignments. Their statewide and heterogeneous constituencies, moreover, compel them to develop interests in a wide band of issues. In contrast, the influence of the individual member in the House is largely determined by effectiveness in the committees; on the floor an individual's influence is slight. The difference in size contributes to a committee-dominated House; the Senate is more individualistic and free-wheeling.

Types of Congressional Committees

The only way that Congress can come to terms with the avalanche of bills and resolutions introduced each session is through its committee system. The "work horses" of Congress are the *standing* committees— the substantive committees to which legislation is referred for consideration. An indication of their importance for congressional decision-making can be gleaned from the following statistics. In the Ninety-fourth Congress (1975–76), 16,982 bills were introduced in the House and referred to its committees; only 985, or less than six percent, were reported out for floor consideration.[10] Clearly, one of the important functions of committees is to cull out proposals.

Established by the rules of each chamber, their jurisdictions set forth in some detail, standing committees continue from one Congress to another. Each chamber, of course, controls the number and the jurisdiction of its standing committees. It can eliminate or combine them, augment or decrease their jurisdictions. Over most of the history of Congress it has been much easier to create new committees than to eliminate or absorb old ones, for the simple reason that committee memberships are part of the currency of congressional power. Committee jurisdictions represent policy turf. No member, and particularly no chairman, is anxious to see his influence diminished by a reorganization of the committee system in which he loses more than he gains. The ultimate loss, of course, is the rare abolition of a committee and the transfer of its policy jurisdiction to another committee.

Interest groups may also oppose a reordering of the committee system. They are accustomed to working with it as it is. They know its ins and outs, its nooks and crannies. They know the members and have special

---

[10]Commission on Administrative Review, U.S. House of Representatives, *Scheduling the Work of the House*, 94th Cong., 2d sess., 1976, p. 24.

Table 3.1 The Standing Committees of Congress (95th Congress, 1977-78)

House	Senate
Agriculture	Agriculture, Nutrition, and Forestry
Appropriations	Appropriations
Armed Services	Armed Services
Banking, Finance, and Urban Affairs	Banking, Housing, and Urban Affairs
Budget	Budget
District of Columbia	Commerce, Science, and
Education and Labor	Transportation
Government Operations	Energy and Natural Resources
House Administration	Environment and Public Works
Interior and Insular Affairs	Finance
International Relations	Foreign Relations
Interstate and Foreign Commerce	Governmental Affairs
Judiciary	Human Resources
Merchant Marine and Fisheries	Judiciary
Post Office and Civil Service	Rules and Administration
Public Works and Transportation	Veterans' Affairs
Rules	
Science and Technology	
Small Business	
Standards of Official Conduct	
Veterans' Affairs	
Ways and Means	

access to at least some of them. When the Senate was considering a reorganization of its committee system in 1977, for example, the President of Common Cause testified:

> [Congress has] policymaking by interest group veto . . . Special interests view the present committee system as holy writ. They have mastered it. They have a stake in it. They will make an all-out fight to retain their advantage.[11]

Currently there are twenty-two standing committees in the House and fifteen in the Senate, as shown in Table 3.1. An ambitious attempt to reorganize the Senate committee system in 1977 by eliminating a large number of standing, select, and joint committees and by rationalizing their jurisdictions was only modestly successful. Six committees of various types, including three standing committees (Aeronautical and Space Sciences, District of Columbia, and Post Office and Civil Service) were abolished and their duties transferred to other committees.[12] Numerous jurisdictional changes were made, such as transferring legislative responsibility for the

---

[11]*Hearings* before the Temporary Select Committee to Study the Senate Committee System, 94th Cong., 2d sess., 1976, p. 6.

[12]Under the terms of the reorganization plan, several additional select and joint committees were slated for termination at a later date.

school lunch program from the Labor and Public Welfare Committee to the Agriculture Committee, but most were not of large significance. The most important jurisdictional change involved changing the name of the Interior Committee to that of Energy and Natural Resources, giving it control over most energy legislation while retaining the bulk of Interior's jurisdiction. Prior to this change, energy policy sprawled over the domains of more than a dozen standing committees.

Committee reorganization has two large characteristics: it is never neutral and it is always sticky. Some legislators are sure to lose, others are sure to win. Not many will get everything they want, save perhaps those whose jurisdictions emerge unscathed. Changes are never easy to make because of the rivalries between committees over certain policy jurisdictions. In addition, while all chairmen are apprehensive over the possible loss of jurisdiction, some are not anxious to gain new territory, particularly if it means that their committees will inherit seemingly intractable policy problems as well as the accompanying pressures from sharply conflictual interest groups (e.g., business vs. environmentalists).

Thus, the reorganization and realignment of committees invariably produce extraordinary political scrambling by legislators and interest groups to preserve their advantages. The tone of this activity is shown by the following comments, made by members of the Senate during the drive to alter the committee system:

> It's a fight over power. What's happening now is predictable. Losers of jurisdiction fight tooth and nail, and the gainers shrink less they appear possessive.

> You could destroy all your reorganization if you're going to take the veterans on. (The original plan called for the abolition of the Veterans' Affairs Committee. Responding to intense pressure from veterans' groups and their legislative spokesmen, the Senate retained the committee.)

> Wiping out the select and specialized committees and reducing the number of subcommittee assignments, while giving the outward appearance of tidying up the Senate operation, not only fails to accomplish its purpose, but results in something that I am not certain anyone wants—that is: Citizens with particularized interests, such as small business groups and veterans' groups, will find their access to the legislative branch severely restricted. (The Select Small Business Committee was also retained.)

> It's strictly turf. You fight much harder to avoid losing something you've got than to get something you never had before. There isn't a traceable ideological dispute on this, or a traceable partisan dispute.[13]

A second type of committee is the *select* committee. Ordinarily these

---

[13]*New York Times*, January 10, 1977.

committees are created to conduct studies or investigations and to report their recommendations to the chamber; only rarely are they empowered to draft and report legislation. Unlike standing (or permanent) committees, the duration of a select committee is the duration of a Congress. In practice, however, it is not uncommon for a select committee to be renewed over a number of Congresses. On occasion, the importance of a select committee, buttressed by the lobbying power of its clientele, dictates its transformation to the status of a standing committee. In the potpourri of select committees of recent Congresses have been such panels as Aging (House and Senate), Small Business (Senate), Intelligence (Senate), Assassinations (House), Congressional Operations (House), and Narcotics Abuse and Control (House). Select committees are sometimes established for the principal reason of placating interest groups that contend Congress has been unresponsive to their needs.

Joint committees are units formed from the membership of both chambers and, like other committees, from both parties. They are essentially study committees, charged with reporting their findings and recommendations to the chambers or, as in the case of the Joint Committee on Taxation, to the relevant standing committees (i.e., House Ways and Means and Senate Finance Committees). The theory behind joint committees is that they are useful instruments for coordinating policy analysis in a bicameral system. In practice, joint committees sometimes founder because of rivalries between them and the standing committees on whose jurisdictions they seem to poach or, more commonly, between the chambers.

One of the most important units in the committee spectrum is the *conference* committee. A form of joint committee, a conference committee is composed of members drawn from both chambers to reconcile differences when the House and Senate have passed different versions of the same legislation. Since virtually all major bills ultimately arrive in a conference committee, it is obvious that these committees play a critical role in policymaking. No bill can be sent to the president for action unless it has been passed in identical form by both houses. The task of the conference members, termed conferees or managers, is thus to resolve the disagreements between the chambers by shaping settlements that will be supported by their respective chambers. This is often perplexing, given the range of differences and the intensity of convictions within the houses.

Several rules and practices govern the formation and proceedings of conference committees. In the first place, each house may appoint as many conferees as it likes, although the number is almost always less than a dozen. The conferees are formally appointed by the Speaker of the House and the presiding officer of the Senate, following the recommendations of the chairman and the ranking minority member of the committee that reported the bill. The typical conferee is a senior committee or subcommittee member, though occasionally junior members are selected. A majority of the conferees of *each* house must accept the conference report before it can be transmitted to the chambers. Although there is a presumption that conferees are limited to working out specific differences between the two chambers, they sometimes smuggle entirely new material into the conference bill.

Managers are expected to support the majority viewpoint of their chamber in negotiations. On occasion the House or Senate may specifically instruct their conferees to hold to the position of their chamber; as it happens, this appears to have relatively slight effect on conference outcomes. Disregarding instructions may be the only means of gaining a compromise between the chambers. If conferees substantially disregard their instructions, the chamber can of course defeat the conference report. This happens only rarely.[14]

The formalized and customary rules of the conference process disclose little about the politics of the engagement. As in all of politics, there are winners and losers. Studies have shown that conference committee decisions on appropriations, tax, and trade legislation tend to be closer to Senate than to House versions, while on Social Security legislation the viewpoint of the House usually prevails.[15] But it is also common for winning and losing to be mixed—for one house to get its way in some respects and to lose in others, as these interesting observations reveal:

> The overriding ethic of the conference committee is one of bargaining, give-and-take, compromise, swapping, horse-trading, conciliation, and malleability by all concerned. Firm positions are always taken, and always changed. Deadlocks rarely occur to the degree that the bill is killed. Someone gives a little, perhaps after an impressive walkout, in return for a little; compromise is the cardinal rule of conference committees. Small wonder that each side claims victory; because almost everyone does win—something, somehow, sometimes.[16]

The most numerous type of committee in Congress is the *subcommittee*. During the last several decades the number of these committees has grown sharply. The typical contemporary Congress will have 250 or more subcommittees spread among its standing and select committees. Subcommittees represent the smallest and most specialized units for the consideration of legislation and for the conduct of investigations. Most standing committees of the House and Senate have from six to eight subcommittees;

[14]See Walter J. Oleszek, "Conference Committee Procedure and Reform," a paper prepared for the Temporary Select Committee to Study the Senate Committee System, *Appendix to the Second Report with Recommendations* (Washington, D.C.: Government Printing Office, 1977), pp. 35–48.

[15]See Richard F. Fenno, Jr., *The Power of the Purse: Appropriations Politics in Congress* (Boston: Little, Brown & Company, 1966), especially Chapter 12, and John F. Manley, *The Politics of Finance: The House Committee on Ways and Means* (Boston: Little, Brown & Company, 1970), pp. 269–94.

[16]Manley, *The Politics of Finance*, p. 271. Also consult John Ferejohn, "Who Wins in Conference Committee?," *Journal of Politics*, 37 (November 1975), 1033–46.

the Appropriations Committee in each house generally has more than a dozen. Subcommittees are typically of the *standing* variety; that is, they have established jurisdictions and continue from one Congress to the next. Occasionally *ad hoc* subcommittees will be created to consider legislation of a specific type.

The proliferation of subcommittees in Congress is the logical extension of the quest for specialization, of the need for the institution and its members to get a better "handle" on government. Subcommittee development encourages this, as at least some members develop exceptional expertise in relatively narrow fields of legislation. Similarly, they come to know a great deal about certain executive agencies—"where all the bodies are buried"—thus promoting to some extent Congress's capacity for effective oversight of the bureaucracy.

But this is only part of the story. There are also important political reasons for their creation. Subcommittee chairmanships increase the influence of those who gain them; they offer prestige, widened opportunities for gaining publicity and claiming credit, and, concretely, an increase in staff assistance:

> Some subcommittees have been set up for the reason that [Senator Goldwater] alluded to; that is for publicity for the chairmen or publicity in regard to a pet issue. Another reason is to get staff. Some subcommittees exist, I think, for that sole purpose. It is often the only way that Senators have found to acquire the additional staff that they need very, very badly.[17]

> We become badge happy around here. Everyone wants to become a subcommittee chairman and wear a badge.[18]

> Once a congressman gets a subcommittee, he has to come up with some plan for the betterment of mankind. Or else he will go back to campaign and his opponent will say, "He's chairman of a subcommittee and what legislation has he brought out—nothing."[19]

Finally, a subcommittee may be created largely for the purpose of rewarding a certain committee member with a chairmanship. With a minimum of resources for exerting control, party and seniority leaders manipulate the committee system and committee assignments as a means of gaining support and expanding their bases of power.[20]

---

[17]*Hearings* before the Temporary Select Committee to Study the Senate Committee System, 94th Cong., 2d sess., 1976, p. 56. The statement is by Senator Alan Cranston (D., Calif.).

[18]*New York Times*, January 16, 1977. The statement is by Congressman David R. Obey (D., Wis.), Chairman of the House Commission on Administrative Review.

[19]As quoted by Richard F. Fenno, Jr., *Congressmen in Committees*, p. 113.

[20]For a study of the manipulation of committee assignments by the majority party leadership, see Louis P. Westefield, "Majority Party Leadership and the Committee System in the House of Representatives," *American Political Science Review*, 68 (December 1974), 1593–1604.

Subcommittees are tailored to the measure of the members' ambitions, interests, and pursuit of reelection—not to the efficiency of congressional operations. Their sheer number poses difficulties for the member as well as for the integration of the institution. In practice it has been common for members, particularly in the Senate, to slight some subcommittee assignments in order to concentrate on others, as these observations make clear:

> . . . I have so many [subcommittees] that some I never attend. I confess that I have so much else to do and so many others that I make a choice among the top three in importance, in my mind, to decide which one I will go to that morning. The others I pass up or send a staff man to monitor it and tell me what went on.[21]

Despite the problems that multiple assignments present, it has not been easy to reduce them:

> We all know that there are too many committees. The fact that we can't get ourselves to this meeting or get the witnesses here is the best testimony in the world of how we are snafued up. But we touch a lot of issues, fray a lot of people's nerves when you start to dismantle anything because each of us has some kind of little area that we have carved out for our domain and we don't want to give that up. We want to change everything, but don't bother the one that I have carved out for myself.[22]

Perhaps the most significant feature of the Senate committee reorganization in 1977 was the reduction in the number of committee and subcommittee assignments to which each member could lay claim and the number on which he might serve as chairman. Prior to the reorganization, the average senator held eighteen committee and subcommittee assignments and some held many more. Under the terms of the reorganization, the maximum number of assignments was reduced to eleven (three committees and eight subcommittees), still a substantial number and larger than the number recommended by the select committee that prepared the plan. In addition, each senator was limited to the chairmanship of one standing committee and of two subcommittees—a victory of significance for younger senators since it contributed to the further distribution of chairmanships.[23] Subcommittees pose a lesser problem for the individual member of the much larger House, since representatives have fewer such assignments.

The most important aspect of congressional subcommittees is not

---

[21]*Hearings* before the Temporary Select Committee to Study the Senate Committee System, p. 19. The statement is by Senator Frank E. Moss (D., Utah).

[22]*Ibid.*, p. 55. The statement is by Senator Lawton Chiles (D., Fla.).

[23]For a summary of the provisions of the Senate committee reorganization, see *Congressional Quarterly Weekly Report*, February 12, 1977. pp. 279–85.

their number, extravagant as it is, but rather their emergence as independent and largely autonomous centers of power. Changes in the relationship between committees and their subcommittees have been particularly dramatic in the House, largely because of decisions by the Democratic caucus in the early and middle 1970s. Sharply altering the balance between committee and subcommittee powers, the new rules include such provisions as the following: no member can serve as chairman of more than one legislative subcommittee; the Democratic caucus of each committee is empowered to select subcommittee chairmen and to provide for subcommittee jurisdictions and budgets; all bills referred to the full committee must be sent promptly to subcommittees; the chairmen of subcommittees are authorized to hire their own staff; all committees with more than twenty members must have at least four subcommittees; and the chairmen of the subcommittees of the Appropriations Committee must be approved by the House Democratic caucus.[24]

The new balance of power distinctly favors the subcommittee system. Under the "Subcommittee Bill of Rights" the powers of House committee chairmen are curtailed. They manage their full committees, but they do not dominate them as they did in the past. Indeed, in some committees virtually all of the "action" is in the subcommittees, as these comments by a committee chairman suggest:

> I didn't pay much attention to subcommittee chairmen before—I did it all myself. Now, the subcommittee chairmen handle bills on the floor. They know that when they're answering questions on the floor they had better know what they're talking about. They really study the legislation now; they're much better prepared and more knowledgeable. Now we go to conference and they do the talking—the Senators never open their mouths. Their staffs are the only ones who know anything. So we're more effective with the Senate.[25]

The growth in subcommittee autonomy and in the powers of subcommittee chairmen has intensified the argument over the decentralization of power in Congress. The subcommittee reforms have diluted the opportunities for committee chairmen to dominate proceedings, strengthened the norm of specialization, reduced the influence of congressional elders, and hastened the rise of younger members to positions of power in the subcommittee system. Just as certainly, the reforms have contributed to the

---

[24] For further details of the "Subcommittee Bill of Rights," see *Congressional Quarterly Weekly Report*, November 8, 1975, pp. 2407–12.

[25] As quoted by Norman J. Ornstein, "Causes and Consequences of Congressional Change: Subcommittee Reforms in the House of Representatives, 1970–73," in *Congress in Change: Evolution & Reform*, ed. Norman J. Ornstein (New York: Praeger Publishers, 1975), p. 108. Also see David W. Rohde, "Committee Reform in the House of Representatives and the Subcommittee Bill of Rights," *The Annals*, 411 (January 1974), 39–47.

further fragmentation of congressional power. While the obvious losers have been the committee chairmen, the party leadership—the strongest force for centralization and coordination—has also been weakened. Party leaders (including the president) now have more bases to touch, more individuals with power in their own right to be accommodated, more units of influence with which to reckon. Congressional party management, in a word, has become more difficult.

Committee Assignments
and the Goals of Members

The range and significance of committee activities make the assignment of members to committees one of the most important internal decisions made in Congress. Charles L. Clapp shows the impact of committee assignments on members of the House:

> Not only is the fate of most legislative proposals determined in committee: to an important degree the fate of individual congressmen may be decided there too. A person's congressional career may rest largely on the kind of committee post he is given. A "good" assignment may greatly enhance his value to his constituents and provide unusual opportunities to publicize his activities in Congress; here he can develop the expertise and the reputation as a "specialist" that will enable him to influence his colleagues and important national policies. This is not to say that a "bad" assignment is an irretrievable setback, since effective work on an unimportant committee can identify a new man as a "comer" and lead to a better assignment. Indeed, it usually does. But being named to a committee in which he has little interest defers the day when a congressman can begin to acquire seniority on a committee of his choice.[26]

Committee assignments are made by party committees ("committees-on-committees") in each chamber. Numerous criteria are taken into consideration by each party's committee-makers in making them, including the member's seniority, constituency, personal preferences, ability, experience, reputation as a legislator, and, at times, ideological orientation.

Committees vary in exclusiveness and prestige. Some committee assignments are much more attractive than others, and members, supported by their state delegations and prominent politicians, actively lobby to win seats on them. In contrast, other committees may have trouble in securing a full complement of members. Party leaders may have to offer inducements to members to get them to serve on them. A seat on the House District of Columbia Committee, for example, is anything but a coveted assignment for the typical member; its jurisdiction is narrow and

---

[26]Charles L. Clapp, *The Congressman: His Work as He Sees It* (Washington, D.C.: The Brookings Institution, 1963), p. 183.

lacks relevance for the member's own constituents.[27] In general, the more exclusive the committee, the greater the attention committee-makers give to the selection of "appropriate" new members.

As a result of changes in committee assignment practices, the newly elected member of Congress today has a better chance than ever of securing the committee assignment he or she requests, or at least of receiving an acceptable substitute. Since the early 1950s, Senate Democrats have followed the "Johnson Rule," which stipulates that each new Democratic member shall be given at least one major committee assignment. Senate Republicans now follow a similar rule. Committee assignments in the House, one recent study shows, have become routinized to the point that, in the main, each party's committee-on-committees matches preferences with vacancies, at times recommending the expansion of certain committees in order to accommodate the requests of members. There will nevertheless always be some first-term members, perhaps about one-third, who fail to receive appointments to the committees they most prefer. For them there is statistical comfort in the fact that by the beginning of their third term nearly all will have succeeded in transferring to their preferred committees.[28] The significance of committee accessibility should not be lost: as in other respects newer members do not have to stand in line nearly as long in order to gain influence in Congress.

The committees of Congress not only differ widely in terms of influence and autonomy, but also in the kinds of members they attract. Richard F. Fenno has shown that House members have three basic goals: *reelection, influence within the House,* and *good public policy.* The opportunities to achieve these goals are variable according to committee. Representatives who seek membership on the "money" committees—Appropriations and Ways and Means—are primarily in search of power and prestige—that is, influence within the House. Members who request assignment to the Interior Committee are essentially motivated to help their constituents and thus to win reelection; the jurisdiction of this committee, with its

---

[27]To persuade members to fill six vacancies on the District Committee at the opening of the Ninety-fifth Congress, the Democratic caucus lifted its membership rules to permit members to serve on this committee in addition to their regular committee assignments (one major or two nonmajor committees). None of the forty-eight new House Democrats had volunteered to serve on the District Committee. *Washington Post,* January 27, 1977. Similarly, only two freshman Democrats applied for seats on the much more prestigious Judiciary Committee, which had five vacancies. The controversiality of the Judiciary Committee's jurisdiction (including busing, abortion, gun control, and school prayers) may have been a deterrent. *Washington Post,* January 20, 1977.

[28]Irwin N. Gertzog, "The Routinization of Committee Assignments in the U.S. House of Representatives," *American Journal of Political Science,* 20 (November 1976), 693–712. Also see Charles S. Bullock, III, "Committee Transfers in the United States House of Representatives," *Journal of Politics,* 35 (February 1973), 85–120; and Malcolm E. Jewell and Chu Chi-hung, "Membership Movement and Committee Attractiveness in the U.S. House of Representatives, 1963–1971," *American Journal of Political Science,* 18 (May 1974), 433–41.

emphasis on federal projects, is particularly conducive to achieving this goal. As one western representative explained: "You take a look at the problems of Interior and you have a list of the problems of my district: Indians, water, mines, parks. I have to stay on at least until I get that water bill through."[29] Finally, members of the Education and Labor and International Relations Committees report that they are mainly concerned with the public policy that falls within the jurisdictions of these committees. A conservative Republican explained his request for assignment to Education and Labor as follows:

> I've had some experience in both fields. My first position in politics was as a member of the city school board. And I own a business; so I understand the management point of view. I'm the kind of person who jumps right into these hot spots. So I figured if this was the most controversial committee in the House, I'd like to get on it. And I thought the management point of view would be good for the Committee.[30]

The committee assignment that pleases one member may not please another. The character and interests of the member's district (or state) heavily influence his or her requests for assignments or transfers. Nevertheless, there is an overall pattern in the prestige, and thus the attractiveness, of House and Senate committees. The best evidence of this is in the requests of members for committee transfers. Studies have shown that those committees whose jurisdictions encompass national or broad-scope matters dominate the transfer process. Thus the elite committees are Foreign Relations, Finance, and Appropriations in the Senate, and Rules, Ways and Means, Appropriations, and International Relations in the House. The least prestigious committees—those to which members seldom transfer—are those such as Veterans' Affairs, Post Office and Civil Service, and Merchant Marine and Fisheries in the House, and Rules and Administration in the Senate.[31] Until its abolition in the 1977 committee reorganization, the Senate District of Columbia Committee ranked as least attractive of the Senate panels.

[29]Fenno, *Congressmen in Committees,* p. 6.

[30]*Ibid.*, p. 11. The congressional committees studied by Fenno were each characterized by a single overarching member goal: power within the chamber, reelection, or good public policy. Eighty percent or more of the members shared a common goal in each of the committees he studied. A recent analysis of the House Committee on the Judiciary, not included in the Fenno study, finds it to be a "mixed goal" committee. For this committee, the distribution of primary member goals was as follows: reelection, forty-seven percent; good public policy, thirty-four percent; career beyond the House, sixteen percent; and influence within the House, three percent. Lynette Palmer Perkins, *Member Goals and Committee Behavior: The House Judiciary Committee* (Ph.D. Dissertation, University of Pittsburgh, 1977).

[31]See George Goodwin, *The Little Legislatures: Committees of Congress* (Amherst: University of Massachusetts Press, 1970), pp. 114–15; and Barbara Hinckley, "Policy Content, Committee Membership, and Behavior," *American Journal of Political Science*, 19 (August 1975), 543–57.

Committees, Chairmen and the Seniority System

As it relates to the committee system, seniority is quite simple. It provides that the member of the majority party with the longest uninterrupted service on a committee becomes the chairman. In popular analyses of congressional politics, seniority is usually viewed as an incubus—an oppressive system for obstructing majority party rule, for giving some sections of the country advantages over others, for keeping younger members in their place, for rewarding mediocrity at the expense of competence, and for institutionalizing the rule of a handful of elders. And until recently a good case could be made for the accuracy of these allegations. The two most important criticisms of seniority have been that, because of the power of committee chairmen over legislation, it militates against effective control by the majority party and, closely related, that it has benefited the South at the expense of the rest of the nation.

Table 3.2 shows the distribution of committee chairmanships among the four principal regions of the country during the Eighty-seventh Congress (the Kennedy administration) and the Ninety-fifth Congress (the Carter administration). The comparison is dramatic. In 1961–62, more than sixty percent of the chairmanships in both houses were held by southerners; in 1977–78, only twenty-seven percent of the House chairmen and thirty-eight percent of the Senate chairmen were from southern states. While the South was heavily overrepresented in chairmanships in previous

Table 3.2 Committee Chairmanships: The Decline of the South in the Democratic Party

| Region | 87th Congress 1961-62 | | 95th Congress 1977-78 | |
	% of Members	% of Chairmanships	% of Members	% of Chairmanships
House				
East	26	25	28	32
Midwest	19	10	23	23
South*	42	60	31	27
West	13	5	18	18
Senate				
East	14	0	23	25
Midwest	18	0	21	12
South*	37	63	30	38
West	31	37	26	25

*The South is defined as the eleven states of the Confederacy plus Kentucky and Oklahoma.

years, the region now holds a number that is roughly equivalent to its proportion of seats in the Democratic party in each house.

Two principal explanations account for the decline in southern power. The first is that southern Democrats no longer constitute as large a proportion of the Democratic party as formerly—a condition that results from the growing strength of the Republican party in the South and the Democratic party in the North. The Democratic party is now more of a northern party than at any time in this century. The second is that there are now many more safe Democratic seats in the North—roughly twice as many—as in the South. Safe seats, of course, are linked to seniority, which in turn is linked to chairmanships. Long disadvantaged by the seniority principle, northern Democrats now stand to be rewarded by it, though it is unlikely that their dominance will ever be as great as that previously enjoyed by members from southern states.

Table 3.3 shows that the seniority principle has not only conveyed regional advantage but also ideological advantage. For as long as any of us can remember, the conservative core of the Democratic party has been the southern contingent in Congress. And with few exceptions the most conservative of all southern Democratic members have been the committee chairmen who, holding different philosophies and responding to a different constellation of interests, frequently vote with Republicans against a majority of their own party. As Table 3.3 shows, southern committee chairmen in the House are about four times as likely to vote against a majority of their party as are eastern or midwestern chairmen; party desertions by southern committee chairmen in the Senate occur with similar frequency. What this shows concretely is that the seniority principle has elevated to positions of power members who are notably out of step with a

Table 3.3   Opposition to Their Own Party Majorities by Democratic Committee Chairmen in Floor Voting, 1976*

Region of Chairmen	Average Percentage of Votes Cast Against Own Party	
	House	Senate
East	10%	17%
Midwest	9	14
South	44	58
West	15	16

*These percentages are computed from data on member support and opposition scores for the second session of the 94th Congress (1976). The chairmen are those serving in the 95th Congress (1977-78). Opposition scores reflect the percentage of votes cast by chairmen with a majority of the opposition party (Republican) against a majority of their own party. *Congressional Quarterly Weekly Report,* January 15, 1977, p. 66.

majority of their party. Perhaps more than any other factor in recent decades, the seniority system has served to check the development of a congressional party system under which the majority party could be held responsible for a program of public policy.

But Congress is changing. For one thing, although the winds of liberalism are still not very strong in the South, there are more liberal and moderate Democratic members from that section today than in the past—at least in the House.[32] This may prove significant in the future. The most important changes, however, involve the committee system and the seniority principle. Two developments have occurred: (1) the influence of committees and committee chairmen has been reduced while that of subcommittees and subcommittee chairmen has been augmented, and (2) the seniority rule has been weakened as a result of changes introduced in both houses by Democratic majorities.

The first change comes down to this: a committee chairmanship is not worth as much as formerly because the influence of the chairman has been diminished. Autocratic committee chairmen are a thing of the past. There are no committees in Congress today in which a chairman runs things in any fashion he chooses, tightly controlling the agenda, the subcommittees and their staffs and, ultimately, the committee's legislative output. Such control was common scarcely more than a decade ago. Committee power is now dispersed. Subcommittees have won a large measure of freedom from their parent committees, and subcommittee chairmen now assume many of the responsibilities previously held by committee chairmen. They are likely to appear before the Rules Committee to negotiate for a rule (in the House), to manage committee legislation on the floor, and to assume a leadership role in conference committee meetings. Subcommittees and their chairmen have a major, independent impact on virtually all legislation.

Changes in the seniority rule have contributed to a lessening of the powers of committee chairmen. Under the current rules of the House Democratic caucus, seniority no longer conveys a presumptive right to the chairmanship of a committee. Instead, at the opening of each new Congress all chairmen are subjected to a secret ballot by members of the caucus as are the chairmen of the Appropriations subcommittees. They can be dismissed or retained. In 1975 the Democratic caucus voted to remove three standing committee chairmen from their positions. In 1977 the caucus voted to remove the chairman of the Military Construction Subcommittee of the Appropriations Committee, a southern congressman who

---

[32]Lawrence C. Dodd and Bruce I. Oppenheimer, "The House in Transition," in *Congress Reconsidered*, eds. Lawrence C. Dodd and Bruce I. Oppenheimer (New York: Praeger Publishers, 1977), p. 24.

had been censured the previous year for conflict of interest. Senate Democrats now follow a rule that provides for a secret ballot election on any chairmanship if requested by twenty percent of the Democratic members.

These changes in seniority practices, dramatized through the ouster of several House chairmen, represent a significant reordering of the structure of congressional power. In the first place, they reestablish the control of the party caucus over committee leaders. Second, they eliminate the automatic succession to chairmanships afforded by seniority. Third, they warn committee chairmen that they can be removed if they are insufficiently responsive to committee members and to their party colleagues at large. Fourth, they dictate that committee chairmen be cooperative and prudent in their relations with other party members.

Although the net result of these alterations is to diminish the influence of committee chairmen, it is important not to overdraw the case. Seniority still matters. It will doubtlessly continue to govern the selection of the vast majority of committee chairmen. No one should expect to see wholesale removals of chairmen. For chairmen with substantial expertise in a policy field and authentic political skills, the new seniority rules pose no serious threat.[33] These chairmen will continue to have a major role in directing committee activities and in shaping congressional policy-making.

It remains to be said that none of the reforms of the committee system guarantee a more effective Congress, one better able to cope with the extraordinary complexities of policy-making. What they do provide and promise is a different structure of decision-making, one in which far more members than previously hold elements of congressional power. They tilt the scales toward further dispersal of congressional power, offset only to the extent that party leaders can manage this unwieldy apparatus in the interest of developing a unified, overall program.

THE CONGRESSIONAL PARTIES

The congressional party is the principal agency for drawing together, or centralizing, legislative power. Yet as a mechanism for the control of the legislature and for shaping public policy, it is often found wanting. Whether Democratic or Republican, the congressional party tends to be neglected by all members some of the time, by some members much of the time, and by a few members virtually all of the time. Outside observers typically

---

[33]Bruce I. Oppenheimer, "Subcommittee Government and Congressional Reform," *DEA News* (Summer 1976), 10. *DEA News* is a publication of the American Political Science Association.

demean party in Congress—that is, when they take account of it at all. The problem is that the congressional system does not provide a fertile soil for the cultivation of strong parties. The parties must compete with powerful and insistent forces, including the constituencies of the members, well organized interest groups, the media, committee and sub-committee leaders, diverse personal and committee staffs, sectional spokes-men and interests and, not the least by any means, the president and the bureaucracy. As a result of the competitive environment of Congress, party leaders face difficult problems in assembling their members to function as a collectivity. They have no more than a loose rein on the behavior of fellow party members, and their formal powers are not impressive.

Under one guise or another the member's primary allegiance is to his constituency and to the elements within it that have leverage on him—that can, in other words, help reelect him. It is therefore not surprising that the parties are only partially successful in taking hold of the government for the purpose of enacting a legislative program. In a legislative system in which power is widely dispersed, where the members' interests are not identical to the group's, it could scarcely be otherwise.

These introductory observations are not meant to suggest that the parties, particularly the majority party, are simply ineffectual or that their activities carry little meaning for their members. Each house is organized by the majority party through its caucus or conference. It selects the leader-ship, which in turn manages the legislative process itself. (The minority party elects a similar array of leaders who, because of their party's minority status, may do little more than stand in the wings, waiting for things to happen.)[34] The point is that Congress could not function with any degree of coherence without the organization that parties bring to the chambers. And they do more than that. The majority party serves as a bridge between the executive branch and the legislature, when the same party controls both branches, and as a critic when the executive branch is controlled by the other party. The party leadership is also a source of policy proposals, a source of information for members in search of voting cues, and an interpreter of congressional activities to the media. What cannot be said, however, is that the parties control the legislature in such a way as to dominate policy outcomes. The party is but one element among many that contribute to the fashioning of public policy—and often not the most important at that.

To understand why parties are uncertain structures for directing Congress, it is necessary to look at the elements of which they are com-posed, beginning with the caucus, the basic unit of party organization.

---

[34]See a study by Charles O. Jones of the political conditions, both internal and external, that shape the role of the minority party in Congress. *The Minority Party in Congress* (Boston: Little, Brown and Company, 1970).

The Caucus

The party caucus, or conference, is a traditional institution in American legislatures used for the purposes of electing leaders, adopting rules, devising strategies, gaining internal agreement, and shaping party positions on legislation. Typically the members of the caucus (all members of the party) are most comfortable when their task centers on the election of leaders (a responsibility that cannot be avoided in any case) and least comfortable when the matter at hand is the development of a party position on a major piece of legislation. When legislation is involved, party leaders follow a counsel of caution and moderation, recognizing the inclination of members to view "grand" questions in a parochial light, in particular to weigh policy changes in terms of their probable consequences for their constituencies.

The caucus has never been particularly strong in the Senate, though it has been at times in the House. Following the revolt against Speaker Joe Cannon in 1910–11, which sharply reduced the powers of the Speaker, the House was dominated by the Democratic caucus for almost a decade. Under the reign of an independent "King Caucus," party loyalty and language became the idiom of the House, manifested in frequent meetings of the caucus and in binding instructions on its members. But the practice of binding caucuses led to the institution's undoing, and before long members began to assert their right to vote on legislation according to their own lights. The caucus became an instrument confined largely to the selection of party leaders, its work limited to the opening days of a new Congress.

The caucus remained a relatively weak agency of party for the next half century. The Democratic party began to revive its caucus in the late 1960s, chiefly in response to initiatives from liberal members who felt thwarted by the powers of committee chairmen. More frequent meetings of the caucus were held, and in the early and middle 1970s it adopted a number of procedural reforms designed to bring committee chairmen under its control. The seniority system was gradually altered, culminating in a rule that requires each chairman to be subjected to a secret ballot at the opening of each new Congress. When three chairmen were voted out of office in 1975, the caucus staked a solid claim to its superiority over committee leaders. Among other changes that year, the caucus awarded the authority for making committee assignments to the party Steering and Policy Committee (depriving the Democratic members of the Ways and Means Committee of this power), empowered the Speaker to nominate the Democratic members of the Rules Committee (thus bringing this crucial agenda-setting committee under his influence), and provided that any committee with more than twenty members must establish no less than four subcommittees. Committees and their chairmen were now more firmly harnessed to the party system and the leadership than at any time since the latter part of the Woodrow Wilson administration.

The decisions of the Democratic caucus in the 1970s have led to fundamental changes in the structure of House decision-making. Procedures have been altered to increase the prospects for intraparty democracy and to diminish the possibilities for arbitrary rule by committee chairmen. As observed by House Majority Leader Jim Wright:

> The day is ended when any committee chairman can run his domain like a feudal barony, oblivious to the wishes and sensitivities of other members. All now have been put on notice that their colleagues will hold them accountable for their stewardship. The office of committee chairman must now be regarded no longer as a right but a privilege . . . and those who give also can take away.[35]

The rejuvenation of the House Democratic caucus does not presage a return to the days of "King Caucus," when members were tightly controlled by its decisions, even to the point of being instructed how to vote on the floor. The independence of today's members, their concern over protecting their own policy turf, and their attentiveness to the impact of legislation on their constituencies make them reluctant to accept central direction on major or sensitive issues. The caucus may on occasion instruct committees to report certain bills to the floor as well as to debate major issues and to vote on them as a means of alerting members to party positions, but it is not apt to go beyond that. Most members, it appears, do not want the caucus to encroach on the legislative domain of committees. The comments of several northern Democratic members are instructive:

> If policy questions continue to come up at caucuses, you'll find more and more people voting to defer the issue.
>
> When the caucus votes on resolutions, it gives many members, especially southern members, trouble back home. People misconstrue the resolutions.
>
> If [the caucus] started pronouncing on all substantive matters, especially before the committees considered the matters, the caucus would then be intruding on the jurisdiction of committees.
>
> If the purpose of a caucus action is to give House members the opportunity to vote on an issue, then that's an appropriate use of the caucus. Committees are not inhibited by the caucus from exercising their own judgment on bills.[36]

[35]*New York Times*, March 20, 1977.
[36]The quotations are drawn from the *Congressional Quarterly Weekly Report*, May 3, 1975, pp. 911–12.

The Policy Committees

In addition to the caucuses (or conferences), each party in each chamber has a policy committee. Acting as executive committees of the caucuses, the much smaller policy committees meet regularly to discuss and seek agreement on party positions involving major policy questions. The parties have organized their policy committees somewhat differently, with the Democratic party having made their committees more clearly an arm of the party leadership. In contrast to the Republican arrangement, which distributes party positions among more members, the Democratic party has made its elected leaders (Speaker of the House, floor leader of the Senate) the chairmen of these committees.

While the policy committees can sensitize members to party positions, provide policy guidance, and contribute a measure of integration, they cannot bind members to a course of action. Like the caucuses, the policy committees have been neglected about as often as they have been followed by the individual member. They can do very little to shape legislation under consideration in committees. Rather, they serve as forums for instructing members and identifying and testing party sentiments.[37] The policy committees have never been sources for the development of comprehensive legislative programs. The disarray of the congressional parties limits the opportunities for centralizing policy formation in any party entity.

The Party Leadership

The most important element in the party structure of Congress is the formal leadership of the majority party, centering in the Speaker and the floor leaders of the House and the Senate. Viewed more broadly, the leadership takes in other positions as well, including the president pro tempore of the Senate (the senior member of the majority party), the whip or assistant floor leader (plus deputy or assistant whips), the chairmen of the caucuses and policy committees, and committee chairmen. And for the minority party, of course, there are counterparts to these positions. The key figures

---

[37]See a recent analysis of the majority policy committee in the Senate by John G. Stewart, "Committee System Management," *Appendix to the Second Report*, Temporary Select Committee to Study the Senate Committee System, 94th Cong., 2d sess., 1976, pp. 14–15. Also consult earlier studies by Hugh A. Bone, "An Introduction to the Senate Policy Committees," *American Political Science Review*, 50 (June 1956), 339–59; Ralph K. Huitt, "Democratic Party Leadership in the Senate," *American Political Science Review*, 55 (June 1961), 333–44; and Charles O. Jones, *Party and Policy-Making: The House Republican Policy Committee* (New Brunswick, N.J.: Rutgers University Press, 1964).

in the leadership are the Speaker of the House and the majority floor leaders in each chamber.

The Speakership of the House has had a checkered history. In the earliest years of the House, the Speaker was no more than the presiding officer of the chamber. But as the legislative parties grew in strength, the Speaker's prominence as the leader of the majority party also grew. Around the turn of the twentieth century, the office had become extraordinarily powerful. Autocratic Speakers, such as Joseph G. Cannon (1903–11), used the full range of the office's powers (including the powers of recognition and of appointing committee members) to dominate the proceedings and policy outcomes of the House.

Eventually, the accumulation of grievances among members led to the "revolution" of 1910–11. The structure of Speakership powers, carefully put together by Cannon and a few predecessors, was dismantled by frustrated members. Among their principal actions were those to remove the Speaker from the chairmanship of the Committee on Rules and to abolish his power to appoint members and chairmen of standing committees. This revolt against arbitrary rule left the Speakership sharply reduced in formal authority; and it left power in the House markedly decentralized.

The problems created by this constriction of the Speaker's powers have been lessened by actions of the Democratic caucus in the 1970s. Two important changes have occurred. The Speaker was made chairman of the party Steering and Policy Committee, thus giving him a stronger voice in the development of party positions on legislation and in the allocation of committee assignments. And second, the Speaker was given the authority to name the party's members on the Rules Committee (subject to caucus approval), thus increasing the probability of close cooperation between his office and this key unit for controlling major legislation on its way from committee to the floor.

The refurbishing of the Speaker's powers falls well short of guaranteeing that he can lead the House. Much depends on his leadership qualities—his sense of purpose, his political deftness, and his persuasiveness. Robert L. Peabody makes a good argument:

> That Speakers like Nicholas Longworth (R., Ohio) and Sam Rayburn (D., Tex.) from time to time have operated effectively has been attributed more to their strong personal characters and persuasive abilities rather than to the limited formal powers available to them. What seems to distinguish strong Speakers from the more mediocre ones has been a willingness to use their limited legislative powers to the hilt, at the same time exploiting other more personal forms of influence with skill and subtlety. They must initiate actions without getting too far out in front of a majority of their followers. They must operate with "controlled partisanship." A Speaker must function in two roles

almost simultaneously—first, as the neutral presiding officer to protect the rights of *all* members, majority and minority alike, and second, as partisan leader of the majority party to seek ways to advance the party's policy objectives and continued control of the Congress.[38]

The temper of the times has also helped to define the role of the Speaker, altering his relations with the members of the House. Leadership is now much less command than persuasion and negotiation. The current Speaker, Thomas P. ("Tip") O'Neill, observes:

> Old Sam Rayburn couldn't name 12 new members of Congress, and he was an institution that awed people. Only on the rarest of occasions could a Congressman get an appointment to see him. And when he called the Attorney General and said, "You be in my office at 3 in the afternoon," that Cabinet officer was there at 3 in the afternoon. Politics has changed. I have to deal in dialogue, in openness; if someone wants to see me, they see me. And of course they're highly independent now. You have to talk to people in the House, listen to them. The whole ethics question has changed. Years ago you'd think nothing of calling Internal Revenue and saying that this case has been kicking around for a couple of years, and it ought to be civil instead of criminal. You'd think nothing of calling a chairman of a committee and saying, "Put this project in, put this dam in." Well, you can't do that now.[39]

The Speaker's powers are fashioned from six elements: parliamentary powers, legislative discretion, information, scheduling, appointments, and exchange. Among his parliamentary duties are those of presiding over the House, referring bills to committee, approving the journal, putting questions and votes, and naming members to preside in his absence. Concerning bill referral, a recent change permits the Speaker to send a bill to more than one committee (jointly or sequentially), to split up a bill, or to send parts of it to different committees. He has considerable discretion in deciding who will take control of the floor through his power to recognize (or not to recognize) members. He is also at the center of the House information network, an advantage that is especially important when his party is in control of the presidency. Simply put, information is power, and no member can rival the Speaker's sources of it. Control over the scheduling of legislation rests largely with the Speaker and majority leader. He appoints members to a number of joint, select, and special committees. Finally, drawing on the previous powers, the Speaker is in a particularly good position for exchanges with members. He can assist them in gaining a desirable committee position, advance legislation in which they have a special interest, give them counsel, arm them with useful information, and

---

[38]Robert L. Peabody, *Leadership in Congress: Stability, Succession, and Change* (Boston: Little, Brown and Company, 1976), pp. 41–42.
[39]*New York Times*, April 5, 1977.

promote their reelection chances by heightening their visibility to constituents, at times even campaigning on their behalf. Members understand the relationship: the Speaker expects their support when it is needed—though "the emphasis is on general exchange over time rather than explicit *quid-pro-quos.*"[40]

Like the Speaker, the majority floor leader in each house assembles his powers from bits and pieces. Indeed, the floor leader draws power from the same well as the Speaker: from the advantages that attach to the office, such as superior information sources and superior access to the president and the media, and from the credits he earns by advancing and protecting the interests and careers of members. His initiatives can make life easier for party colleagues, especially newer members, whether they are concerned with gaining better committee assignments, scheduling and moving their "pet" legislation along, securing increased appropriations for their committees or subcommittees, climbing up the congressional party ladder, or simply securing information in order to reduce risks and to shape their own plans. Members need his assistance (or intervention) in a manner similar to his need for theirs; ultimately his effectiveness depends on their support and their willingness to accept his leadership. The sum of it is that the majority leader and members are tightly meshed in a network of favors and rewards, mutual interests, and personal and political interdependencies. The opportunities for establishing cooperative relationships are limited only by a failure of imagination—on his part or on theirs.

The chief power of congressional party leaders is simply the power of persuasion. No leader rules, but all bargain and negotiate. No leader expects to get his way all the time. The current majority leader of the House, Jim Wright (D., Tex.), offers an apt description of the leader's role: "The majority leader is a conciliator, a mediator, a peacemaker. Even when patching together a tenuous majority he must respect the right of honest dissent, conscious of the limits of his claims upon others."[41] Because members' interests differ and because no member has more than a partial claim on any other member, congressional leadership requires exceptional intelligence and purpose, bolstered by a broad range of political skills. Naturally these qualities are not always found.

Ranking below the floor leader is the whip. Each party in each chamber selects a whip plus a number of deputy or assistant whips. The Senate Democrats have a whip and eight assistant whips drawn from different sections of the country. The much smaller Republican delegation has a whip and sixteen assistant whips. Substantially more elaborate is the whip organization of the House, especially in the majority party. House

---

[40]This paragraph is based on Peabody, *Leadership in Congress*, pp. 42–47. (Quotation on p. 46.)

[41]*Congressional Quarterly Weekly Report*, December 11, 1976, p. 3293.

Democrats have a whip, a chief deputy whip, three deputy whips, and thirty-two assistant whips whose positions are allocated by zones or at large. The whip organization of the House Republicans is composed of a whip, four regional whips, and twelve assistant whips divided among the regions.

The importance of the whip system derives from its functions as a transmission belt for communications between the leadership and the rank-and-file members and as an instrument for gaining information on which to base floor strategy. Major legislation often brings the whip system into action. The leadership needs to know how party members intend to vote and it needs supportive members to be present when the vote is taken. To learn members' intentions, the whip's office may conduct a poll of the entire party contingent. In the process they may learn that certain provisions of the legislation are troublesome for members, and that if amended will increase the number of supporters. They also learn which members can be counted upon, which are uncertain, and which are opposed to the legislation—valuable pieces of information to the leadership as it seeks to pick up a few votes here and there to form a majority. If the poll discloses that the outlook for the legislation is dim, the leadership may decide to delay floor consideration, giving them more time to put it in a form that is likely to be acceptable and to apply pressure on certain members. The whip's office takes particular pains to make sure that members friendly to the legislation are on hand for the vote.[42]

Informal Party Groups
and State Delegations

In addition to the formal party offices and agencies, there are several informal party groups—resembling "parties" within parties—that have been formed in the House of Representatives. Bearing names such as the Acorns, Chowder and Marching Club, and Wednesday Club (all Republican), and the Democratic Study Group (Democratic), these groups meet to discuss legislation, share information, and plan strategies on major legislative matters. The importance of these groups is that they are central sources of legislative information for their members. At the same time, they increase the cohesion of like-minded congressmen, enhancing their bargaining positions as well as their impact on public policy outcomes.

The best known and by all odds the most powerful of these groups is the Democratic Study Group. The DSG was formed in the late 1950s by liberal Democrats in a move to offset the conservative power of southern

---

[42]See an analysis of the whip system in Randall B. Ripley, "The Party Whip Organizations in the United States House of Representatives," *American Political Science Review,* 58 (September 1964), 561–76.

Democrats. Today the DSG has a membership of over 200, an elected chairman and executive committee, a professional staff, and a whip system that functions on important legislation. Issuing fact sheets and weekly legislative reports, the DSG concentrates its efforts on meeting the information problems of its members and in turning them out for floor votes. From its uncertain and awkward launching in the 1950s the DSG has emerged as a substantial liberal force in the House. A number of the most important House reforms of the 1970s are directly credited to the inspiration, leadership, and activities of the DSG.[43]

State party delegations also influence political behavior in the House of Representatives. Some state party delegations, such as the California and Texas Democratic delegations, have regular weekly meetings to discuss matters of interest to their members. Other state delegations meet irregularly, though their members may have a considerable number of informal contacts with each other. Still other delegations, such as those of both parties in New York, rarely meet and have little cohesion.[44]

Cohesive delegations are a major source of information for their members, as these comments suggest:

> We're so busy we have to find shortcuts. If you talk to someone on the delegation, you can find out the inside things—which parts were controversial and who was on which side. The workload is impossible.

> We have good committee spread. The man on the committee takes the lead, keeps the rest of us informed about what's going on. We get pretty good intelligence that way.[45]

A cohesive state party delegation is valuable to members in several respects. The delegation helps new members to learn their way around the House and to learn their jobs. Delegations can also be helpful in lobbying for good committee assignments for their members. Delegation members are a convenient and time-saving source of information for congressmen

---

[43]See an account of the DSG by Arthur G. Stevens, Jr., Arthur H. Miller, and Thomas E. Mann, "Mobilization of Liberal Strength in the House, 1955–1970: The Democratic Study Group," *American Political Science Review*, 58 (June 1974), 667–81. For a study of the group's early years, see Kenneth Kofmehl, "The Institutionalization of a Voting Bloc," *Western Political Quarterly*, 17, (June 1964), 256–72.

[44]This analysis of state party delegations is based largely on Barbara Deckard's study, "State Party Delegations in the U.S. House of Representatives: A Comparative Study of Group Cohesion," *Journal of Politics*, 34 (February 1972), 199–222. Also see Barbara Deckard, "State Party Delegations in the United States House of Representatives—An Analysis of Group Action," *Polity*, 5 (Spring 1973), 311–34; Richard Born, "Cue-Taking within State Party Delegations in the U.S. House of Representatives," *Journal of Politics*, 38 (February 1976), 71–94; and John H. Kessel, "The Washington Congressional Delegation," *Midwest Journal of Political Science*, 8 (February 1964), 1–21.

[45]Deckard, "State Party Delegations in the U.S. House of Representatives: A Comparative Study of Group Cohesion," 210.

hard-pressed to discover those things they need to know. Cohesive delegations help to structure voting and to facilitate bargaining, particularly in the interest of state or district projects. But in one sense they make the House more difficult for party leaders to manage, for the members of cohesive delegations are less dependent on the leadership for information and voting cues. In addition, members of these delegations have more strength in bargaining with leaders than they would have as individuals. The broad point to recognize is that while cohesive state party delegations are useful for the members, they contribute to the decentralization of power in the House and to the parochial cast of some of its activities.

Party and Policy-Making

American political parties, in Congress as elsewhere, are not teetering on the brink of oblivion, but they are not in the best of shape. Their role in political campaigns has been eroded as the influence of the mass media, public relations specialists, and campaign management firms has grown. Campaigns have become more and more candidate-centered, relegating the party organizations in many jurisdictions to positions somewhere near the sidelines. With increasing frequency individual candidates stake out their independence from party in campaigns, at times appearing to campaign as much against their own party (the "machine") as against other candidates. Among voters the number of independents grows, while the number of strong party identifiers declines. The disillusionment of the public with the parties shows up again and again in public opinion surveys. The American party system has become an object of concern for those who believe that parties and democracy are tightly intertwined and an object of dismay for those who like tidy, patterned, and predictable politics.

The fact that the American people lack enthusiasm for party does not diminish two important facts concerning this basic institution for the popular control of government. The first is that most voting decisions in congressional elections are based significantly, though not flatly, on the party affiliations of the candidates. The parties win elections where they are expected to win—even though weakened, party affiliation is still a critical variable in the election of members of Congress. And second, even though weakened, party affiliation is still the most important variable in influencing the voting behavior of members of Congress.

An appropriate point of departure for examining the role and influence of political parties in Congress is to consider the extent of party voting over time—that is, the proportion of votes in which the members of one party oppose those of the other. Various definitions of party voting have been used. Between 1921 and 1948, one study shows, about seventeen percent of the roll call votes taken in the House of Representatives were

Table 3.4   Party Voting in the U.S. House of Representatives, 1861-1974

Congresses and Years		Percentage of All Roll Call Votes with Majority Against Majority
37th-41st	(1861-71)	74%
42nd-46th	(1871-81)	73
47th-51st	(1881-91)	67
52nd-56th	(1891-1901)	63
57th-61st	(1901-11)	74
62nd-66th	(1911-21)	54
67th-71st	(1921-31)	55
72nd-76th	(1931-41)	65
77th-81st	(1941-51)	47
82nd-86th	(1951-61)	50
87th-91st	(1961-71)	43
92nd-93rd	(1971-74)	34

Source: Jerome M. Clubb and Santa A. Traugott, "Partisan Cleavage and Cohesion in the House of Representatives, 1861-1974," *Journal of Interdisciplinary History,* 7, no. 3 (Winter 1977), 382-83 (as adapted). The percentages shown are the averages for the five Congresses of each decade. This study should also be consulted for other tests of party voting.

"party votes"—defined as ninety percent of one party opposed to ninety percent of the other party.[46] Using this definition, a later study covering the years 1950 through 1967 finds no session of Congress in which more than eight percent of the roll call votes were party votes; in some sessions the proportion was well under five percent.[47]

A much less constrictive definition of party voting used in a recent study depicts the same trend. Table 3.4, adapted from the work of Jerome M. Clubb and Santa A. Traugott, shows the percentage of roll call votes in which a *majority* of the members of one party opposed a *majority* of the other party in all Congresses, grouped by decade, between 1861 and 1974. The table shows that the level of party voting has substantially declined in the twentieth century. Fewer and fewer conflicts occur between the parties. In recent Congresses, only about one-third of the roll call votes have yielded alignments in which a majority of Democrats opposed a majority of Republicans—and this, of course, is far from a stern test of partisan cleavage, such as the "ninety percent versus ninety percent" standard.

The reasons for the decline in party voting are not easily weighed for significance. But many can be identified. The weakening of the parties in the electorate, marked by a growing number of independents and a massive increase in ticket-splitting, is, of course, a partial explanation. Changes in Congress have also contributed to party devitalization. Beginning with the

[46]Julius Turner, *Party and Constituency: Pressures on Congress* (Baltimore: Johns Hopkins Press, 1951), p. 23. The original Turner study was revised by Edward V. Schneier, Jr., in 1970.
[47]*Ibid.,* p. 17.

revolt against Speaker Cannon early in the twentieth century, the powers of the congressional party leadership were steadily weakened—at least until the early 1970s. The consolidation of the seniority rule served to establish an alternative set of leaders, the committee chairmen, who have often been at odds with the elected leaders and with a majority of their party. The increase in the power and autonomy of committees, and later of subcommittees, has made party management of Congress increasingly difficult. And the presence of a large number of members who were elected to Congress mainly as a result of their own initiatives—who owe little to district or state party organizations and who enjoy their independent status—has undoubtedly softened congressional party organizations. The leaders of the congressional parties understand the independence of members as well as anyone. It prompts them to shape party strategies and positions with one eye on the desirable and the other on the possible. If party members stray off the reservation, voting regularly with the other party, there is not much that they can do about it.

The decline in the frequency of party voting in Congress does not mean that partisan cleavages rarely occur on matters that count. Certain kinds of public policy questions regularly produce conflicts between the parties—or at least between large majorities of each party. Taken as a group, Democratic members are much more likely than Republicans to favor social welfare programs (and increased appropriations for the agencies that administer them), job programs through public works, tax revisions that aid lower income families, government regulation of business, and new and expanded federal programs. The conservative alternative posed by Republican members often prescribes smaller expenditures for various programs, general fiscal prudence, state rather than federal administration or implementation, and policy formulations that favor business over labor or higher income groups over lower income groups.[48] When viewing the economy, Republicans worry more about inflation, Democrats more about unemployment.[49]

---

[48]The legislative issues on which the Chamber of Commerce and the AFL-CIO Committee on Political Education each ranked members are generally similar and occasionally identical. A few examples will suffice. In the Ninety-fourth Congress, COPE favored legislation providing for no-fault insurance, increased food stamp coverage, the right of federal employees to participate in partisan political campaigns and to run for local, state, or federal office, increased funding for federal housing projects, the creation of jobs through public works, support for federally funded day care centers serving low-income families, and federal educational grants for disadvantaged children. The Chamber of Commerce opposed job-creating public works projects and more restrictive clean-air requirements, while favoring an easing of antitrust laws and a limitation on the eligibility for food stamps of persons engaged in striking or in other labor disputes. For a complete listing, see the *Congressional Quarterly Weekly Report*, February 5, 1977, pp. 223–35.

[49]See Edward R. Tufte, *Political Control of the Economy* (Princeton, N.J.: Princeton University Press, 1978), especially Chapter 4.

Figures 1 and 2 capture the essence, though not the totality, of the differences between the parties in Congress. They also reveal something of the problems of disunity that perplex each party. Figure 1 shows the positions of senators, lodged in regional groups, on legislation of interest to the Chamber of Commerce of the United States, the best known of all business groups. Two important conclusions are readily drawn from it.

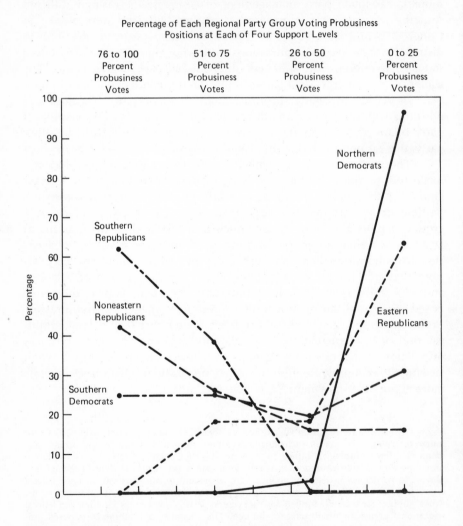

Figure 1. Support for Probusiness Positions by Party Groups, U.S. Senate, 94th Congress, 2nd Session. *Source:* The data are drawn from the *Congressional Quarterly Weekly Report,* February 5, 1977, p. 222. Each senator is ranked in terms of the percentage of votes which he cast in agreement with the positions of the Chamber of Commerce of the United States. "Noneastern" Republicans are all northern members except those from the eastern states.

First, although the parties are not tightly cohesive, there are genuine differences between the parties on legislation that attracts the concern of organized business. A strong majority of Democrats shows slight sympathy for the legislative objectives of the Chamber of Commerce while most Republicans rally to its banner. Nearly all of the members of the largest of the party groupings, northern Democrats, are found in the lowest quartile of support for probusiness legislation. The strongest supporters of business are the southern Republicans, clearly the most conservative contingent in the Senate, followed by noneastern (midwestern and western) Republicans. Figure 2 shows the other side of the coin: support for pro-labor positions in the Senate. The voting behavior of the members is reversed, with northern (i.e., non-southern) Democrats voting heavily in agreement with the AFL-CIO side and Republicans (except for those representing eastern states) voting strongly in opposition.

Second, the problem of party disunity is chiefly a regional phenomenon. Eastern Republicans and southern Democrats, particularly the former, have the least in common with a majority of their own party and the most in common with the other party. As they desert their parties on labor-management questions, cohesion and party voting decline. Southern Democrats present a particularly interesting case. They are arrayed in roughly equal numbers at all levels of support in both figures, suggesting a wide range of ideological positions among the members of this regional set. A few southern Democrats, such as Bumpers (Ark.) and Hollings (S.C.), are almost as likely to take the liberal side of labor or management issues as the average northern Democrat. A liberal Democratic party in the South is not imminent, but there are clearly more liberals and moderates in the southern "branch" of the party today than at any time in recent decades. At the same time, a number of eastern Republicans have become increasingly restive over the conservative thrust of their party. Such Republican senators as Javits (N.Y.) and Mathias (Md.) have voting records on labor-management questions that are scarcely distinguishable from those of their northern Democratic counterparts. Overall, it is plain that the "maverick" members of the congressional parties have discovered ways to satisfy their constituencies that do not include voting with a high degree of party regularity and, in the case of some southern Democrats, a high degree of sectional unity.

The evidence of party disunity takes on more significance when another congressional element is brought into view, the conservative coalition—a durable voting alliance of southern Democrats and Republicans that has been in existence since the late 1930s.[50] When party lines break in either house, there is a good chance that the emergent voting pattern will show Republicans and southern Democrats in opposition to

---

[50]See a recent study of the conservative coalition by John F. Manley, "The Conservative Coalition in Congress," in *Congress Reconsidered*, eds. Lawrence C. Dodd and Bruce I. Oppenheimer (New York: Praeger Publishers, 1977), pp. 75–95.

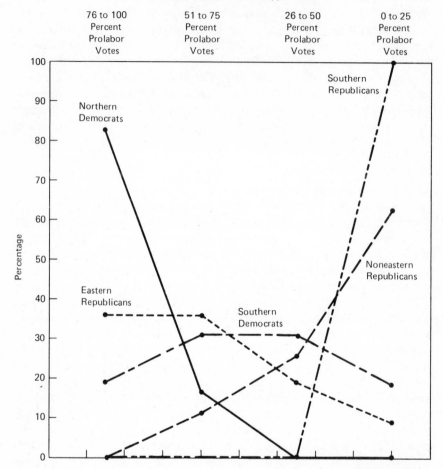

Percentage of Each Regional Party Group Voting Prolabor
Positions at Each of Four Support Levels

| 76 to 100 Percent Prolabor Votes | 51 to 75 Percent Prolabor Votes | 26 to 50 Percent Prolabor Votes | 0 to 25 Percent Prolabor Votes |

Figure 2. Support for Prolabor Positions by Party Groups, U.S. Senate, 94th Congress, 2nd Session. *Source:* The data are drawn from the *Congressional Quarterly Weekly Report,* February 5, 1977, p. 222. Each senator is ranked in terms of the percentage of votes which he cast in agreement with the positions of the AFL-CIO Committee on Political Education. "Noneastern" Republicans are all northern members except those from the eastern states.

other Democrats. And of more importance, there is a good chance that, once formed, this biparty coalition will win.

Table 3.5 shows the incidence and the success of the conservative coalition on floor votes from 1965 through 1977. Although the coalition fared poorly in 1965—the first congressional session of President Lyndon Johnson's "Great Society" administration—it has done remarkably well since then. Typically the coalition comes together on about one-quarter of all roll call votes and wins perhaps sixty percent of the time—a formidable

Table 3.5   The Effectiveness of the Conservative Coalition in Congress, 1965-1977

Year	Percentage of Coalition Recorded Votes	Percentage of Coalition Victories House	Senate	Total
1977	26%	60%	74%	68%
1976	24	59	58	58
1975	28	52	48	50
1974	24	67	54	59
1973	23	67	54	61
1972	27	79	63	69
1971	30	79	86	83
1970	22	70	64	66
1969	27	71	67	68
1968	24	63	80	73
1967	20	73	54	63
1966	25	32	51	45
1965	24	25	39	33

Source: Congressional Quarterly Weekly Report, January 7, 1978, p. 4. A conservative coalition vote is any vote on which a majority of voting southern Democrats and a majority of voting Republicans are opposed to a majority of voting northern Democrats. Included in the southern states are Alabama, Arkansas, Florida, Georgia, Kentucky, Louisiana, Mississippi, North Carolina, Oklahoma, South Carolina, Tennessee, Texas, and Virginia. All other states are considered to be "northern."

achievement. There have been occasional sessions in which the coalition has won over eighty percent of the votes on which it appeared. Bolstered by the White House, the coalition was especially potent during the first term of President Richard Nixon.

THE PROFESSIONAL STAFFS OF CONGRESS

The Congressional bureaucracy is the third major component in the internal power structure of Congress. Congressional employees now number about 18,000 persons. Included in this number are about 10,000 aides who work in lawmakers' personal offices and about 3,000 who hold committee and subcommittee staff appointments.

The Development of Professional Staffs

The growth in professional staffs has been phenomenal in recent years. In 1960, for example, the number of personal staff aides in the Senate was 1,418, an average of 14 aides per office; by 1976 the total had reached 3,122, an average of 31 per office. The smallest personal staff in the Senate in 1976 had 13 members, while the largest had 71. Staff allowances for members of the Senate are calculated on the basis of state population; they vary from a minimum of about $450,000 (for members from states with less than two million population) to about $900,000 (for members from states with populations over 21 million). Each member of the House is entitled to a personal staff of 18 members. Staff allowances for House and Senate committees have also increased dramatically in recent years, due partially to the growth in the number of subcommittees.[51]

Although the rapid growth in congressional staffs is a source of worry for some sectors of the press and for some members of Congress as well, there are reasonable explanations for it. In the broadest sense, it traces from the increasing complexity of American society and from the accompanying growth in the complexities of lawmaking and of legislation. Major issues are more appropriately described as bundles of issues—tangled, interrelated, and complicated:

> Complexity in lawmaking mirrors the complexities in American society at large. It is a commonplace that our world has become more interrelated and interdependent, and it is therefore increasingly difficult to cordon off a particular issue for isolated consideration. Agricultural policy, for example, is increasingly tied to the foreign policy of the United States, but it also reaches to community and rural development, income assistance for the poor, health and nutrition, and other issue areas. The city and countryside are linked in policy by population flows, employment opportunities, investment strategies, environmental quality, and many other things. It is becoming more and more difficult to consider an important policy question without reckoning with spillovers to other areas. . . .[52]

The development of professional staffs has been one congressional response to the growing complexity of lawmaking.[53] No member can be an expert in everything that comes before his chamber, not even an expert in most things he must consider. The demand for additional professional staff is thus a recognition of the need for expert assistance and counsel and a strategy for organizing the legislature and equipping its members to deal with the complexities of policy-making.

[51]See Susan Webb Hammond, "The Operation of Senator's Offices," a paper prepared for the Commission on the Operation of the Senate, *Senators: Offices, Ethics, and Pressures*, 94th Cong., 2d sess., 1977, pp. 4–18.

[52]Allen Schick, "Complex Policymaking in the United States Senate," a paper prepared for the Commission on the Operation of the Senate, *Policy Analysis on Major Issues*, 94th Cong., 2d sess., 1977, p. 9.

[53]For a comprehensive analysis of congressional staffs, see Kenneth Kofmehl, *Professional Staffs of Congress* (West Lafayette, Ind.: The Purdue University Press, 1977); and Harrison W. Fox, Jr., and Susan Webb Hammond, *Congressional Staffs: The Invisible Force in American Lawmaking* (New York: The Free Press, 1977).

Three additional explanations for the increasing importance of congressional staffs need to be taken into account. One is that the quest for staff is a quest for self-sufficiency on the part of members as well as on the part of Congress. Both the institution and the members need their own sources of information and policy analysis as a means of offsetting the influence of executive agencies and private organizations. Ultimately the independence of Congress rests on its capacity to acquire and organize information and to fashion policy options apart from those readily available to it from external sources. Professional staff assistance is an important component of legislator and legislative independence.

The second explanation is readily understood and often cited by members of Congress. It is that the volume of interactions between members and their constituents has become so great that staff assistance to deal with it has become indispensable for the functioning of congressional offices. One indication of this, for example, is that the quantity of mail addressed to members of the House by constituents has increased from 14 million pieces in 1969 to 42 million in 1975—an increase of 300 percent in only six years.[54] For every letter that comes into Congress, one or more usually go out. And that is only part of the story. Constituents want solutions to problems that confront them. Their problems create casework for the members. The importance of staff in handling constituent matters is indicated in these observations by a member of the Senate:

> More than half of my total staff time is devoted not to the substantive issues that we are sent here to deal with, but to casework problems—resolving individual difficulties that have developed between citizens and their government—and to responding to the mail. We all know that we have to deal with the casework and respond to the mail in order to be able to remain here to do the other things that we want to do.[55]

Finally, congressional staffs have grown in size and influence because they are able to perform so many activities that promote the member's main objective of winning reelection. On the whole, the personal staffs of members spend relatively little time on purely legislative matters, such as legislative research and bill drafting. Rather, the major portion of their time is allocated to casework problems, to meeting with constituents and lobbyists (in the constituencies as well as in Washington), to answering letters, to writing letters or newsletters designed to increase constituent awareness of the member's activities and accomplishments, to dealing with the media in pursuit of publicity for the member, and to the drafting of

---

[54]Commission on Administrative Review, U.S. House of Representatives, *Scheduling the Work of the House*, 94th Cong., 2d sess., 1976, p. vii.

[55]*Hearings* before the Temporary Select Committee to Study the Senate Committee System, 94th Cong., 2d sess., 1976, p. 56. The statement is by Senator Alan Cranston (D., Calif.).

speeches. In one way or another, virtually all members of Congress use their staff personnel to keep them in the public eye, to drum up electoral support, to monitor political developments at home, and to deal with all the forms of constituency and Washington politics that bear on their reelection. Astute, energetic staffs provide incumbents with an incalculable advantage over their opponents.

The staffs of congressional committees are lodged at the hub of legislative policy making. Although their quality and contributions vary from staff to staff and from committee to committee, it is plain that the overall influence of congressional staffers has grown markedly and that much of the legislation passed in any session bears their heavy imprint. It could hardly be otherwise: their influence on policy is a function of what they do. They gather and analyze information for committee members, thus constructing the intelligence base on which public policy is fashioned; they plan and administer public hearings (including the selection of witnesses) and investigations; and they draft legislation and committee reports, thereby helping to structure the issues and alternatives to be considered. "Some committee staffs are more innovative than others, and on these committees, staff members may be as likely as committee members themselves to initiate legislation."[56]

The scope of staff involvement in decision-making is shown in the following observations:

> [Their] ability to run committee investigations, the results of which they can skillfully leak to the media, gives them influence over the items Members choose to put on the legislative agenda. Once something is on the agenda, the staff works to assemble a coalition supporting a specific piece of legislation. As it sets up committee hearings, the staff will reach as broadly as possible without sacrificing the goals the chairman, often at their urging, has adopted. Then, when a bill is "marked up" (amended and passed in committee), the staff will be expected to reconcile competing interest-group demands. When conflicts cannot be resolved, the Members may then learn enough about the details to weigh the political costs of compromise. But if the major differences raised by the normally vocal interest groups can be settled otherwise, most Members will be content to leave the details to the staff, as well—details that can frequently mean everything to whole industries or groups of people.[57]

The information and policy analysis requirements of Congress, the need for specialized skills and knowledge, and the desire to strengthen the legislature in its relationship with the executive branch have all contributed

---

[56]Samuel C. Patterson, "Staffing House Committees," a paper prepared for the Select Committee on Committees, U.S. House of Representatives, *Committee Organization in the House*, 93rd Cong., 1st sess., Vol. 2 of 3, Part 3 of 3, 1973, p. 676.

[57]Michael J. Malbin, "Congressional Committee Staffs: Who's in Charge Here?," *The Public Interest*, Number 47 (Spring 1977), 17–18. ©1977 by National Affairs, Inc. See also Michael Andrew Scully, "Reflections of a Senate Aide," *The Public Interest*, Number 47 (Spring 1977), 41–48.

to an increase in the policy-making role of congressional staffs. Despite the controversy that occasionally swirls around them, this is not likely to change.

Staffs, Politics, and Policy

The congressional bureaucracy attracts criticism for four principal reasons. The first is the increasing cost of maintaining Congress. In 1968 the budget for Congress and its supporting services was less than $300 million, but by 1977 it had climbed to nearly $1 billion—tripling in size in about a decade. The need for staff support tends to be obscured by the sheer scope of Congress's expenditures on itself. The chairman of the House Commission on Administrative Review explains:

> Congress is damned if you do and damned if you don't. If you don't increase your capability, you're ridiculed as being the sapless branch. If you do something, you're rapped for being a $1 billion Congress.

> We're dealing with a lot more than we did 30 years ago when old Charlie came here and worked three days a week until Labor Day. I'm not concerned about the fact that the budget for Congress is growing. It should. It's long overdue. I am concerned about the fact that the growth of staff is around an outdated committee structure.[58]

The partisanship of committee staffs is sometimes a point of dispute, particularly within Congress. There are members who believe that all committee staffs should be sternly nonpartisan and others who believe that partisanship in staffing is essential as well as inevitable because policy is made (at least in some committee jurisdictions) on the basis of differences in party philosophies. Some committee staffs, such as that of the divisive House Committee on Education and Labor, have become known for the partisan orientation of their members. A role of limited partisanship, however, is the norm for the staffs of most congressional committees.[59] In recent years House Republicans have steadily sought to change the chamber's rules to provide that up to one-third of the funds designated to committees for staff appointments be assigned to the minority party. Their efforts have thus far failed.

A third line of criticism focuses on the misuse of staff by members. At issue are the committee staffs, whose members are sometimes diverted from the committee work for which they were hired to assignments in legislators' offices, handling casework, serving as general legislative aides,

---

[58]*New York Times*, January 16, 1977. The statement is by Congressman David R. Obey (D., Wis.).

[59]Samuel C. Patterson, "The Professional Staffs of Congressional Committees," *Administrative Science Quarterly*, 15 (March 1970), 31.

and doing a variety of political chores (including campaign activities). Perhaps one-third of the members of the Senate, the *Washington Post* has estimated, have used their committee staff members for business unrelated to their committee assignments. Members justify this in terms of their need to take care of the problems of their constituents:

> It's true that not everybody uses staff as well or as effectively or for proper purposes as they should. . . . The point is that, if you've got staff in one area— whether it's the subcommittee area or the full committee area—and inadequate staff in another area of your legislative responsibility, the tendency is to try to use whatever staff you've got to cover the legislative responsibilities for which you have to be answerable to your constituents.[60]

Of all the criticisms lodged against congressional staff members, clearly the most important is that they have come to exercise too much influence in policy-making, leading some members to conclude that staff have usurped the authority of the elected representatives. The impact of staff on policy-making is widely recognized, but it is particularly nettling to conservative members of the minority:

> Members are so burdened with other duties that an increasing amount of committee work is being delegated to staff personnel. As a result, professional staffers are assuming too much power, and in some cases, are making policy rather than merely helping with the technical problems as was intended.[61]

> Many times . . . I have complained that too much authority—important authority—is left in the hands of congressional staff members who have no right, and in many cases, no ability, to exercise it. I'm not saying that every member of a staff—whether the staff is that of an individual Senator, a House member, or a committee—is inefficient. Far from it. Most staffers are extremely able. But this does not alter the fact that they have been given far too much power by members who are too busy or too lazy to exercise it themselves. This is not right. Nor is it . . . in keeping with the governmental structure envisioned by the Founding Fathers, because these staff members often exercise the power of decision-making on matters affecting millions of Americans, although they were never elected to do so.[62]

The public policies that emerge from Congress are the result of a mix of influences. To the internal factors of committee, party, and staff must be added the external factors of chief executive, interest group, and constituency. We turn to these in Chapter 4.

[60]*Hearings* before the Temporary Select Committee to Study the Senate Committee System, p. 292. The statement is by Senator Edmund S. Muskie (D., Maine). See an excellent series on the congressional bureaucracy by Stephen Isaacs in the *Washington Post*, issues of February 16–23, 1975.

[61]*Hearings*, p. 117. The statement is by Senator Robert Dole (R., Kan.).

[62]Barry Goldwater, *The Coming Breakpoint* (New York: Macmillan Publishing Co., Inc., 1976), pp. 84–85.

External Pressures

4

There is anomaly in the legislative process as in everything else. Consider the formal position of Congress. The Constitution places it firmly in charge of national policy-making by granting it "all legislative powers." But there is much less to this constitutional authorization than meets the eye. Other political actors draw heavily and steadily on the powers of Congress. Their involvement in the legislative process is a natural outgrowth of the openness of the institution, its numerous points of access, and its lack of strict hierarchy. Congress is an institution vulnerable to invasion by others. The three principal external forces that interact with Congress, seeking to move it along lines congenial to their interests, are the chief executive (including the bureaucracy), interest groups, and constituencies.

PRESIDENT AND CONGRESS

The Constitutional Basis of Executive-Legislative Relations

The Constitution of the United States provides only a bare framework for the involvement of the president in the legislative process. Unless it is read carefully, in fact, it is easy to miss the grants of "legislative" powers to the president. There are only three. He is empowered to recommend measures for the consideration of Congress, to veto legislative acts, and to convene either or both houses in special session.

The key to the Constitution is not its specific authorizations of power but rather its adaptability. It permits, even encourages, changes to take place. Using the message and veto powers, modern presidents have been able to establish a firm legal basis for entering the legislative process. Often tentative in the nineteenth century, executive interaction with Congress has become well institutionalized in this century. All members of Congress, what is more, have come to expect it—which is not to say that all welcome it.

The power to call special sessions is no longer of much importance, since Congress now works virtually year-round in regular session. The last president to invoke this power was Harry S. Truman in 1948. Shortly after his nomination, he called the Republican-controlled Eightieth Congress back to Washington to consider his program, which had fared badly in the regular session. As anticipated, Congress gave it short shrift. But its inactivity gave him an issue—the "do-nothing" Congress—which he exploited to the maximum in the presidential campaign.

The power to recommend measures is much more important. The president prepares three major messages for Congress: the State of the Union message, as required by the Constitution, and the Budget and Economic Report messages, as required by acts of Congress. From the perspective of the president, these messages are more opportunity than obligation. They invite him to lay his program before Congress and the nation. In addition, he regularly sends special messages to Congress, outlining his views and recommendations on particular policy problems, such as taxation, welfare, or foreign policy. To a marked extent, the recommendations in his messages become the major items on the congressional agenda. Congress, of course, will not pass all of them, perhaps not even a majority, but it does consider most of them.[1]

The veto is at times an important presidential weapon—a means by which he can resist change, weed out legislation he deems inappropriate, and contain congressional power and initiative.[2] Its large impact, especially when invoked on major bills, is to limit congressional control over the

---

[1] A president who secures the passage of 50 percent of his legislative proposals is doing reasonably well with Congress. Among recent presidents, Lyndon Johnson leads in the proportion of administration bills gaining congressional approval. In 1965, more than seventy percent of his proposals were adopted. Neither Richard Nixon nor Gerald Ford reached the level of fifty percent in any session of Congress, and at times fell much below that. Yet the proportion of administration bills passed is not a sharply accurate test of executive influence, since legislative measures vary greatly in their significance. Moreover, the proposal-passage ratio reveals nothing about the president's priorities: he wants some enactments much more than he wants others. See William J. Keefe and Morris S. Ogul, *The American Legislative Process: Congress and the States* (Englewood Cliffs, N.J.: Prentice-Hall Inc., 1977), pp. 381–83.

[2] The president also possesses a "pocket veto." If he refuses to sign a bill passed in the last ten days of the session, it dies. The significance of the pocket veto has declined since Congress is now in session virtually all year.

policy-making process. The all-time leader in the use of the veto is Franklin D. Roosevelt, who vetoed 631 bills during his lengthy tenure in office. Only nine of his vetoes were overridden. The other two modern presidents to use it frequently were Harry S. Truman and Dwight D. Eisenhower. Truman exercised the veto 250 times and suffered twelve losses in Congress; Eisenhower vetoed 181 bills and was overridden just twice. Since Eisenhower, only one president, Gerald R. Ford, has vetoed more than fifty bills. In his brief term as president, Ford vetoed 66 bills and was overridden twelve times.

Out of the nearly 3,000 vetoes cast by all presidents, less than 100, or about three percent, have been overridden. These statistics nevertheless exaggerate the significance of the veto. Perhaps ninety percent of all vetoed bills have been minor in character, many involving private bills such as immigration permissions or pension claims. Moreover, the president rarely returns a major tax or appropriations bill to Congress, preferring to lobby vigorously for acceptable provisions while the bill is still under consideration; even if these measures fall short of his preferences, he usually signs them. Finally, presidents view the veto with some trepidation. No president has an endless stream of political capital; what he has can be depleted through the excessive use of the veto. He runs the risk that a certain veto may provoke Congress to retaliate on other administration bills. Use of this power is thus more circumscribed than might appear at first glance.[3]

The president may also employ the threat of a veto to prompt Congress to revise pending legislation to meet his objections. Ordinarily presidents are prudent in the use of this threat, since Congress can ignore it. Indeed, the threat of a veto may goad Congress into writing legislation even less satisfactory to him. Short of examining individual cases, about the most that can be said about this tactic is that it sometimes works. The threat of a veto probably carries less weight with the more independent members of today's Congress than it did with members in previous years.

Conflict between
President and Congress

Relations between the president and Congress are both complex and variable. Some presidents have had relatively smooth relations with Congress, while others have been steadily embroiled in conflict with it. As a rule, prospects for harmony between the branches are greatest when the president makes no great stir and lodges no more than minimal demands

---

[3]This paragraph is based mainly on Thomas E. Cronin, *The State of the Presidency* (Boston: Little, Brown and Company, 1975), pp. 76–79.

on Congress. The president who elects not to play the role of "chief legislator," who regularly defers to and conciliates Congress—as President Dwight Eisenhower did over most of his two terms in the 1950s—ordinarily will succeed in getting along with most elements in the legislature.

In contrast, the president who chooses to recommend major legislative proposals and to mobilize support for their passage is sure to arouse congressional opposition, particularly if his proposals challenge long-standing congressional dispositions or produce uncomfortable reverberations in the constituencies of the members. His success in moving his program through Congress is likely to depend on the vigor and skill with which he pursues his initiatives, the size of his party's congressional majority, his support among the public at large and, at times, his ability to put together bi-party coalitions for specific proposals. Of course even under the most favorable circumstances, there is no assurance that his objectives will be attainable in Congress, an institution with large powers in its own right.

Relations between the executive and legislative branches in recent decades have been characterized more by conflict than by harmony. Why the president and Congress find it hard to get along, to work in harness, is not hard to uncover. The foundation for the conflict is the system of separation of powers and checks and balances. The Constitution not only makes the branches independent of each other, but also provides for their sharing of functions and powers. This structural arrangement—of independence mixed with sharing—is an invitation to conflict, as each branch, responding to the claims pressed upon it, pursues its conception of good public policy.

A second factor promoting disagreement is that modern presidents, not content with the administration of laws passed by Congress, have tended to regard the initiation of public policy proposals as a central function of their office. Congress, of course, sees itself as the lawmaking power; it is seldom satisfied simply to place its approval on proposals emanating from the executive branch. It is, moreover, zealous in defending its independence. When, for example, relations between the Carter administration and Congress were strained by the failure of the president to consult adequately with key legislators concerning both policies and personnel, Speaker Thomas "Tip" O'Neill stated bluntly:

> With the War Powers Act and the new budget process, Congress is proving that it is capable of operating on an equal footing with the executive. Common sense and the Constitution demand that Pennsylvania Avenue remain a two-way street.[4]

Third, the constituencies that elect the president and Congress are radically different. Chosen by a large and heterogeneous national electorate,

[4]*Congressional Quarterly Weekly Report*, February 26, 1977, p. 361.

the president owes his election to the support of many kinds of organized groups and many kinds of voters. Those who support the president have special claims upon him. He hears claims, moreover, that barely register on Congress. One element in the tension between executive and legislature is found in the ideological tilt of their followers: the constituency of the president, whether Democrat or Republican, is usually more liberal than that of the typical member of Congress. When this is the case, policy conflicts along liberal-conservative dimensions are the result.

While the president is elected by perhaps 40 million votes, the average member of the House is elected by not much more than 100,000 votes. Only a few members of the Senate receive as many as 1 million votes. A great many congressmen are elected from "one-party" districts distinguished for the homogeneity of their populations. Often lacking serious opposition in elections and securely supported by the dominant combination of interests in their districts, these members have scant incentive to support presidential initiatives if by doing so they risk upsetting their electoral followings. It is a major truth about Congress that all members have a large investment of emotional and political capital in their constituencies, and when there is apparent conflict between presidential and local priorities, local priorities usually win out.

A fourth reason for the persistence of legislative-executive conflict traces from the party system in Congress. There is abundant evidence that neither the Democratic nor the Republican legislative party organizations are cohesive. On certain kinds of issues each party is inclined to fly apart. The member who opposes the leadership of his party, including the president, is rarely subjected to any form of party discipline. He knows that if he satisfies the general run of voters and the organized elements in his constituency he can be reelected again and again. Indeed, he may strengthen his position with constituents by openly opposing the president. Congressional careers have sometimes been built on a foundation of persistent opposition to the chief executive.

The weakening of the parties in the electorate, moreover, has diminished the president's role as national party leader. He can no longer count on powerful party leaders and organizations in states and cities to help marshal support for his legislative program and to bring recalcitrant legislators into line. The significance of party organizations has declined at all levels under the press of new social forces—television, widespread education and affluence, and population mobility—and new forms of campaigning and electoral behavior—the rise of professional campaign management firms, the increase in the number of so-called independent candidates, and the increase in ticket-splitting and in the number of independent voters.

The erosion of party influence in the electorate has also contributed to the independence of members of Congress. Owing election more to their own resourcefulness and efforts than to those of their party's, they have gained a larger measure of freedom to establish their own legislative priorities, quite apart from the urgings of the president, and to work out policy positions designed to promote continuing support within their constituencies.

Fifth, congressional structure and organization contribute to tension between the branches. Power in Congress is lodged in nooks and crannies, making decentralization the most important characteristic of the institution. The customs, rules, and practices of Congress support the member inclined to resist the president's legislative proposals. Even if the congressional party leaders are firmly in league with the president, there are limits to what they can do to promote and protect his legislation in committee. As Mike Mansfield, former majority leader of the Senate, described his position: "I'm not the leader, really. They don't do what I tell them. I do what they tell me . . . The brains are in the committees."[5]

The terms of legislation are set largely in committee. Elevated to their positions through the seniority rule, committee chairmen have substantial power to influence committee choices, and they use it steadily to shape legislation. Many of the classic disputes of American politics have occurred between a "liberal" president, impatient to see one of his major legislative proposals adopted, and a "conservative" chairman, bent on delaying, revising, or defeating it. Seniority, the independent status of committees, the power of committee and subcommittee chairmen, and the rules that may be invoked to delay action (such as the "unlimited" debate rule of the Senate) usually serve to diminish the influence of the chief executive on the legislature.

Finally, conflict occurs because the members of Congress and the president are governed by different timetables. The activist president is usually in a hurry, anxious to establish a legislative record, and worried about his reelection. In contrast, no one is ringing a bell for the member of Congress. Unencumbered by a two-term limitation, he is likely to remain in Congress for many years, no matter how the president's legislative program fares. The reality of the political timetable was aptly described by President Lyndon Johnson:

> You've got to give it all you can, that first year. Doesn't matter what kind of majority you come in with. You've got just one year when they treat you right, and before they start worrying about themselves. The third year, you lose votes; if this war goes on, I'll lose a lot of 'em. A lot of our people don't belong here, they're in Republican seats, and the Republicans will get them

[5]As quoted by James A. Robinson, *Congress and Foreign Policy-Making* (Homewood, Ill.: Dorsey Press, 1962), pp. 215–16. ©1962 by the Dorsey Press.

back. The fourth year's all politics. You can't put anything through when half the Congress is thinking how to beat you. . . .[6]

Whether conflict between the president and Congress serves the best interests of the nation is a contextual question as well as a matter of opinion. Conflicts may contribute to stalemates and to missed opportunities, but they also contribute to the clarification of issues and to the sharpening of the public's awareness of the matters at stake. The important point to recognize is that most conflicts occur not because of the short-sightedness, pettiness, or truculence of either branch, but because there are serious disagreements over the thrust of public policy. Conflict, after all, is a feature of all democratic politics. Neither branch has an exclusive or superior claim to represent the "public interest." It should be emphasized, finally, that despite the opportunities for conflict built into the system, there is nonetheless substantial cooperation between the branches.[7]

Executive-Legislative Interactions: The President's Advantages

Among the standards by which pundits and political historians measure the "greatness" of presidents is their capacity for leading Congress in the formation of public policy addressed to critical problems. Those presidents who have an instinct for the preservation of inherited patterns, or who shrink from engagement with Congress to bring about change, ordinarily fare poorly in their evaluations.

The bearing of the Constitution on the president's role in legislation is important. Its significance is not to be found in the specific legislative responsibilities and powers it awards the president, such as the veto. Its principal contribution is rather more elusive and incalculable. Through its specific grants of legislative authority in Article II, the Constitution places the president's initiatives in a recognized context of legitimacy. The Constitution frees the president to be as active in the legislative environment as he chooses or as political realities permit—or to invoke Woodrow Wilson's

---

[6]Harry McPherson, *A Political Education* (Boston: Little, Brown and Company, 1972), p. 268.

[7]Cooperation occurs because responsibility is shared. Analyzing executive-legislative relations in foreign affairs, Holbert N. Carroll writes: "Friction, tension, uncertainty, a tug of war, the jockeying for power, position, and prestige, maneuvers to protect or to advance particular interests—all of these normal and publicized features of . . . executive-legislative relations tend to obscure the significant feature of the American system that, while powers and functions are separated and dispersed in varying degrees, responsibility is shared." *The House of Representatives and Foreign Affairs* (Boston: Little, Brown and Company, 1966), p. 349.

allusive phrase, "to be as big a man as he can." For the activist president, the "legislative" powers that count are more likely to be informal than formal, political than legal.

In his encounters with Congress the president has formidable advantages. They stem from the nature of his office and from the nature of Congress. For purposes of analysis, they are grouped into six categories: (1) expectations of presidential leadership, (2) information and expertise, (3) visibility, (4) dominant trader in a trading system, (5) party leader, and (6) fragmentation of congressional power. At the outset, it needs to be emphasized that neither singly nor in combination do these advantages guarantee that, when strongly contested in Congress, the president's side will win. Far from it, the president is often fortunate simply to break even— to gain some of what he wants while losing on other things. This, of course, is a characteristic of American politics: few participants get everything they want, few lose completely, and most get at least something.

Expectations of Presidential Leadership. The president's advantages begin with the expectations that others have about his leadership role in the nation's political life. It is not easy to show the sources of these expectations, but two stand out. Severe crises, such as the Great Depression and World War II, undoubtedly helped to extend the reach of the modern presidency. Looking for solutions to these emergencies, the public came to focus on the president. His capacity for leadership, more than Congress's, seemed to promise relief from these national troubles. And of more than passing interest, national emergencies not only have shaped popular conceptions of the presidency, to the benefit of the president, but have also contributed to the expansion of the presidential establishment, as shown by the creation and augmentation of agencies and staffs to assist the president in meeting major problems.

National political campaigns have also illuminated the importance of the presidential office. The extraordinary coverage of presidential elections offered by the media, particularly television, has widened the opportunities for candidates to capture the attention of the public and to advertise their policy wares and positions; the result has been to heighten public expectations for presidential initiative in the adoption of certain legislation. Evidence from survey research bears on this. It has been shown, for example, that voters absorb more information about presidential candidates than they do about congressional candidates; of more importance, the policy views of voters are more in line with their presidential choice than with their choices for either congressman or senator. The significance of this, John Kessel points out, is that "there is far better reason to say that the president receives an issue mandate from the voters than there is to make such a claim for Congress."[8]

---

[8]John H. Kessel, *The Domestic Presidency: Decision-Making in the White House* (North Scituate,

Expectations of presidential leadership are not confined to the public. They are also found in Congress.[9] Party leaders know, for example, that their effectiveness is increased when the president lends his prestige and assistance to their efforts. He helps them win just as they help him win. Moreover, Congress has passed numerous acts that enlarge the president's responsibilities and increase his capacity to shape the national agenda and the direction of public policy.[10] Consider two of the major acts of this century. The Budget and Accounting Act of 1921 is well known for its institutionalization of the executive budget, inviting the president each year to set forth his program for Congress, together with its estimated costs. The budget, it needs to be remembered, ultimately determines what government is all about. The Employment Act of 1946 provides another large opening to legislative policy-making, since it requires the president to take stock of the economy and to submit an annual Economic Report to Congress; this document is replete with recommendations to meet the economic problems that confront the nation.

The broad point is that although Congress sometimes becomes aroused over executive aggrandizement, the fact is that it has created at least some of the conditions under which it becomes possible—by augmenting executive responsibilities and executive expertise (typically, as noted, to meet critical problems), by regularly calling for his assistance, by its own

---

Mass.: Duxbury Press, 1975), p. 115. For the data in support of this argument, see Barbara Hinckley, C. Richard Hofstetter, and John H. Kessel, "Information and the Vote: A Comparative Election Study," *American Politics Quarterly*, 2 (April 1974), 131–58.

[9]But if there are expectations that the president will lead, at least some of the time, there are also expectations that he will consult, all of the time. Presidents who fail to consult usually run into trouble with Congress. Quite early in his administration, President Carter announced his intention to eliminate funding in the budget for a number of water resource projects (mainly dams), contending they were wasteful or jeopardized the environment. His announcement provoked a storm of protest in Congress. The projects not only were essential, members contended, but the process by which the decisions were reached had demeaned Congress. Members whose districts or states were affected had not been consulted, some learned of his intentions only two or three days in advance of his announcement, and some learned of the action only through the newspapers or television. Nothing that occurred in the early months of the new administration did more to impair relations between the president and Congress. "This is motherhood. Carter picked the wrong issue for a showdown with Congress," one legislative aide remarked. The Senate majority leader was reported to have written an indignant letter to the president, pointing out that "the road can be smooth or the road can be rough. . . . There's a great sense of frustration, the feeling here on the part of members that they have not been consulted, brought into decisions before they were made." In the culmination of this imbroglio, each side won something—the funds for some projects were restored, the funds for others were deleted. The quotations are drawn from the *Congressional Quarterly Weekly Report*, March 19, 1977, p. 481.

[10]Evidence of the desire of Congress to constrict the president's powers can also be found. Increasingly in recent years Congress has employed a procedure, the "legislative veto," that reverses executive and legislative roles and responsibilities. One form of this procedure permits the president to advance a proposal which will go into effect *if not disapproved* by one or both houses within a particular period of time (e.g., thirty or sixty days). Controversy over the legislative veto has grown as its use has become more widespread, particularly in restricting presidential actions in foreign policy, such as the sale of warplanes to foreign nations.

inattention to matters of national priorities, or by dodging problems it is disinclined or unable to solve by itself.[11]

Information and Expertise. In all political systems the rewards for information and analysis are large. In the evolution of the presidency, particularly since Franklin D. Roosevelt, few changes appear in bolder relief than its extraordinary institutional growth. Over the last forty years Congress after Congress—usually prompted by distinguished citizens' committees, commissions, and task forces appointed by the president—has struggled with the development of means for helping the chief executive to do his job. The solutions, in one form or another, have centered on increasing his resources in agencies and staffs—in a word, increasing the expertise on which he can draw. Between 1932 and 1972—from Roosevelt to Nixon—the White House staff grew from 37 to 600, the staff of the Executive Office (created in 1939) from zero to many thousands.[12] Comparable developments occurred throughout the bureaucracy as new programs were launched and old ones enlarged.

The net result of the enlargement of the presidential establishment (including the formation of a congressional relations office)[13] has been to expand the president's opportunities for pursuing policy initiatives in Congress. The congressional bureaucracy has also grown dramatically, especially in recent years, as Congress has sought to guarantee its survival as an independent branch, but its expansion has been nothing on the scale of that found in the executive branch. Of course it is also true that congressional staff are used at least as fully on constituent and political business as they are on policy questions. The fact of the matter is that there is no way that Congress can equal the president's information resources[14] and staff expertise.[15]

[11]See the evidence of the "swelling" of the presidency by Cronin, *The State of the Presidency*, especially pp. 121–24.

[12]Stephen Hess, *Organizing the Presidency* (Washington, D.C.: The Brookings Institution, 1976), p. 9.

[13]See an analysis of the legislative liaison forces of the executive branch in Abraham Holtzman, *Legislative Liaison: Executive Leadership in Congress* (Chicago: Rand McNally & Company, 1970).

[14]As used here, information resources are taken to include the capacity for *analysis* of information. To quote a member of the Senate: "I have no problem with it (information). I have too much information. There is no scarcity of any information that I've found on any of my committees. I can't keep up with all of the material that is already available." What is lacking is the time and capacity to cull out irrelevant information and to assemble useful information that bears on complicated public policy alternatives. See Norman J. Ornstein and David Rohde, "Resource Usage, Information and Policymaking in the Senate," a paper prepared for the Commission on the Operation of the Senate, *Senators: Offices, Ethics, and Pressures*, 94th Cong., 2d sess., 1977, pp. 37–46. The quotation is drawn from p. 43.

[15]And consider the proposition that a highly developed information system, available to members in general, may not be everywhere welcomed in Congress, because of its larger consequences for the internal distribution of power. During the Bolling Committee hearings in the 93rd Congress, Congressman William Steiger (R., Wis.) identified this problem: "Anything we do which enables the individual member to obtain more relevant information

Although Congress is sometimes stirred by a vision of research and information parity with the executive, its members recognize keenly their disadvantages. While a member of the Senate, Walter F. Mondale observed:

> I have been in many debates, for example on the Education Committee, that dealt with complicated formulas and distributions. And I have found that whenever I am on the side of the Administration, I am surfeited with computer print-outs and data that comes within seconds, whenever I need it to prove how right I am. But if I am opposed to the Administration, computer print-outs always come late, prove the opposite point, or always are on some other topic. So I think one of the rules is that he who controls the computers controls the Congress, and I believe that there is utterly no reason why the Congress does not develop its own computer capability, its own technicians, its own pool of information. I would hope that we do so.[16]

Visibility. The president also draws power from the fact that he is the most visible politician in America, with a wealth of opportunities for focusing public attention on the White House and on his program. While individual legislators, including leaders, strain for occasional newspaper coverage, the president is the center of correspondents' attention. The massed drums of public relations and press announcements, bolstered by the steady fare of newspaper, radio, and television commentary, make the president the visible sign of national power and purpose. Although some of the president's exposure appears as nothing more than going through the motions that keep him in the public eye, other occasions take on genuine importance. Crisis dramatizes his responsibilities and increases his influence.

By contrast, Congress never speaks with a single, distinct voice. All members, as it were, play a role in explaining what the legislature will do or has done. The result is frequently a cacophony of conflicting voices.

Television has become a powerful weapon in the political arsenal of presidents:

> In the realm of videopolitics, the networks' news policies have traditionally favored the President, by allowing him access to television to address the Nation virtually whenever he requests it while regularly televising his White House press conferences in full. By contrast, the networks as a matter of news policy provide regular news coverage only of congressional committee proceedings and usually turn down requests by designated congressional spokesmen for airtime to reply to televised Presidential addresses. Thus, network news policies—with respect to providing special news coverage—encourage Presidents to set national agenda on television, to champion their programs,

---

makes that member a potential or real threat to the committee that historically has preserved unto itself its prerogatives, its information." Panel Discussions before the Select Committee on Committees, U.S. House of Representatives, *Committee Organization in the House*, 93rd Cong., 1st sess., Vol. 2 of 3, Part 2 of 3, 1973, p. 314.

   [16]Quoted in Charles O. Jones, "Why Congress Can't Do Policy Analysis," *Policy Analysis*, 2 (Spring 1976), 256.

and where, in apparent conflict with a majority in Congress, to undermine public support for the positions of the congressional opposition.[17]

The president's public standing, Richard Neustadt has suggested, conditions congressional responses to his initiatives, tending "to set a tone and to define the limits of what Washingtonians do for him, or do to him."[18] When the president's prestige is high, it can serve as a source of influence for him—and also for others who need his leverage. When it is low, it makes him more vulnerable; the costs of opposing him seem relatively slight.

The president's popularity takes on special significance when he takes his case to the people, seeking to rally their support for his program in Congress. Although this strategy is sometimes effective, it has serious limitations. Teaching the public what he thinks it needs to know is a hard task. Rousing it to action is even more difficult. And congressional opponents naturally view the strategy with less than enthusiasm. If the public, whose interest in politics so easily flags, ignores his appeals, the president's professional reputation may be damaged.

The Dominant Trader. In the president's reach for influence, he often resorts to trading with members of Congress. Based on discreet exchanges, but not on illusions, trading is a way for the president to gain support for his program. What the president wants on administration measures are votes; what members of Congress want in return are advantages. The bargains struck are of great variety. Members want federal projects for their constituencies, patronage for their supporters, help with their own "pet" legislation, help with legislation that benefits a major industry or commodity at home, defense contracts for their districts or states, the president's support (and perhaps involvement) in their bids for reelection, and recognition. The president can often supply these. Overall, he is in a better position to logroll with legislators than they are with themselves.

Among the currencies in the president's trading system are negative sanctions—threats to withhold favors from members who fail to go along. In explaining his opposition to the Vietnam War, Senator Frank Church (D., Idaho) once showed President Johnson an article on the war by Walter Lippmann. "All right," Johnson remarked, "the next time you need a dam for Idaho, you go ask Walter Lippmann."[19]

---

[17]Denis S. Rutkus, "Television Network News Coverage of Senate Committees," a paper prepared for the Temporary Select Committee to Study the Senate Committee System, *Appendix to the Second Report with Recommendations* (Washington, D.C.: Government Printing Office, 1977), p. 112. See also Michael J. Robinson, "Television and American Politics: 1956–1976," *The Public Interest*, Number 48 (Summer 1977), 3–39.

[18]Richard E. Neustadt, *Presidential Power: The Politics of Leadership* (New York: John Wiley & Sons, Inc., 1976), p. 155.

[19]As quoted by Louis W. Koenig, *The Chief Executive* (New York: Harcourt Brace Jovanovich, Inc., 1975), p. 125.

The subtle or "soft sell" by presidents is more common than the blunt threat. One Republican congressman explained President Nixon's approach when his administration was pressing for an extension of the surtax:

> It was interesting. He's very skillful. He started by asking us what we thought, and we all told him. Then he said, "I don't want you to vote against your conscience but here's the way I see it from where I sit. I'd appreciate it if you could go along." If he'd said, "You'll lose a dam in your district," you'd say, "Hell with you, you dirty politician." But it's awful hard, the way that he did do it.[20]

The temper and mood of trading characterizes some administrations more than others. As much as anything, it is a matter of the president's personal tastes, since the opportunities are always there, awaiting exploitation. Louis Koenig has observed that Franklin D. Roosevelt "excelled at the art of congressional gratification."[21] Lyndon B. Johnson was perhaps equally adept in this complicated art. Jimmy Carter may be something of an anomaly: "I am not much of a trader," he professed early in his administration. "That is one of my political defects for which I have been criticized a great deal."[22]

Party Leader. Another source of power for the president is his position as national leader of his party. Ordinarily when his party has control of both branches of Congress by heavy majorities, the president can exploit his position as party leader to secure some of his legislative objectives. Benefited by a lopsided party advantage in the Eighty-ninth Congress (1965–66), for example, President Johnson was able to secure enactment of the vast bulk of his "Great Society" program; the defections of many conservative Democrats, mainly southerners, only narrowed the margins by which his proposals passed. Thin party majorities in the legislature, however, will not do the job, since some members invariably join the opposition. President Kennedy was repeatedly confounded by the loss of support among the southern wing of the Democratic party; earlier, at a time when the Republicans narrowly controlled Congress (1953–54), President Eisenhower's sharpest critics were conservatives in his own party. As both Kennedy and Eisenhower learned two decades ago, and Carter learned recently, the president cannot get what he wants from Congress simply by dealing with party colleagues. Some members of the opposition party are more likely to be allies of the president than some members of his own party. Both Kennedy and Eisenhower devoted long hours to nurturing

---

[20]As quoted by John W. Kingdon, *Congressmen's Voting Decisions* (New York: Harper & Row, Publishers, 1973), p. 187. Copyright ©1973 by John W. Kingdon. By permission of Harper & Row, Publishers, Inc.

[21]Koenig, *The Chief Executive*, p. 169.

[22]*Congressional Quarterly Weekly Report*, April 16, 1977, p. 691.

support among the opposition party and, in varying measure, both received it.

The twentieth century has been hard on American political parties. The introduction and consolidation of the direct primary has made it much more difficult for the parties to control the nominating process. Congressional candidates of all ideological stripes regularly win nominations in each party's primaries, leading to intra-party conflict in Congress. The problem lies in the disparities between presidential and congressional electorates. "Without convergence at the stage of nomination," Neustadt observes, "there will be severe constraints on party loyalties at the stage of legislation."[23]

And there are other reasons for the decline of congressional parties. Patronage, which has sometimes been the cement of executive-legislative party relations, has dropped sharply in the face of merit system extensions. The institutionalization in Congress of the "conservative coalition"—a heady mixture of southern Democrats and Republicans—has provided an alternative to government by party majority, much to the disadvantage of Democratic presidents. The weakening of the parties in the electorate—revealed in rampant ticket-splitting and in the growth in the number of independents—not only has contributed to candidate- rather than party-centered campaigns, but also to the frequency of divided government. Between 1952 and 1980 half of all national elections yielded governments with one party in control of the presidency and the other in control of Congress. Under conditions of divided party control, the president is forced to try his hand at splicing together bi-party coalitions for his legislation.

Against this backdrop of reality—a party system in disarray—the president attempts to inject energy into the legislative party apparatus to promote his objectives. He knows that he cannot bank on a large and receptive party audience in the electorate and that members of Congress are preoccupied with their own problems. He also knows that members have large loyalties to interests other than the president's. He thus works with the resources available. He uses his formal powers, he lobbies, he trades, he wheedles, he scolds, he dramatizes issues, he identifies or manufactures crises, occasionally he threatens. If his popularity is high, some members will want his assistance in their off-year bids for reelection. And when the president runs for reelection, some members may gain "unearned" votes from his coattails. Perhaps only implicit, quid pro quo is nevertheless present in the mix of presidential and congressional campaigning: the president expects support from those he assists.

And undergirding all relationships is the factor of party loyalty: sometimes deep, sometimes shallow, it carries some weight with all members

---

[23]Neustadt, *Presidential Power: The Politics of Leadership*, p. 68.

whose party controls the presidency. The comments of two Republican congressmen during the Nixon administration make the point:

> As a party matter, this means a great deal to the administration, and it's *my* administration. If there would be something that I was sure they were wrong on, I'd go against them. But when in doubt, I don't want to see the administration embarrassed.

> It would have been good politics for me to vote for it. But the administration is trying to resist this budget-busting. So it would be bad politics for the administration. I ended up going along with the administration. It has become clear that the crowd on the other side of the aisle is doing this over and over again. They want to bust the budget and embarrass the administration, and I won't be sucked in by that.[24]

The leading edge of congressional support for the president is the party leadership in each chamber—when the same party controls both branches. There have been times, of course, when certain leaders have been hardly more than observers of the president's legislative initiatives or, worst yet from his perspective, actively opposed to them. But ordinarily the leaders work closely with the president, conscious of their stakes in his and their party's successes. What limits the congressional party leadership is what limits the president: a scarcity of political resources. Their principal power, like his, is the power of personal persuasion; their principal limitation, like his, is the independence of their followers. Strong leadership, moreover, does not guarantee as much as formerly:

> The institution of party has been the traditional bridge between the competing interests of the legislative and executive branches. The majority leader has been viewed traditionally as the man in the middle, representing the Senate's concerns to the White House and functioning as a principal spokesman for the president on Capitol Hill. But as party identification among the voters has weakened and as individual Senators have been elected with a minimum of obligation to party, the extent to which party, as such, can bridge these differences has declined. And it has become more difficult for the majority leader to carry out his two-sided existence.[25]

> The Senate itself is different. It is no longer an establishment kind of place. And every generation of young Senators who have come along have changed it a little bit. . . . The war and other issues have changed the Senate. It is no longer made up of men who are willing to be part of a hierarchical arrangement with the leader at the top of the pyramid and everybody else in his proper place waiting to climb and all the rest of it. The institution just has been opened up too much. . . . Just as in all aspects of American life there

---

[24]As quoted by Kingdon, *Congressmen's Voting Decisions*, pp. 172–73.

[25]John G. Stewart, "Committee System Management," *Appendix to the Second Report*, Temporary Select Committee to Study the Senate Committee System, 94th Cong., 2d sess., 1976, p. 17.

is no such thing as blind followers any more in this country—blind acceptance of political leaders and institutions. And the same thing is true here. . . .[26]

Congressional Power.   The fragmentation of power in Congress affects the legislative role of the president. It is at once an invitation to the president to lead and a barrier to his leadership. Power is lodged at all points of the legislative compass—in party leaders, party agencies, committees and subcommittees, committee and subcommittee chairmen, conference committees, interest blocs, regional blocs, bipartisan coalitions, informal party groups (e.g., DSG), prestigious members, and individual members. No one controls Congress because power is shared—by different members with different commitments and purposes.

The diffusion of power means that Congress is vulnerable, or even hospitable, to initiatives and leverage from outside its chambers. Chief among these external forces is the president. Whether the president succeeds in winning acceptance for his proposals is not the main point. What he does best, particularly when his party controls Congress, is to focus legislative attention on problems he has identified, at the same time providing a stimulus for their resolution. The principal items on the congressional agenda, at almost any point in almost any session, are those of the president—when, of course, his party holds a majority in Congress. Agenda-setting, it should be emphasized, is not an activity found at the margins of politics. Quite the reverse, it lies at the creative center of policy-making in all institutions.

Congress is "our slow institution."[27] Part of the reason for this is its size. An institution of 535 varied individuals, Nelson W. Polsby reminds us, is not "designed to be fast on its 1,070 feet."[28] Structure also plays a part. Under a bicameral form, both houses must agree if legislation is to be adopted. That power is fissiparous, rather than consolidated, is a third explanation for the inability of Congress to act more rapidly. Finally, the increasing openness of Congress, so characteristic of the institution in recent years, has served to slow down the process of lawmaking. "The greater the fragmentation of influence," Richard F. Fenno, Jr., observes, "the harder it is to develop or assert internal leadership. And the more open

[26]The statement is by a member of the Senate, as quoted by Robert L. Peabody, *Leadership in Congress: Stability, Succession, and Change* (Boston: Little, Brown and Company, 1976), pp. 8–9.

[27]Richard F. Fenno, Jr., "Strengthening a Congressional Strength," in *Congress Reconsidered*, eds. Lawrence C. Dodd and Bruce I. Oppenheimer (New York: Praeger Publishers, 1977), p. 263.

[28]Nelson W. Polsby, *Congress and the Presidency* (Englewood Cliffs, N.J.: Prentice-Hall, Inc., 1971), p. 13.

the internal operation, the easier it is for external groups to interpose their wishes at all stages of the process."[29] A principal beneficiary of the sluggishness of Congress is the president. James L. Sundquist writes:

> The inherent slowness of Congress gives the president infinite advantages as policy leader. Only the president, indeed, can be trusted with power where quickness of decision and action is imperative. This has been recognized not only in time of war but also to a degree in peacetime when the government must be able to respond quickly to events beyond its control. In foreign relations, therefore, the president has often been granted broad latitude to commit the nation, and the War Powers Resolution appears to acknowledge a continuing if limited authority even for the use of military force. The president has been granted discretionary powers in such domestic matters as price and wage controls. . . . Presidents can procrastinate, too, but unlike Congress they are not compelled to by any institutional structure. When their minds are made up, they can act within the limits of their statutory power.[30]

Although power diffusion in Congress invites presidential involvement in the legislative process, it does not create the conditions necessary for a one-way flow of presidential directives. In a real sense, in fact, the wide distribution of congressional power is a residual source of legislative independence. The permeability of Congress may result in preferments for outsiders, such as the president, but there are no guarantees. No one can take Congress for granted because in the last analysis no one knows what Congress will do. Congress itself must wait to know what it will do, if anything, until it has done it—in both houses.

Congress is not a neat and orderly institution. The lack of predictability in its behavior is a consequence of its lack of hierarchy, its competing "whirlpools" of influence, its many stages where legislative proposals can be discarded or undone and reworked. Such an institution has great strengths in its own right. Allen Schick makes a cogent argument:

> Congress and the executive branch are different. The executive has the comparative advantage of putting things together, coordinating a variety of actors and problems, concentrating power in a few hands. The comparative advantage of a legislature is in the sharing of power, in the necessity that many wills be satisfied in order for one law to pass. Viewed from this perspective, the fragmentation and disarray of the legislative process are functional; they certainly are not aberrations that must be remedied away if Congress is to become an effective policymaking institution. A legislature is not just a multi-member executive, nor does it exist only for the purpose of separating

[29]Fenno, "Strengthening a Congressional Strength," p. 263.
[30]James L. Sundquist, "Congress and the President: Enemies or Partners?," in *Congress Reconsidered*, eds. Lawrence C. Dodd and Bruce I. Oppenheimer (New York: Praeger Publishers, 1977), p. 233.

governmental power into two compartments. Its large purpose is to diffuse power where the other branch concentrates it.[31]

President and Congress:
A Summary View

Although there is difficulty in reconciling myth and fact in assessing the president's leadership in legislative policy-making, there are several summary arguments that can be made. The first is that his advantages must be placed in context. Faced with a Congress controlled by the opposition party, or with a bi-party majority such as the conservative coalition, the normal advantages of the president dwindle. The antipathies toward the chief executive and the bureaucracy that always reside in Congress come into play. Congress asks more questions, launches more inquiries into administrative behavior, takes oversight more seriously, generates more policy ideas of its own, and proceeds more at its own pace. Stalemates are common. The president is inclined to resist unwanted congressional initiatives through the exercise of his veto.

Second, even when the same party holds both branches, Congress is not necessarily the weaker partner. In dealing with the administration, Congress interacts with others besides the president. Through its committee system in particular, it maintains strong links to elements throughout the bureaucracy. In advancing the interests of certain agencies—at the same time serving the interests of its own members—Congress may in fact be working at cross-purposes with the president. Moreover, Congress is as concerned with the decisions of the bureaucracy as it is with those of the president. The activities and decisions of bureaucrats not only affect the lives of constituents but also members' careers. With good reason, members believe that they can earn credit with the voters by bringing federal money into their states and districts. Hence, there is substantial interaction between members and the bureaucracy over the awarding of defense contracts and the location of federal installations such as veterans' hospitals, military bases, and agency field offices.[32] For the most part, the president is more a witness than a participant in congressional-bureaucratic exchanges.

Stimulated by dissatisfaction over the Vietnam War, the events of Watergate, and the weakening of the presidency, Congress has become more assertive in defending traditional legislative prerogatives, such as the power of the purse and the power to declare war. Aroused by the president's vigorous prosecution of the Vietnam War, Congress adopted the War

---

[31]Allen Schick, "The Supply and Demand for Analysis on Capitol Hill," a paper prepared for the Commission on the Operation of the Senate, *Policymaking Role of Leadership in the Senate*, 94th Cong., 2d sess., 1977, p. 74.

[32]See an analysis by Randall B. Ripley and Grace A. Franklin, *Congress, the Bureaucracy, and Public Policy* (Homewood, Ill.: The Dorsey Press, 1976).

Powers Act of 1973. Under its terms, the president can still commit armed forces to military actions without a congressional declaration of war. Congress, however, must be immediately apprised of his action. More important is the provision for a "legislative veto": unless authorized by Congress, the troops must be withdrawn within sixty days, though an extension of the deadline for thirty days can be granted if required for the safe withdrawal of the troops. If it chose to do so, Congress could at any time during this period order the removal of these forces. It remains to be seen how much this legislation will inhibit presidential discretion as well as what other consequences will result from it. But it is clearly a step in the direction of increasing congressional influence in matters of war and peace.

The other large act to be passed by Congress in seeking to redress executive-legislative imbalances is the Congressional Budget and Impoundment Control Act of 1974. The presidential practice of impounding funds—that is, of refusing to spend program funds already appropriated by Congress—is about as old as the nation itself. Virtually all presidents have impounded funds—often with the acquiescence of Congress—but none did so on the scale of President Nixon. In response to his unprecedented use of this power, frequently exercised to shortchange social programs, provisions were placed in the 1974 Act to require congressional concurrence with impoundment orders.

The most important features of this legislation are those that provide for a congressional budget. In adopting the first thoroughgoing reform in budgetary processes since 1921, Congress charged itself with the responsibilities of establishing broad fiscal policies and of determining budget priorities. Until Congress sought to put its budgetary house in order, it had never paid steady attention to the coordination of expenditures and revenues. Parcelled out among its many committees, the president's budgetary proposals were handled on a piecemeal basis; the final expenditure levels were nothing more than the sum of all the individual programs for which funds had been appropriated. The total budget was anyone's guess. The new provisions place a much tighter rein on the scattered actions of Congress.

The budget reform act established a budget committee in each house, a Congressional Budget Office to provide analytical support services, and an elaborate timetable to govern the stages of the budgetary process.[33] Before acting upon individual spending bills, Congress must adopt (by May 15) a concurrent resolution that fixes spending targets for the coming fiscal year. Decisions on spending enactments then begin. When this process is

[33]See an analysis of the new budget process by John W. Ellwood and James A. Thurber, "The New Congressional Budget Process: The Hows and Whys of House-Senate Differences," in *Congress Reconsidered*, eds. Lawrence C. Dodd and Bruce I. Oppenheimer (New York: Praeger Publishers, 1977), pp. 163–92. This article is especially valuable for its analysis of the strategies of the two budget committees.

completed by mid-September, Congress is required to reconcile spending and revenue, taking into account the actions of individual committees as well as changes in the economy, and to adopt a second resolution that becomes in effect a binding budget. From that point on, the overall ceiling on expenditures cannot be exceeded. If individual budget categories, such as national defense or agriculture, are altered upwards, corresponding cuts must be made elsewhere, or else Congress must vote expressly for higher taxes or a larger deficit.

The significance of the new budget process should not be lost. It affects both relations within the institution and between it and the president. Within Congress, it is a force for centralization, for the first time a means for determining priorities and gaining coherence in its spending programs. It makes the overall budget somebody's business, not an accident of unrelated committee and subcommittee actions. It also represents an assertion of legislative independence, an effort to recapture the power of the purse. Plainly, it moves Congress closer to parity with the president, simply because the most important element in all policy-making is money. And finally, when party conditions are right—when the same party bridges the executive-legislative gap—it holds out the possibility for coordination of presidential and congressional perspectives on what government is to do and how it is to do it. Of course when party conditions are wrong, it promises conflict all out of the ordinary.

Our concluding proposition on presidential-congressional relations is simply that they are often unpredictable, sometimes unfathomable, and always complex. Factors of great variety enter the calculus of relationships. Congressional policy-making, moreover, is an unusually complicated phenomenon. Who leads and who follows in the process is seldom clear to outsiders and often not to insiders as well. Dominance at one point in the legislative process may be followed by acquiescence at another, making the final outcome a blend of victories, losses, and accommodations for each branch. And finally, this is the comfortable ambiance that Americans apparently prefer: "a shared, multiple-leadership form of government, in which no institution is permitted unrestrained dominance."[34]

INTEREST GROUPS
AND CONGRESS

Congress, like other American legislatures, provides a friendly environment for political interest groups to make claims on government. Public policies

---

[34]Cronin, *The State of the Presidency*, p. 107.

are their main interest. Because of the nature of their interests, some groups spend their major efforts in defensive lobbying, seeking to resist (or soften) policy changes that would prove injurious to them. Groups that have been earlier "losers"—who feel disadvantaged by existing policy settlements—mobilize their resources for the adoption of new legislation whose terms will be more favorable. Lobbying designed to protect existing law is normally much easier, and more likely to be successful, than that designed to undo existing arrangements. Policy change, even of modest significance, rarely comes easily.

The Access of Groups to Congress

Congress is built to order for interest-group politics. It does not necessarily succumb to their pressures and blandishments—any more than it does to those of the president—but it does provide substantial access for them. In the first place, the organization of Congress is conducive to interest-group involvement in policy-making. The standing committees of Congress are organized around functional categories, such as agriculture, labor, or judiciary. Interest groups gravitate toward those committees that write legislation involving their well-being. Organized labor monitors carefully the activities of committees that deal with labor-management questions, civil rights groups interact with the judiciary committees, and farm organizations are attentive to the work of the agriculture committees. The relatively small size of committees, moreover, facilitates negotiation and bargaining, not to mention logrolling, among major interests; agreements can be arranged in committee that could never be worked out in the chamber as a whole.

The committee selection process further smooths the way for interest-group participation in legislative affairs. Members are attracted to committees whose policy jurisdictions are important to their districts or states. And they listen carefully to the claims advanced by major groups within their constituencies. A member of the House and a senator's legislative assistant comment on the peculiar importance of committee assignments:

> I was attracted to [Interior and Insular Affairs], very frankly, because it's a bread and butter committee for my state. I guess about the only thing about it that is not of great interest to my state is insular affairs. I was able to get two or three bills of great importance to my state through last year. I had vested interests I wanted to protect, to be frank.[35]

[35] As quoted by Richard F. Fenno, Jr., *Congressmen in Committees* (Boston: Little, Brown and Company, 1973), p. 6.

When you've got a fast-growing state with millions of people, you've got a lot of eggs in the appropriations basket—military installations, flood control, urban renewal, rivers and harbors, reclamation, agricultural research, and so forth. People I have never heard of before come in here with their tin cups looking for dollars. Public officials—county supervisors, city councilmen, game wardens, and so forth—write to us all the time. That's why the Senator wanted to get on the Committee—so perhaps they'll all remember us and do us a favor at election time. That's the selfish motivation that guides most men on Appropriations.[36]

The decentralization of power in Congress is also a boon to interest groups. They help to fill the void created by the weakness of the congressional party. If members cannot defy party leaders with impunity, they nonetheless can often go their own way, supporting legislation that seems likely to satisfy their constituencies, including the organized elements in them. The member's party, moreover, can do relatively little to protect his career during elections. He is on his own. In working out his strategy for reelection, he is likely to accept support—endorsements, campaign contributions, workers, and counsel—where he can find it. Major interest groups are there to provide it, but not by light of altruism. What they want is access, a friendly hearing of their claims and, at times, a commitment to support their objectives.

The nature of the legislative process undoubtedly serves the welfare of many groups, especially those that are opposed to large changes in public policy. The dominant characteristic of the congressional policy process is its incrementalism. New policies tend to be overlays of old ones, introduced more at the margins than at the center of existing law. Support for new approaches to meeting public problems is not easily secured. The beneficiaries of minimal change are of course all those groups that gain advantages from the status quo.

The difficulty in making major changes in public policy cannot be attributed simply to the conservatism of Congress. The process itself inhibits change. Lawmaking comes in stages. Each stage is a point of access for groups bent on obtaining the best outcomes open to them. Bargaining and accommodation dominate the process, thus reducing the possibilities for fashioning comprehensive or distinctly new ways of addressing public problems. James L. Sundquist writes:

> Except in [the] one field of fiscal policy, there remains no regular institutional structure in either house to deal effectively with matters that cut across the jurisdictions of two or more committees. With its power dispersed, Congress remains organized to deal with narrow problems but not with broad ones. Its structure impels it to think parochially. It can skirmish for limited objectives but it cannot think strategically.[37]

[36]*Ibid.*, p. 143.
[37]Sundquist, "Congress and the President: Enemies or Partners?" p. 240.

Finally, many interest groups find Congress a congenial environment because of its devotion to the distributive ethic. As a rule, it is much easier for Congress to pass legislation that is distributive in character (e.g., agricultural subsidies, public works, or water resource projects) than it is to pass proposals that are regulatory (e.g., pollution control, strip mining, or consumer protection) or redistributive (e.g., civil rights or labor-management issues such as common-site picketing or the minimum wage). The outstanding characteristic of distributive policies is that they award discrete benefits to particular groups or constituencies without producing *obvious* costs or disadvantages for others. Distributive policies are easy politics: groups and localities (often linked in curious logrolling alliances) win advantages and legislators earn credit.

Lobbies and Lobbyists

It would be difficult to exaggerate the variety of groups that ply their trade in Washington. At any one time there are 1,500 or more groups and individuals registered as lobby organizations or as lobbyists. Their character, scope, and legislative interests are highly diverse, as the following sample helps to indicate:[38]

Organization	*Legislative Interests*
Citizens Committee for the Right to Keep and Bear Arms	Conservation, recreation and firearms legislation
Common Cause	Employment, education, health, consumer protection, environment, family planning, law enforcement . . . and reordering of national priorities and governmental reform
National Abortion Rights Action League	Opposed to all restrictive legislation dealing with abortion
Tenth Pro-Life Congressional District Action Committee (Bronx, N.Y.)	Human life amendments
Delmarva Poultry Industry, Inc.	Income tax legislation affecting poultry business
Colt Firearms Division	Firearms matters
Northrop Corporation	All matters pertaining to Department of Defense and military matters
Solargen Energy Systems	Alternate energy systems
Uncle Ben's Foods	Rice industry
Amalgamated Clothing & Textile Workers Union	Legislation affecting working people
American Bar Association	Matters of general interest to the legal profession

[38]These lobby registrations are taken from the *Congressional Quarterly Weekly Report*, June 11, 1977, pp. 1169–74.

Organization	*Legislative Interests*
Calorie Control Council	Ban on saccharin
Independent Petroleum Association of America	Petroleum industry
National Association of Manufacturers	Regulatory matters, consumer protection, and antitrust
National Education Association	Public education
Sisters of Charity (Cincinnati, Ohio)	Claims against Communist China on behalf of the Sisters of Charity
American Association of Blood Banks	Health care, including blood banking
Centre National Interprofessional De L'Economie Laitiere (Paris, France)	Opposed to proposed dairy inspection and labeling bills

The largest and most powerful lobbies maintain headquarters in Washington, and many have impressive research staffs as well as professional lobbyists. Small and narrow-gauge organizations, on the other hand, may have nothing more than a part-time lobbyist to represent their case. The most numerous lobbies are those that represent corporations and trade associations. Professional associations, such as the American Medical Association or the American Osteopathic Association, are also fairly numerous. In recent years there has been a sharp increase in lobbying activity by environmental groups, as environmental problems have come of age, and by citizens' groups, such as Common Cause, Congress Watch or the National Organization of Women (NOW). Not so well known is the fact that there are many state and local government associations that carefully monitor the activities of Congress and lobby for legislation, such as revenue sharing, to benefit their jurisdictions. The best known in this group are the National Governors' Conference, the National Conference of State Legislatures, the U.S. Conference of Mayors, and the National League of Cities.

Some members of Congress have earned reputations for being "inside" lobbyists for certain interests. Strongly committed to the objectives of these groups, they introduce legislation desired by them, help to move it through committee, defend it on the floor, and lobby other members to support it. Members sharply oriented to labor, farm, business, or section of the country—to take leading examples—are important cogs in the representation of group interests in Congress. Consider this account:

> For the most part the Colorado River Bill was not lobbied in the conventional sense. Large industry organizations and trade associations did not become intimately involved. Rather . . . the Members of Congress from the states in the Colorado River Basin were the primary lobbyists for the Colorado River Bill.[39]

[39]*Congressional Quarterly Weekly Report*, November 1, 1968, p. 3020. Quoted by Fenno, *Congressmen in Committees*, p. 40.

The influence of lobbies in the legislative process depends heavily (but not exclusively by any means) on their resources and their willingness to commit them to political action. Although no neat formula exists by which to assess the comparative influence of groups, the general outlines of group power are easy enough to distinguish. The central factors are: (1) the size of the group, (2) its financial resources, (3) the cohesiveness of its membership, (4) the skills and expertise of its leadership, (5) its prestige, (6) the geographical distribution of its membership, (7) its tenacity and intensity,[40] (8) its capacity to arrange alliances with other groups, and (9) the compatibility of its purposes with the traditional values of the society. Some groups score high on virtually all counts, other groups on only a few. Deficiencies in certain resources may be offset by the imaginative exploitation of those available.

Lobbies and Lawmaking

All stages of the legislative process are of interest to lobbies and lobbyists—from the introduction of legislation by a friendly member to the vote on its passage. Except for minor legislation, few bills emerge from Congress in the same form as they were introduced. Quite the contrary, changes are steadily made as bills move from subcommittee to committee, to the floor, and through conference committees. Each stage of the process presents the opportunity for interest groups to press for the inclusion of favorable provisions or the deletion or modification of unfavorable ones. Nothing about the process is automatic. A victory at one point may be undone at another. A favorable settlement in committee may be offset by a damaging amendment adopted on the floor. A loss in one house may be restored, partially or completely, in the other.

The willingness of sponsors and strategists to accept alterations, even in major provisions, is often the key to a bill's success. That is why groups shape their policy objectives with one eye on the desirable and the other on the attainable. Something is probably better than nothing!

Lobbyists pay particular attention to the activities of committees. Most legislation is lost there. In recent sessions of the House of Representatives, for example, only five or six percent of all bills introduced have been reported out of committee. Moreover, the overwhelming majority of bills that clear the committees eventually become law. The importance of

[40]Groups opposed to abortion provide a good example of the power of intense convictions. Following the defeat of his bill to remove the ban on the use of Medicaid funds for abortions, Senator Robert Packwood (R., Ore.) commented on the antiabortion groups: "They are a very significant force. To politicians, they are a frightening force. They are people who are with you 99 percent of the time, but if you vote against them on this issue, it doesn't matter what else you stand for." *New York Times*, July 1, 1977.

committee decisions to lobbyists is thus obvious. An adverse decision at the committee stage is difficult to reverse.

The centrality of committees to policy formation makes both their structures and membership of concern to interest groups. Thus when the Senate undertook to reorganize its committee system in 1977, the AFL-CIO opposed the abolition of the Joint Economic Committee, which among other things studies unemployment and strategies to achieve full employment, and the Post Office and Civil Service Committee, a panel of great importance to postal workers. It also opposed a number of jurisdictional shifts that would diminish labor's access in the Senate. The membership of committees can be of similar concern to groups, as the following account shows:

> With one exception in the last few years, John McCormack [former Speaker of the House] and Andy Biemiller [Director of the AFL-CIO Legislative Department] have decided who gets on [the Education and Labor Committee]. Last year, for example, they picked all six members. A year ago in January, Adam Powell got up at our legislative conference and said, "Here are the names of the six new members of the Education and Labor Committee." Then he read the names from a slip of paper and said, "I got this slip from Andy Biemiller, so they are all right." That wasn't too bright, saying that with so many newspapermen around. But we do that. The only exception was _____. John came to us and said, "I've got to put one southerner on. You've already got a good working majority." So we said, "OK, give us one that won't do anything." And he did.[41]

The Techniques of Lobbies

The broad objective of all political interest groups is to influence the decisions of government. Their activities, as lobbies, are inextricably bound up with the strengthening or preservation of their advantages and of those with whom they identify. They engage in two main forms of lobbying: direct contact with members of Congress (including their staffs and committee staffs) and grass-roots lobbying. The latter form refers to all those activities designed to stimulate constituents to contact their representatives on legislation of concern to the group. The broad outlines of these interactions are shown in Figure 3.

Lobbyists' interactions with members of Congress cover a wide sweep. An important part of their role, in fact, consists of providing services that many members find useful in meeting their own responsibilities. Lobbyists collect and organize data, fashion arguments, produce speeches,

[41]As quoted by Fenno, *Congressmen in Committees*, p. 34.

trade information, join members in devising strategies, arrange for meetings with other interested parties, and assist in the drafting of legislation. They have frequent contacts with personal and committee staffs as well. Save perhaps for the party leadership, no one is more interested than

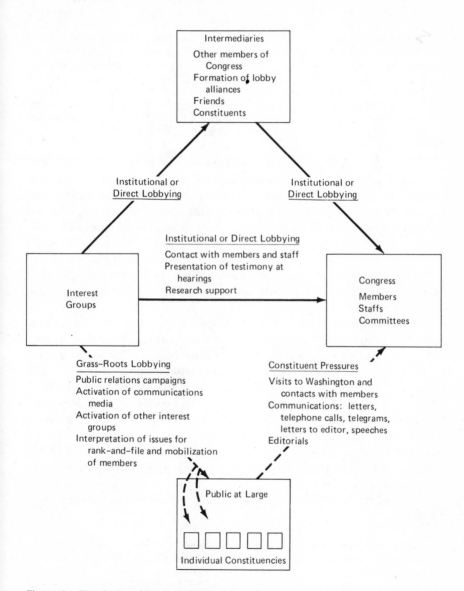

Figure 3. The Paths of Interest Group Influence

lobbyists in the "head count"—a tabulation of the voting intentions of members. The following account, reported by John Kingdon, shows why:

> If you're interested in the machinery, we have meetings of all the lobbyists and compare notes. On something major like this, we coordinate very closely. We went down the list of congressmen, and each guy took his assignment. Each guy took members that he worked with. Maybe he's been dealing with him through his work with his committee, or maybe he has a good political association. Then we'd call back in, when we had a good reading on what the guy was going to do. We'd start filling in the list—definitely for, definitely against—and the list of undecideds narrows. Then we start to go to work on them. All this time, we've been getting people back in their districts to write— telegrams, phone calls, delegations, everything. We particularly put it to the undecideds. Then we get down to a couple of days before the vote and we had only 20 or 30 still to work on. We crank it up on these guys.[42]

The task of forming a majority in committee or on the floor is never particularly easy, even on bills of middling significance. One tactic that lobbyists find effective is to use intermediaries—close friends of the congressman, a constituent, or a fellow congressman—to intercede on behalf of the lobby's position. Since members often discuss legislation with their colleagues, the use of fellow members as "lobbyists" is a natural opening for extending lobby influence. One study of decision-making in the House of Representatives has shown that congressmen's floor votes are influenced more by fellow members than by anyone else.[43] Lobbyists appreciate this fact.

Interest groups look for allies wherever they can find them. Two important lobbies in support of a position are more influential than one, and half-a-dozen are considerably more influential. For this reason groups search steadily to find the common denominators in policy proposals that invite the formation of alliances. The coalitions put together may owe their origins to a more or less common ideology and common set of legislative objectives or to nothing more than agreements to logroll. Many alliances are simply ad hoc—temporary coalitions that come together on a specific issue and dissolve when it is settled. Some alliances have been remarkably durable, such as that between certain powerful agricultural and business groups, joined to promote conservative policies. The influence of alliances, especially when distributive legislation is under consideration, is difficult to mistake:

> Take the highway lobby. It is really pervasive. It includes truckers and those you'd think of. But it also includes construction people, gravel pit operators,

---

[42]As quoted by Kingdon, *Congressmen's Voting Decisions*, pp. 154–55.
[43]*Ibid.*, especially pp. 16–23 and 69–102.

state and local officials, the AAA. A lot of jobs and money are involved in highways. And they really turn it on. They plant newspaper articles, they can generate terrific volumes of letters and telegrams.[44]

Interest groups recognize that policy preferments do not come easily. Claims must be registered and pressed, using whatever resources are available. A central point of interaction between groups and legislators is found in political campaigns, particularly in their financing. Many candidates for Congress depend on the contributions of organized groups to defray significant portions of their campaign expenses. The chief point to recognize about this nexus is that interest groups contribute money selectively, to those candidates most likely to view their legislative aims sympathetically.

A rough indication of the involvement of interest groups in elections can be gained from Table 4.1, which shows the twelve largest group contributors to House and Senate campaigns in 1976.

There is nothing quixotic about campaign donations. Interest groups provide money with the practical aim of influencing legislation. Candidates accept it because they need it: campaigns are expensive. All that is plain enough. Less clear is what interest groups derive from their contributions. In the broadest sense, groups attempt to secure a favorable legislative climate—a disposition on the part of members to consider their proposals.

Table 4.1   Interest Group Gifts to Congressional Campaigns, 1976

Group	Total Contributions
American Medical Associations	$1,790,879
Dairy committees	1,362,159
AFL-CIO COPEs	996,910
Maritime-related unions	979,691
United Auto Workers	845,939
Coal, oil, and natural gas interests	809,508
National Education Associations	752,272
National Association of Realtors	605,973
Financial institutions	529,193
International Association of Machinists	519,157
United Steelworkers of America	463,033
American Dental Associations	409,835

Source: Congressional Quarterly Weekly Report, April 16, 1977, p. 710. The data on contributions, based on campaign finance reports filed by the groups, were tabulated by Common Cause.

[44]*Ibid.*, p. 146.

In a more specific sense, groups give money in order to gain "access" to members. Campaign money helps to open doors:

> . . . What contributors buy is not as tangible as is often supposed. Mostly what they buy is "access." Politicians who get the money, along with solicitors who raise it and contributors themselves, state invariably that in return for his funds a contributor can get, if he seeks it, access to the party, legislative or administrative officials concerned with a matter of interest to him. One lobbyist called it "entree" and another called it "a basis for talking". . . . The number of cold bargains that are struck for campaign funds are negligible.[45]

> When the lobbyists themselves are asked to define the chief value of campaign contributions in their work, they frequently reply with one word: access. The campaign donation, they say, helps them obtain access to the legislator so they can present their case. . . . Since it would be unrealistic to expect the lobbyist to describe his campaign contributions as attempts at influence, the "access" explanation may be, in some cases, a cover story. In the majority of instances, however, it is probably the truth or close to it. Senators and Representatives are busy men, and the competition for their attention is keen. The lobbyist who makes a campaign donation—or arranges for one to be made by his client—frequently is doing nothing more than meeting the competition and creating good will, to insure that he, too, will be heard.[46]

The invasion of public campaigns by private money is open to serious abuses. The Watergate affair is as much a story of illicit campaign money as it is of breaking and entering, dirty tricks, and cover-ups. Congress unfortunately has also had its share of seamy episodes involving campaign money. It was disclosed in late 1975 that the Gulf Oil Corporation had illegally contributed, over a period of a decade, some $5 million in corporate funds to dozens of members of Congress. No action was taken against the members, who for the most part denied knowing the illegal nature of the money. A year later came the South Korean scandal, a case involving a South Korean businessman, Tongsun Park, who had given large sums of cash to certain members of Congress and entertained many members lavishly, presumably to build congressional support for military assistance for his country.

An important point to recognize about these scandals is that they are intimately related to the private financing of congressional campaigns. Whatever its merits, private financing encourages dissembling and corner-cutting, leaves at least some members vulnerable to seduction or

---

[45]Alexander Heard, *Money and Politics* (New York: Public Affairs Pamphlet No. 242, 1956), p. 13. Copyright ©1956 by Public Affairs Committee, Inc. Used with permission.
[46]James Deakin, *The Lobbyists* (Washington, D.C.: Public Affairs Press, 1966), p. 101.

exploitation, prompts some political operators to try to buy influence, and occasionally takes a toll on the public standing of Congress. There is no doubt that public financing of congressional elections would sharply diminish the use of illicit money in campaigns.

The other major method for influencing legislators is known as indirect or grass-roots lobbying. It owes much to the techniques of mass marketing. Interest groups that engage in this form of lobbying, as virtually all the major ones do, concentrate on influencing or "educating" the public to accept the goals of their organizations. Their assumption is that a reservoir of good will among the public toward the organization, coupled with sympathy toward its objectives, makes the task of influencing legislators more manageable. When indirect lobbying is successful, as it often is, constituents are inspired to communicate with their representatives on behalf of the claims of the group.

The key to grass-roots lobbying is public relations. Major public relations campaigns are highly expensive, and only large and moneyed interest groups have the capacity to arrange full-scale efforts. A systematically conceived attempt to mold public opinion calls for newspaper and magazine advertisements, radio and television programs and advertisements, press releases, newspaper accounts, editorials, films, speeches, and assorted pieces of literature. Mass mailings, directed toward carefully targeted groups of voters, have become increasingly common in grass-roots campaigns—particularly those designed to promote conservative causes. Interest groups spend millions of dollars each year in efforts to cultivate and arouse public opinion and to convert it into political influence in Congress.[47] The National Right to Work Committee, for example, sends out about 46,000 pieces of mail each day, perhaps 12-15 million letters a year. Located near Washington, its volume of mail is so large that the Postal Service has awarded the committee its own zip code.[48]

On some issues spontaneous, inspired, and direct lobbying are closely linked together. For example, when the Food and Drug Administration proposed a ban on the sale of saccharin—because its use posed a cancer risk—Congress was deluged with mail from indignant citizens. Many of the letters undoubtedly were written by individuals who knew nothing more about the issue than what they had learned from television and newspaper accounts; just as certainly others were stimulated to action through the grass-roots campaigns of groups such as the Calorie Control

---

[47]According to one estimate, lobbies spend $1 billion a year in direct lobbying in Washington and another $1 billion in campaigns to shape public opinion. *Time*, August 7, 1978, p. 15.

[48]*Congressional Quarterly Weekly Report*, July 30, 1977, p. 1606.

Council, an organization associated with Coca-Cola that represents the low-calorie soft drink industry. The response of Congress, not long in coming, was to adopt a bill providing for an eighteen-month moratorium on the FDA ruling. The views of two House members on the issue are instructive:

> I've received more spontaneous mail about the saccharin bill than any other issue that's come before the House during my three years in Congress. . . . I also received an incredible number of letters from every television and radio broadcaster in my district opposing a ban. They said they feared a drop in revenue from advertising for diet foods and drinks if a ban went into effect or we had voted to place warnings on the products, since they would have had to have been repeated in the ads.

> [The saccharin issue] is a clear example of the capitulation of Congress to a combination of pressures from both home and industry. With this bill we're permitting the sale and consumption of a substance that we know to be cancer-causing.[49]

Grass-roots lobbying represents a triumph for merchandising and manipulation. Its remarkable growth has been no happenstance: it came from the realization that the public has been an overlooked source of interest group power. Citizens require stimulation and activation—the essence of the persuasive task in grass-roots lobbying. Although it is impossible to weigh the overall impact of this form of lobbying, unquestionably it is highly important. "Grass roots," a lobbyist for the U.S. Chamber of Commerce has observed, "is the Chamber's stock in trade." When organized labor received an unexpected defeat on its common-site picketing bill in the Ninety-fifth Congress, for example, members supporting labor emphasized the importance of grass-roots lobbying by business interests:

> It was the best-organized, best-financed effort to create the impression that you have grass-roots support for your position that I've ever seen. They used all the new developments in fund-raising and targeting. They targeted the vulnerable members. They blanketed newspaper ads and direct mail, and they picked members' districts where they thought they could create the most heat.

> The Associated General Contractors in particular launched a fantastic mail drive. They even sent employers packets of postcards for employees to send in to members of Congress. I think the business groups surprised themselves by coalescing so successfully and defeating situs picketing.[50]

[49]*New York Times*, October 5, 1977. The first statement was made by Henry A. Waxman (D., Calif.) and the second by Andrew Maguire (D., N.J.). Congressman Maguire also proposed that a label be placed on saccharin products that reads: "Assurance—this product may not cause cancer in the opinion of your congressman although scientific evidence indicates that it does."

[50]*Congressional Quarterly Weekly Report*, July 30, 1977, p. 1602. The statements were made by Congressmen William D. Ford (D., Mich.) and Frank Thompson Jr. (D., N.J.). Common-site picketing would permit a labor union with a grievance against one contractor to picket all contractors on that construction site.

The communications of the public with members of Congress are important in influencing voting behavior but, a major study suggests, only under one condition: a connection with the member's constituency is required. Letters and telegrams from Washington-based lobbies often end up in the wastebasket. "It doesn't make any difference to me unless it is from my district," a congressman is likely to observe. "We get stuff in here all the time from the Washington offices of organizations and I often don't even read it."[51] Mail from the member's constituency is another matter. It counts.

The Impact of Lobbying

The ills of Congress are often attributed to the influence of lobbies. On occasion, of course, lobbies score spectacular victories that appear to have slight association with anything that might be called the "public interest." At times their methods are questionable or even illegal. And at other times legislators simply regard them as a nuisance.[52] Nevertheless, the case against them is usually exaggerated.

Legislative scholars usually attribute three effects to lobbying: reinforcement, activation, and conversion. The most important is reinforcement. Lobbyists pay close attention to members who are generally favorable to their position, reinforcing or "backstopping" them by providing information, arguments, and rationalizations. As a lobbyist points out, "Friendly senators need to be reassured that they will receive credit for their position . . . that they are not forgotten."[53]

The activation of members is a second objective of lobbying. By any standard the members of Congress are harried, pushed and pulled in all directions. The task of the lobbyist is often that of convincing busy members to give more time and energy to the objectives of the interest group. As viewed by one lobbyist:

> Ninety percent of what goes on here during a session is decided on the previous election day. The main drift of legislation is decided then: it is out of our control. There is simply no substitute for electing the right folks and defeating the wrong folks. Our job is a little like that of a football coach. Our

[51]Kingdon, *Congressmen's Voting Decisions*, p. 143.
[52]In a talk given to the American Bankers' Association, Congressman William S. Moorhead (D., Penna.) remarked: "Congress is tired of the squabbling among financial lobbyists that immediately occurs whenever any legislation of substance is proposed. I am tired of being told by every banker, savings and loan official and mutual savings bank president, and now add credit unions to that list, that a particular piece of legislation, if it passes, will mean the end of western civilization as we know it." *Pittsburgh Post-Gazette*, February 28, 1977.
[53]Donald R. Matthews, *U.S. Senators and Their World* (Chapel Hill: The University of North Carolina Press, 1960), p. 191. ©1960 The University of North Carolina Press. By permission of the publisher.

material is given. By careful coaching we can sometimes improve the effectiveness of the material.[54]

Lobbying may also lead to the conversion of members to the side of the interest group or to a neutral position. In fact, however, lobbies devote relatively little energy to this objective, and few votes are changed as a result of lobbying. Conversion is not an attractive strategy because it is difficult, time-consuming, and usually fruitless. As realists, lobbyists concentrate their efforts where they will do the most good: among those members who already agree with them, who are leaning in their direction, or who have not yet made up their minds.[55]

The Regulation
of Interest Groups

The right to lobby is protected by the First Amendment to the Constitution, which gives the people the right to petition their government for redress of grievances. Hence all legislation designed to regulate lobbies encounters a special difficulty: if it is too restrictive, it is likely to be challenged as an intrusion on First Amendment freedoms. Proposed regulatory legislation also encounters questions concerning its political feasibility. Is it reasonable? Can it be passed? What consequences may result from it?

Although several minor laws regulating lobbies were passed in the late nineteenth century and early twentieth century, it was not until 1946 that Congress adopted a wide-ranging lobby law. The Federal Regulation of Lobbying Act contains four main provisions. First, any person or group that solicits or receives money for the *principal* purpose of influencing the passage or defeat of legislation is required to register with officials of the House or Senate. Second, these individuals and groups must keep a record of all contributions and expenditures, including the names of persons who make contributions of $500 or more and to whom expenditures of $10 or more are made. Third, they must provide information each quarter concerning their employers, salaries, expenses, receipts, expenditures, the articles and editorials they have caused to be published, and the legislation

---

[54]*Ibid.*, p. 193.

[55]For evidence on this proposition, see Raymond A. Bauer, Ithiel de Sola Pool, and Lewis A. Dexter, *American Business and Public Policy* (New York: Atherton Press, 1963), pp. 350–57. See also Michael T. Hayes, "The Semi-Sovereign Pressure Groups: A Critique of Current Theory and an Alternative Typology," *Journal of Politics*, 40 (February 1978), 134–61. This article faults the conventional view of political scientists that pressure groups are simply "service bureaus" that members of Congress may heed or ignore as they choose. The influence of pressure groups, Hayes argues, is contextual—that is, it varies according to circumstances, including the nature of the policy issue at hand.

that their employer opposes or supports. And fourth, this information is to be published in the *Congressional Record.*

The broad purpose of the 1946 Act is to remove some of the mystery from interest group activities involving Congress. The specific objectives are to set up controls of *identification, disclosure,* and *publicity.* In upholding the constitutionality of the law in 1954, the Supreme Court noted that Congress "wants only to know who is being hired, who is putting up the money, and how much."[56]

The deficiencies of this act have become apparent over the years. In the first place, under the interpretation of the Supreme Court the reporting requirements of the act apply only to those persons or organizations whose *principal* purpose is to influence legislation. As a result, some individuals and groups that lobby Congress have declined to register, contending that the act does not apply to them. Second, the Court has held that the law applies only to those persons or organizations engaged in *direct* lobbying, thus exempting grass-roots lobbying. Third, the lobbying of executive agencies is not covered by the law. And finally, the implementation and enforcement of the act have been lax.

Widespread dissatisfaction with the 1946 act has increased the prospects for the adoption of new and more comprehensive legislation, but it has been difficult to reach agreement on its provisions; lobbyists, moreover, have not been reluctant to lobby against a new lobby law. One of the most difficult problems to resolve concerns how to "trigger" the registration requirement for lobbies. Some proposals make registration dependent on the amount of money spent by an organization in lobbying during any quarter or on the number of hours spent by employees in lobbying efforts. Other proposals require organizations to register when they reach a certain level of lobbying activity, measured by the number of contacts (oral and written) which they have with members of Congress or the executive branch. The triggering formula has important ramifications for group activity. Certain volunteer and low-budget groups that would be excluded under a money-and-time formula would be required to register under one based on contacts. In addition, use of the contact formula would require extensive record-keeping by all organizations, since they would be required to list all the members whom they had contacted and the nature of their communications or conversations.

Other nettling questions to be decided relate to lobbying of the executive branch, grass-roots lobbying (vastly more important today than in the past), and the extent to which the internal operations of interest groups (including their contributors) should be made a matter of public record.[57]

---

[56]*U.S. v. Harriss et al.,* 347 U.S. 612 (1954).

[57]For additional information on lobby law reform, see various issues of the *Congressional Quarterly Weekly Report.*

Like the 1946 act, the thrust of the new proposals is to disclose the activities of interest groups, not to eliminate them. Interest groups are not outlaws in the political system.

CONSTITUENCIES AND CONGRESS

The first principle in understanding congressional behavior is that constituents and constituencies are of paramount importance to members of Congress. Yet so many words have already been written about constituencies in this book, especially in Chapter 2, that their treatment here can be relatively brief.

The Public's View of Congress

The preoccupation of members with their constituencies is not surprising. It results from their natural inclination to focus on matters that involve their electoral security. But it is also an outgrowth of their awareness that constituents *expect* a great deal of attention to be paid to them and their districts. A nationwide Harris survey commissioned by the House Commission on Administrative Review shows that the public gives highest priority to the representation of district interests. The four most important jobs (duties, functions) of the congressman, in the view of the public, are closely associated with constituents. (See Table 4.2.) Interestingly, tasks that involve the legislative role of the congressman are mentioned spontaneously much less often than tasks that relate to the member's representative or constituent role.

Table 4.3 shows additional dimensions of the district-centeredness of the average citizen. Almost twice as many people believe that a congressman should concentrate on the needs and interests of his district rather than on those of the nation. Moreover, when there is a conflict between his conscience and what he perceives his district wants, by a margin of over two-to-one the public expects him to represent the interests of his district. More than one-fourth of the public, however, adopts an "it depends" position. One inference to be drawn from this evidence is that if constituents monitored carefully the behavior of their representatives—which is not the case—members would find their leeway and discretion diminished.

Table 4.2 The Most Important Jobs of the Congressman—as Seen by the Public

Job, Duty, or Function	Percent Mentioning
Work to solve problems in his district, help people, needs of our area	37%
To represent the people of his district, vote according to the wishes of his district	35
Keep in touch; contact with people; visit district; hold meetings; know constituents	17
Find out what people think, need, want; send out polls, questionnaires	11
Should attend as many sessions as possible; be there to vote	10
Be honest, fair, truthful; keep promises; be a person of good character	10
Working on improving the economy	10
Be knowledgeable, well-informed on legislation	9
Hammer out positions on legislation	8
Use media/newsletters to keep people informed about what he is doing	7
Don't know	10

Source: Report of Louis Harris and Associates to House Commission on Administrative Review, February 3, 1977, p. 5 (as adapted). The question asked was: "Now I'd like to ask you what *kinds* of things you feel it is most important for an individual Congressman to do, not what positions he takes on issues but what he does in his job. What kinds of jobs, duties, or functions do you expect a good Congressman to perform?" The total exceeds 100 percent because of multiple answers.

Table 4.3 The Proper Representational-Role Orientations of the Congressman—as Seen by the Public

If you had to choose, do you think your Congressman should be primarily concerned with looking after the needs and interests of his own district, or do you feel that he should be primarily concerned with looking after the needs and interests of the nation as a whole?

When there is a conflict between what your Congressman feels is best and what he thinks the people in his district want, do you think he should follow his own conscience or follow what the people in the district want?

	Percent		Percent
Own district	57	Follow his own conscience	22
Whole nation	34	Follow his district	46
Not sure	9	Depends on the issue	27
		Not sure	5

Source: Report of Louis Harris and Associates to House Commission on Administrative Review, February 3, 1977, pp. 10-11 (as adapted).

The Scope
of Constituency Service

Members of Congress interact with their constituents through correspondence, visits with constituents in Washington, frequent trips back home, and promoting legislation of interest to them. From one perspective, both houses of Congress have become large service organizations for constituents—or as one congresswoman has put it, "We are the complaint window in the Federal department store."[58] The basis of constituent service is the members' mail. Requests of infinite variety arrive daily. Whether the letters are concerned with social security payments, veterans' benefits, income tax matters, emergency military leaves, government contracts, medicare, immigration, or any of a thousand other things, they have one thing in common: the need for assistance. For the most part the requests— known as "casework"—require the member to intervene with agencies of the executive branch in order to solve problems that citizens are unable to solve by themselves. The casework load in larger states is massive. Senators from California and New York, for example, average between 30,000 and 50,000 cases a year. The office of Senator Edward Kennedy (D., Mass.) handles over 70,000 cases a year.[59]

Involvement in casework is seen by members as a legitimate responsibility of congressional office. Many, in fact, encourage the public to give them their problems, as shown in this newsletter statement by Senator H. John Heinz (R., Pa.):

> Casework is part of my responsibility to ensure that Pennsylvanians get timely and responsive service from the federal government. We are fortunate to have many dedicated people who work in the Senate office full-time on solving your problems. Lost Social Security checks, foul-ups in Black Lung benefits, and problems with military enlistments are just a few of the many problems our 5 in-state Senate offices handle every day. Some problems can be handled quickly, while others take a little more time and persistence. For example, during the Egyptian exhibit at the National Gallery of Art in Washington, we were contacted by the D. T. Watson Home for Crippled Children in Pittsburgh. They wanted to take the children to Washington to see the exhibit but the Gallery had refused their request for a special tour because of the huge crowds. A personal call to the Gallery's Director convinced him of the children's special need and the tour was quickly arranged. It has been a pleasure to represent you in the U.S. Senate during the past year. If you ever need help, please do not hesitate to write or call.[60]

[58]*New York Times*, March 27, 1978.
[59]See Janet Breslin, "Constituent Service," a paper prepared for the Commission on the Operation of the Senate, *Senators: Offices, Ethics, and Pressures*, 94th Cong., 2d sess., 1977, pp. 19–36.
[60]*John Heinz Reports*, April, 1978.

Members of Congress also have frequent contacts with local groups and communities that desire assistance in securing federal grants. Organized constituents can expect their representatives (and office staffs) to assist them with their applications and grant proposals, to intervene with agencies in their behalf, and to try to protect their projects through the review process. The ingenuity of members in providing grant assistance is impressive:

> The computerization of Capitol Hill has also made it much easier for congressmen to provide custom service for their constituents. In Carolina Beach, N.C., Rep. Charles Rose listened to local officials complain about inadequate fire protection when their town's population swelled during the summer from 1,500 to more than 30,000. Rose pulled out an 11-pound computer terminal (about the size of a portable typewriter), hooked it up to a telephone and dialed a data bank in Washington. He played at the keyboard briefly and minutes later got back a list of eleven Federal programs that might provide assistance—from a firebreak built by the Forest Service to fire-fighting equipment on sale cheap from closed military bases. In the end, the town chose a Farmers Home Administration loan to finance a new firehouse.[61]

The handling of routine requests, casework, and projects comprises a large share of the office workload of members of Congress. Quite apart from the satisfaction that members may derive from solving the problems of citizens, constituency service gives them the opportunity to earn the gratitude of voters. Many members believe that a good record of constituency service affords them greater leeway in the positions they take on controversial public policy questions.

Constituency service is a "growth industry" in Congress. It serves the interests of some citizens and of most members. It also serves the interests of the bureaucracy, which hopes to win favor with members by its responsiveness to their requests; presumably an agency that enjoys substantial good will in Congress is likely to fare better in the appropriations process. These linkages, Morris Fiorina argues, constitute the "Washington system":

> [There] is an identifiable Washington system, composed of Congress and the federal bureaucracies operating in a seemingly antagonistic but fundamentally symbiotic relationship. . . . [By] working to establish various federal programs (or in some cases fighting their establishment) congressmen earn electoral credit from concerned elements of their districts. Some federal agency then takes Congress's vague policy mandate and makes the detailed decisions necessary to translate the legislation into operating programs. The implementation and operation of the programs by the agencies irritate some constituents and suggest opportunities for profit to others. These aggrieved and/or hopeful constituents then appeal to their congressman to intervene

in their behalf with the bureaucratic powers that be. The system is connected when congressmen decry bureaucratic excesses and red tape while riding a grateful electorate to even more impressive electoral showings.

Thus congressmen appropriate all the public credit generated in the system, while the bureaucracy absorbs all the costs. The bureaucrats may not enjoy their status as objects of public opprobrium, but so long as they accommodate congressmen larger budgets and grants of authority will be forthcoming. All of Washington prospers as ever larger cadres of bureaucrats promulgate ever more numerous regulations and spend ever more money. Meanwhile, ever fewer congressmen meet electoral defeat. This is the Washington system.[62]

Errand-running for constituents has often been criticized because it preempts the time of members—time that might be spent on lawmaking and other less parochial activities. Most constituent requests can be handled by staff members, but not all by any means. Moreover, the direct involvement of the member in a case heightens the prospects for a satisfactory solution. In addition, there are some members who prefer to concentrate their energies on serving their constituents, generally unmindful of the larger responsibilities that attach to a representative body. A congressional staff member observes:

> Mr. _____ is a pothole congressman. We do constituency services. The constituents do not try to decide whether a matter is local, state, or federal; it all comes to us. It's like continually filling in the potholes in a street. The phrase means constituency service. We are known for our constituency services.[63]

Constituencies and Voting Behavior

The evidence concerning the importance of constituency in influencing the voting behavior of legislators is mixed. One study finds that congressmen have great difficulty in identifying the dominant view in their districts—even on major bills. Consequently, the congressman enjoys considerable freedom to vote according to his own lights.[64] Another study finds that constituency influence is related to the nature of the issue. Civil rights legislation shows a high degree of agreement between the congressmen's

---

[62]Morris P. Fiorina, *Congress: Keystone of the Washington Establishment* (New Haven: Yale University Press, 1977), p. 71.

[63]Lynette Palmer Perkins, *Member Goals and Committee Behavior: The House Judiciary Committee* (Ph.D. Dissertation, University of Pittsburgh, 1977), p. 37.

[64]Lewis A. Dexter, "The Representative and His District," in *New Perspectives on the House of Representatives*, eds. Robert L. Peabody and Nelson W. Polsby (Chicago: Rand McNally College Publishing Company, 1977), pp. 3–25.

votes and the policy preferences of their constituents; in contrast, on questions of foreign involvement congressmen tend to make up their minds in terms of administration positions rather than constituency opinions.[65] Finally, any number of opinion surveys have shown that constituents are poorly informed about the voting records of their representatives, a fact which raises doubts about the direct control of constituencies over members' voting behavior.

A study by John W. Kingdon sheds new light on the impact of constituencies on the voting behavior of congressmen. Based on interviews with a cross-section of the House of Representatives, the study examines the importance of a variety of political actors (constituency, fellow congressmen, party leaders, interest groups, administration, staff, and reading) in influencing the decisions of members on *specific* issues brought up for floor consideration. The broad findings, shown in Table 4.4, are unusually interesting. Of greatest importance in members' voting decisions are constituency and fellow congressmen. Moreover, further analysis (not shown in the table) shows that when the constituency position on an issue is identified, congressmen vote in agreement with it about three-fourths of the

Table 4.4   Actor Importance

Impor-tance	Con-stit-uency	Fellow Con-gress-men	Party Leader-ship	Interest Groups	Adminis-tration	Staff	Reading
Determi-native	7%	5%	0%	1%	4%	1%	0%
Major impor-tance	31	42	5	25	14	8	17
Minor impor-tance	51	28	32	40	21	26	32
Not impor-tant	12	25	63	35	61	66	52
Total %	101	100	100	101	100	101	101
Total n	222	221	222	222	222	221	221

Source: John W. Kingdon, *Congressmen's Voting Decisions* (New York: Harper & Row, Publishers, 1973), p. 19. Copyright ©1973 by John W. Kingdon. By permission of Harper & Row, Publishers, Inc. Some column totals will not be exactly 100 percent, due to rounding error.

[65]Warren E. Miller and Donald E. Stokes, "Constituency Influence in Congress," *American Political Science Review*, 57 (March 1963), 45–56.

time.[66] Thus, under certain circumstances, constituency looms as a major influence in the voting behavior of members. Constituency interests and problems, as shown earlier, dominate the activities of their offices.

In summary, the previous pages have shown that what Congress does is not determined by Congress alone. Far from it. Outside interests affect the pace at which Congress proceeds, the choices that it makes at all stages of the legislative process, and the public policies that it adopts. Many relationships between Congress and other actors are cooperative; others are marked by strains and tensions. Congress is far from predictable. It shifts between receptivity and resistance to the appeals and pressures of outside forces. It meshes outside claims with internal objectives. It uses outside energy to overcome internal inertia. In the end it does what it feels it is necessary to do or simply what it wants to do. What others want from Congress has never been the only valid criterion for the strategies it pursues or the decisions it makes.

[66]Kingdon, *Congressmen's Voting Decisions*, p. 20.

Change
and
Constancy

5

Congress is a changing institution. Congresses of the late twentieth century differ in many ways from those of earlier eras. No new Congress is the same as the previous one. Congresses differ from one session to the next, and in some respects even from one month to the next. Elections, events, deaths and retirements among members—each contributes something to congressional change.

Also contributing to change, advanced in the name of "reform,"[1] are the conscious decisions of leaders and rank-and-file members to develop new ways of organizing their chambers and of transacting congressional business. To be sure, most changes occur at the periphery of the congressional system, all but unnoticed, but some occur at its center. Major rearrangements always carry the possibility of creating a new distribution of power among leaders, members, regions, and blocs. The aim of this concluding analysis is to show the ways in which Congress has changed and is changing and the ways in which, in the midst of change, the institution remains essentially the same.

[1] "Reform" is a convenient word often used to describe congressional change. Its usage, however, is awkward and vague. Proposed alterations in congressional organization or procedures invariably are cast as "reforms" by their sponsors and, typically, by the press. But not all reforms necessarily strengthen institutions. One person's reform may be another's regression. Reforms may also have significant unintended consequences, changing institutions in ways never anticipated by their sponsors. Consistent with the common usage, "reform" as used here refers to self-conscious congressional decisions designed to change the organization or procedures of the institution. There is no assumption that any of the changes have in fact "improved" Congress. See an instructive analysis of legislative reform by Samuel C. Patterson, "On the Study of Legislative Reform," in *Legislative Reform and Public Policy*, eds. Susan Welch and John G. Peters (New York: Praeger Publishers, 1977), pp. 214–22.

CONGRESSIONAL REFORM

Three major reform periods have occurred in Congress during the twentieth century. The first took place in 1910 when a bi-party bloc of Democrats and Progressive Republicans, chafing under the absolute rule of Speaker Joseph G. Cannon (R., Ill.), took drastic actions to curb the powers of the Speaker. The second occurred in the mid-forties, culminating in the passage of the Legislative Reorganization Act of 1946. The most recent period is marked by the passage of the Legislative Reorganization Act of 1970 (which had been under consideration since 1965) and by a number of less comprehensive but important changes adopted in various Congresses of the 1970s.

Congressional reforms serve a variety of purposes. They are advanced, for example, to make Congress more democratic, or more responsible, or more efficient, or more powerful (in relation to other branches of government). A desire to change the thrust of public policy is sometimes at the root of reform proposals. Some reforms are lodged primarily in efforts to redistribute power within the chamber.[2] Regardless of variations in emphasis, the characteristic common to most changes of consequence is that some members stand to gain from them while others stand to lose. Not often neutral, reforms have an uneven impact on positions and careers, contributing at times to an abrasive effect on relations among members.

Institutional change is a matter that counts. Struggles to alter existing arrangements provide attentive outsiders with their clearest glimpses of the political stakes imbedded in congressional organization and procedures.

Revolution of 1910–11

Few if any changes in Congress have been more dramatic or led to more far-reaching consequences than those made in 1910–11. At stake were the powers of the Speaker of the House. In the early years of the republic the Speaker was essentially a presiding officer, with limited opportunity to influence House decisions. Quite early in the nineteenth century, however, the office grew in importance. The Speaker acquired the power to appoint committee members, enabling him to serve the preferences and increase the power of political allies. Inevitably the Speaker was drawn into factional politics, and his office became useful for serving factional purposes. With

---

[2]See the analysis of Walter J. Oleszek, "A Perspective on Congressional Reform," in *Legislative Reform and Public Policy*, eds. Susan Welch and John G. Peters (New York: Praeger Publishers, 1977), pp. 3–10.

the emergence of legislative parties in the first quarter of the nineteenth century, and their consolidation during the 'Jacksonian era, the Speaker came to be the principal party leader of the House.

Supported by their partisans, Speakers of the latter part of the nineteenth century enlarged the powers of the office, often simply by their interpretations of the rules. It remained for the arch conservative Joseph G. Cannon, elected Speaker in 1903, to exploit these powers to their fullest. Leading the House and tolerating no opposition, he appointed members to committees, transferred "unreliable" and offending committee members, named committee chairmen, controlled the House agenda and the flow of legislation through his position as chairman of the Rules Committee, used the Republican caucus to bind party members to policy positions, interpreted House rules in ways designed to serve his and his party's interests, and used his power of recognition (for example, refusing to acknowledge a member requesting to speak) to control business on the floor. Little escaped his attention and no opponents his wrath. Legislation he approved cleared the House, while legislation he opposed was lost. Adroitly manipulating rewards and sanctions, he advanced the careers of faithful party regulars and damaged those of party dissidents.

But arbitrary rule is difficult to sustain—especially in an institution marked by bargaining and accommodation.[3] Led by George W. Norris of Nebraska, a coalition of insurgent Republicans and Democrats came together in 1910 to challenge Speaker Cannon. When the smoke had cleared, and their work on the House rules was completed, the office of Speaker had been sharply changed. No longer would he serve on the Rules Committee or be empowered to appoint committee members and chairmen. His power over the recognition of members was curtailed. These key changes virtually dismantled the structure of power so carefully put together by earlier Speakers.

A convergence of frustrations and political pressures led to this reshaping of the speakership. In the process of combatting Cannonism and redefining his office, the rebellion produced a fundamental transformation of power in the House. The broad result was that the House shifted from a centralized to a decentralized system. The automatic operation of seniority shortly replaced the Speaker's discretion in the selection of committee chairmen. The power to assign members to committees, no longer the Speaker's prerogative, was vested in committees on committees. Perhaps of most importance, committees grew in independence and power.

---

[3]See an instructive account of how and why Cannon went wrong by Charles O. Jones, "Joseph G. Cannon and Howard W. Smith: An Essay on the Limits of Leadership in the House of Representatives," *Journal of Politics*, 30 (August 1968), 617–46.

Increasingly, senior members were able to carve out spheres of their own, protected and encouraged by their committee positions and largely free from party control. Committee policies came to be House policies. Thus the principal legacies of the 1910–11 revolution were a weakening of the formal leadership, a sharp fragmentation of the power of the House, a consolidation of government by committee, and an overall decline in the accountability of the majority party for the decisions of the chamber.

From the revolt against Cannon until the 1940s Congress made only a few significant changes in organization and procedures. A constitutional amendment to provide for the direct election of senators was forwarded to the states and ratified in 1913, thus enhancing popular control over that chamber. In 1917 the Senate adopted its first cloture rule (rule 22), but its "triggering" provisions were so difficult to reach (agreement of two-thirds of the senators voting was required to terminate debate) that it was all but useless as a device for halting filibusters. And in 1921 the Senate cut a wide swath through its tangled committee system, eliminating more than half of the seventy-odd existing standing committees. Yet over most of this period, only limited attention was given to the internal workings of Congress—as is usually the case, system design and procedural arrangements proved less intriguing for members than the politics of shaping new public policies and defending old ones.

Major changes, however, were taking place in the legislative parties. Suffering sharp losses in northern states in 1918 and losing control of Congress, the Democratic party became a southern-dominated party; more than half of its members in most Congresses of the 1920s were southerners. When the party recaptured Congress in 1932, its seniority leaders, hence its committee chairmen, fully reflected southern power. Northerners watched their colleagues from the confederacy, in league with minority Republicans from the late 1930s onward, steadily exploit their committee offices to advance conservative causes and, even more, to hamstring liberal ones. Lacking a firm party rudder in Congress, Democratic presidents (Roosevelt, Truman, Kennedy) often found their programs foundering on legislative shoals. Thus, the conservative coalition prospered, in large part the result of southern-held chairmanships, especially those of key committees, such as the "money" committees and the House Rules Committee. In spite of a steady barrage of criticism of the seniority system, year in and year out, its iron hold over chairmanships was not eased until the 1970s. As for the Republican party, from the New Deal to the present it typically has been in the minority, numerically weak, its capacity to influence legislative decisions ordinarily dependent on its alliance with the southern wing of the majority Democrats.

Legislative Reorganization Act of 1946

Popularly known under the names of its authors, Senator Robert M. LaFollette, Jr., and Congressman Mike Monroney, the Legislative Reorganization Act of 1946 was more important for what it launched than for what it concluded. Its mixed contents included provisions for (1) a sharp reduction in the number of standing committees in both houses (from forty-eight to nineteen in the House and from thirty-three to fifteen in the Senate); (2) an increase in staff assistance for members and committees; (3) a requirement for lobbyists to register and file financial reports; (4) an increase in legislative salaries and the installation of a retirement plan; and (5) the development of a legislative budget designed to promote congressional control over government spending.

Intended to modernize Congress, the act fell far short of expectations. The elimination of many committees did not by any means solve all of the jurisdictional problems present in committee organization; then as now committee chairmen struggled to prevent loss of any of their committee's legislative turf. The regulation of lobbies under Title III of the act proved to be inconsequential, its provisions laced with ambiguities and its applications uncertain. As for the congressional budget, it was tried once and abandoned. Finally, by shoring up committees through the provision of staff, at the same time ignoring the party structure,[4] the act strengthened centrifugal forces and weakened the central leadership.

Congressman Richard Bolling, long the leading advocate of reform in the House, found limited merit in the act:

> The LaFollette-Monroney Act . . . did not propose significant changes. The number of committees was reduced and their jurisdictions consolidated. A budget system was instituted. The most far-reaching improvement may have been simply the establishment of a retirement system for members, which enticed incompetents out of office. Fundamentally, the act touched nothing. If it had done more, it would have trod on the toes of the members of the power structure of the Democratic party in the House.[5]

---

[4]The opposition of the House led to dropping a provision in the reorganization bill to create party policy committees in each chamber. In an independent action in 1947, the Senate established its own policy committees, and not long afterward House Republicans transformed their steering committee into a policy committee. Not anxious to rush into things, House Democrats waited until 1973 to create a policy committee. In truth, the policy committees have proved to be slight threat to the standing committees' control over policymaking.

[5]Richard Bolling, *Power in the House* (New York: E.P. Dutton & Co., Inc., 1968), p. 262.

Congressional reorganization is never the outcome of a coherent vision of what a legislature should look like. It is rather the sum of miscellaneous strands, those which a majority, diverse in its interests, will accept (or tolerate) at a particular time. Although the reorganization of 1946 was legislation designed to satisfy minimalists, it nevertheless left its imprint on congressional politics in three fundamental ways. First, it laid the foundation for an extraordinary expansion of staff, culminating not many years later in a legislative bureaucracy that dwarfs those of other nations. Second, although it reduced the number of committees, it strengthened those that survived; moreover, committee consolidation paved the way for a sharp increase in the number of subcommittees, thereby unraveling the benefits of consolidation. The result was further decentralization of power in Congress, which continues to the present day. And third, even its abortive experiment with a legislative budget proved important, for Congress revived the idea when it passed the Budget and Impoundment Control Act of 1974. For what it introduced, for what it did not do as well as for what it did, for its unintended as well as its intended consequences, the reorganization act of 1946 is of large significance in the history of Congress.

Reform in the 1970s:
A Potpourri

It is not every day that Congress is stirred by the prospects for reform. Quite the contrary. Reform is threatening, so much so that most members are steadily wary of changes that promise major rearrangements in the way things are done, particularly if the changes appear likely to promote the concentration of power. Like all institutions whose memberships change slowly, Congress is more comfortable with familiar landmarks, settled procedures, accustomed relationships—in a word, comfortable with the status quo. Hence, in periods of change, it is not surprising to find scores of members negotiating from defensive postures, concerned to keep the institution in about the same form as they have both known and used it, concerned to keep their positions and prerogatives intact. What change imperils and what the status quo guards, in the broadest sense, is predictability. Yet changes do occur—when the conditions are right.

Politics is the vehicle of change. External politics can be as instrumental as internal politics in prompting institutions to reassess themselves. And reform is contagious. From the late-sixties through the mid-seventies, an extraordinary number of changes were introduced in the American political system. Ostensibly in the interest of participation, openness, representativeness, and other aspects of democratization, the party system was turned inside out, the powers of professionals and regulars diminished, those of amateurs, purists, and citizen enthusiasts augmented.[6] Change came to Congress as well, prompted in part by the same events that played upon the parties. Popular disaffection over the Vietnam War, and Congress's inability (and perhaps unwillingness) to do much about it in the face of presidential power, led to widespread demands for a restoration of congressional initiative and power in matters of foreign relations. Illuminating the possibilities for presidential excesses and corruption, the events of Watergate gave rise to still other demands that Congress assume a larger role in American politics. And finally, of at least as much importance, the general call for the democratization of American political institutions reached Congress about the time it reached the party system. The presence of a large number of younger, more independent members helped to make Congress receptive to these new, if inchoate, demands.

Addressed to small as well as large matters, the recent changes in Congress are a mixed batch.[7] No central conception of the legislative process informs them. They serve the ends of centralization as well as of decentralization, though particularly the latter. A number of changes won acceptance for their presumed contributions to making Congress more democratic, others because they promised to alter executive-legislative power imbalances. For purposes of analysis, the reforms are categorized in terms of their impact on the committee system, the party system, and on Congress as a whole. Changes in one domain, of course, frequently spill over into another.

The most important changes in recent years have involved the committee system. The Legislative Reorganization Act of 1970,[8] the first general reform act passed since 1946, contained a number of provisions affecting committee procedures. Included in the act are requirements for recording and publishing the votes of individual members, advance notice of committee hearings, prompt filing of committee reports, limitations on proxy voting, and biennial committee accounts of their activities. The act empowers committee majorities to call a meeting if the chairman ignores their request for one. Members of the minority party are permitted to call their own witnesses at hearings. The act permits committees, at their discretion, to open their hearings to broadcasting or televising. An important change in the Senate provides that no member may serve on more than one of the four top committees (Appropriations, Armed Services, Finance,

---

[6]Austin Ranney, *Curing the Mischiefs of Faction: Party Reform in America* (Berkeley: University of California Press, 1975).

[7]See a comprehensive analysis of recent reforms by Leroy N. Rieselbach, *Congressional Reform in the Seventies* (Morristown, N.J.: General Learning Press, 1977).

[8]For an instructive analysis of the 1970 act and the politics of its passage, see John F. Bibby and Roger H. Davidson, *On Capitol Hill: Studies in the Legislative Process* (Hinsdale, Ill.: The Dryden Press, 1972), Chapter 8.

and Foreign Relations).[9] Viewed broadly, these provisions were designed to reduce committee secrecy, increase the accountability of members, limit opportunities for arbitrary rule by committee chairmen, and strengthen the position of the minority party.

The 1970 law provided the basis for further and more significant changes designed to open committee transactions to public view. As a result of decisions made in 1973 and 1975, all committee meetings in both houses must now be open to the public unless a committee majority publicly votes to close them; these "sunshine" requirements cover not only regular meetings but also "mark up" sessions (the critical stage where bills are put in final form) and conference committee meetings. For most of the activities of Congress, thus, legislative secrecy has been sharply curtailed. Whether the openness of committee proceedings has improved congressional performance is, of course, another matter, one on which there is no evidence, only impressions. The proponents of "sunshine" provisions may find it humbling that their leading justification for sweeping away secrecy—the need to restore public confidence in Congress—has thus far proved unfounded. As shown by national surveys, the open and accessible Congress continues to be lodged on the outskirts of public affection. The public may neither know nor care that Congress is far more open than in the past.

The committee changes of greatest significance in the 1970s involved the allocation of power within Congress. Of special importance were those dealing with seniority and committee-subcommittee relationships. Under the new party rules, committee chairmanships no longer are tied solely to the seniority system, to be awarded automatically to the majority party member having the longest continuous service on each committee. All four party caucuses (or conferences) now provide that factors other than seniority may be taken into account in selecting chairmen (or ranking minority members). Moreover, chairmen can be removed from office by caucus action, as happened in 1975 when the House Democratic caucus voted to unseat three southern committee chairmen. The opportunity for secret caucus votes makes it easier to depose chairmen who have fallen out of favor with party members on their committees and/or a majority of their caucus.

Even though seniority will continue to govern the selection of most chairmen, the relationship between them and committee members has been fundamentally altered. Chairmen cannot take their positions for granted. They cannot abuse their powers, treat the preferences of members disdainfully, or otherwise run their committees in the manner of feudal baronies. Committee leadership now carries more risks and fewer satisfactions. No chairman is likely to be effective (or secure in his office) who

[9]Incumbent senators were "grandfathered"—that is, exempted from this provision.

fails to "touch bases" and to seek accommodation with fellow party members. What is now required of committee leaders is a new style of politics, based on consultation and persuasion rather than dictation and arm-twisting.

The crimp in the powers of committee chairmen results not only from the seniority reforms but also from basic changes in the provisions governing committees and subcommittees. Both chambers have limits on the number of chairmanships that a member can hold (one) and the number of subcommittee chairmanships that a committee chairman can hold (one in the House, two in the Senate). The House subcommittee limits originated in the Democratic caucus in 1971. Prior to the Senate changes in 1977,[10] some members held as many as eight or ten committee and subcommittee chairmanships. The 1977 Senate reforms also limited the number of committees and subcommittees on which a senator could serve to eleven; incredibly, to at least most outsiders, some members previously held seats on as many as twenty, even thirty, committees and subcommittees. The thrust of these changes was to spread leadership posts and preferred committee assignments around, snatching them from senior members and giving them to more junior members. These limitations not only gave younger (and more liberal) Democratic members a bigger "piece of the action" but also reduced the power of southern committee chairmen, particularly in the House.[11] The limitations also contributed to the further decentralization of power in both houses.

The powers of House committee chairmen suffered new erosion in 1973 when, responding to the initiatives of the liberal Democratic Study Group, the Democratic caucus approved reforms known as the "Subcommittee Bill of Rights." Paring the power of committee leaders to control their subunits, the reforms made provision for such things as firm subcommittee jurisdictions, prompt referral of bills to subcommittees by committee chairmen, assured subcommittee budgets, selection of subcommittee chairmen by the Democratic caucus of each committee (taking into account committee or subcommittee seniority), appointment of subcommittee staff by subcommittee chairmen, and creation of subcommittees in all committees with memberships in excess of twenty. As a result of these changes, the powers of subcommittees are now specified more clearly than ever, thus limiting the opportunities for committee chairmen to manipulate the subcommittee structure for their own ends. The biggest losers in the

---

[10]The changes in the Senate committee system were an outgrowth of recommendations made by the Temporary Select Committee to Study the Senate Committee System, established in 1976 and chaired by Adlai E. Stevenson III (D., Ill.).

[11]Norman J. Ornstein, "Causes and Consequences of Congressional Change: Subcommittee Reforms in the House of Representatives, 1970–1973," in Ornstein, ed., *Congress in Change: Evolution & Reform* (New York: Praeger Publishers, 1975), pp. 102–103.

congressional reforms of the 1970s were the committee chairmen—a fact that helps to explain their growing preference for retirement.

From almost any perspective, these were major changes in the committee system. When analysis is confined to the relationship between committee leaders and committee members, it is not extravagant to contend that the contemporary Congress is indeed a new Congress. Far and away its most notable characteristics are the diffusion of power and the freedom of members from leadership controls, including those so vigorously exercised by committee chairmen in earlier years. Whether viewing Congress at a distance or close up, observers do not find it easy to discover an answer to the question, "Who's in charge here?" Members themselves are not sure.

The rash of "subsystem" reforms in the last decade occurred not because the institution as a whole became markedly hospitable to change, but rather because the congressional parties, operating through their caucuses, took advantage of opportunities to press for new arrangements. The principal agent of reform was the Democratic caucus in the House, under the control of the liberal faction and influenced by a number of impatient new members. The caucus not only clipped the powers of committee chairmen by increasing the autonomy of subcommittees and by placing a harness on the seniority system, but in the process reclaimed power for itself. Assertion of its authority to judge succession to committee posts was but the first step. In 1973, House Democrats adopted a rule that allows a majority of the caucus (on petition of fifty members) to instruct fellow party members on the Rules Committee to permit floor consideration of a certain amendment, even though the Committee had requested a closed rule. In its organizational session in 1975, the caucus stipulated that the subcommittee chairmen of the key Appropriations Committee must be approved by the caucus. Seeking to strengthen leadership control over the committee structure, it transferred the power to make Democratic committee assignments from the Democratic members of the Ways and Means Committee to a party agency created in 1973, the Steering and Policy Committee, headed by the Speaker. Still at work on Ways and Means, it enlarged its size as a means of increasing the number of liberal members. And finally, rounding out this adventure in centralization, it gave the Speaker the authority to nominate the Democratic members of the Rules Committee, subject to caucus approval.

The promise of reform touched Congress as a whole as well as its committees and parties. Congress is not and never was simply the sum of its committees, or of its parties, or of some combination of the two. Committees do not govern everything and congressional parties, of course, encounter difficulty in governing anything. The reformers thus turned to

Congress as a unit, introducing changes designed to make it more democratic and a more nearly equal partner with the president.

The main thrusts of the democratizing reforms were to make Congress more open, its decisions more visible, and its members somewhat more accountable for their actions. One of the more important changes was the introduction of recorded teller votes in the House, as provided by the Legislative Reorganization Act of 1970. Prior to its passage, when using teller votes in the committee of the whole, members would proceed up the center aisle and be counted by tellers; the total yea and nay votes would be tabulated without recording how individual members had voted. The act sharply modified this procedure. Under the new teller system, twenty members may request that a vote be recorded, showing the position of each member. Secrecy is thus diminished and accountability heightened. Other results have been a major increase in the number of record votes and in the voting participation of members at the crucial amending stage. No one doubts that the new system has affected the outcomes of certain votes and reduced the capacity of committees to win their way on the floor. Overall, the fate of amendments has become more unpredictable. For members, recorded tellers represent the loss of a hiding place—one previously used to elude the gaze of citizens and the pressure of lobbyists.

Other far-reaching changes occurred in 1977 when the House and Senate each adopted a stringent code of ethics. The codes cover annual financial disclosure by members, the receipt of gifts from lobbyists, lobbying by former members, office accounts, franked mail, foreign travel, and outside earned income. The range of requirements and prohibitions imposed by the codes can be seen in the following provisions: (1) All members (and principal staff employees) are required to file an annual financial disclosure statement showing earned income, other income, honoraria, the source and value of gifts, financial holdings, real estate holdings, securities and commodities transactions, and personal liabilities. (2) The amount of outside income that can be earned by members is limited to fifteen percent of their official salary; at the current salary of $57,500, members thus may earn as much as $8,625 in outside income. (3) Honorarium payments, such as for making a speech or writing an article, are limited to $1,000 for members of the Senate and $750 for members of the House. (4) Private, unofficial office accounts ("slush funds") used to pay for official expenses are outlawed as is the use of campaign funds for personal expenses. (5) Members are prohibited from accepting gifts from lobbyists of more than $100 in aggregate value in any year. (6) Members seeking reelection are prohibited from sending franked mass mailings less than 60 days before a primary or general election. A House member is limited to annual franked mailings equal to six times the number of addresses in his district, and one who is a candidate for statewide office is prohibited from sending franked mass mailings to residents outside his district. (7) Foreign travel at government expense is prohibited for lame-duck members. (8) Senators are prohibited from lobbying in the Senate for one year after leaving office.[12]

The new codes of ethics were not passed because lines of citizen reformers had taken over the streets, demanding that Congress do something about the conduct of its members. Active, widespread public support for institutional change is never easily mobilized. Rather the codes won acceptance because of the need for both houses to counteract the publicity flowing from a continuing run of scandals among members. Included in the train of dingy episodes were cases involving illegal corporate political contributions, kickbacks from staff, submission of false information on financial reports, diversion of campaign funds for personal use, free hunting trips from defense contractors, false claims for travel expense reimbursements, solicitation and acceptance of bribes, acceptance of money and gifts from Korean influence peddlers, and a spectacular brouhaha involving a mistress on the congressional payroll.[13] Aimed at these scandal zones, the codes were seen as a means of restoring public confidence in Congress. Common Cause, the professed citizens' lobby, bolstered by the media, contributed heavily to the pressure for Congress to act. And it was difficult not to act, not only because opposition to "ethics" is perceived as risky but also because members had just received an exceptional pay raise of $12,900. A quid pro quo, something for the public, was required.

Shaped to deter conflict of interest practices, the most controversial regulations have been those relating to the disclosure of members' assets and the limitation on earned income from outside sources. The personal financial activities of all members have become public business, permitting other members and observers to make judgments about the extent to which the private finances of officeholders have become intertwined with their public responsibilities.[14] Although many members resented this intrusion on their private lives, only a few openly criticized the disclosure requirements. Some members chose retirement rather than compliance with disclosure or acceptance of the limitation on outside earned income. And doubtlessly many agreed with a New York congressman who declared:

[12]See detailed accounts of the codes in the *Congressional Quarterly Weekly Report*, issues of March 5 and April 2, 1977.

[13]*Congressional Quarterly Weekly Report*, October 30, 1976, pp. 3105–10.

[14]The first disclosure reports, filed in 1978, carried a vast assortment of information about the wealth and financial activities of members. Evidence that members had used their offices to enrich themselves was not immediately apparent, but a *Congressional Quarterly* analysis of the members' committee assignments in relation to their financial holdings indicated possible conflicts of interests for some members. For example, as Chairman of the Senate Finance Committee, Senator Russell B. Long (D., La.) played an important role in the 1978 drive to deregulate natural gas prices; at the same time, he reported ownership of $1.1 million in oil and gas leases. *Congressional Quarterly Weekly Report*, September 2, 1978, p. 2314.

Having fought and voted for years against people having their phones tapped, their mail opened, their tax returns publicized, their bank accounts examined and for their right of privacy, I am expected to give up all of my own. Public servants are people, too. I would rather give up my public life and get out of the goldfish bowl.[15]

From the outset, the congressional pay raise and the limitation on outside earned income were closely linked—the one serving to make the other more palatable. Nevertheless, for many members the financial losses promised to be large. Not a few members earned $15,000 to $25,000 or more a year in honoraria.[16] Lucrative private law practices, producing income far in excess of the amount permitted, were not uncommon. Some members found it especially nettling that the limitation on outside income applied only to that which was earned; income received in dividends from stocks, bonds, or trusts or from family farms or businesses was exempted, mainly to the advantage of members of substantial wealth. The rationale for the limitation was that the public was entitled to representation by full-time members, free from the distractions of outside work and from the appearance of conflict of interest.

Few political ideas are as appealing as democratization. When the idea spread to the Senate in the 1970s, it renewed prospects that the chamber's cloture rule could be modified to make it easier to terminate debate and thus to halt filibusters. Under the provisions of the 1959 cloture rule (rule 22) the termination of debate required the agreement of two-thirds of those present and voting, thus 67 votes if all members were present. Under this stringent requirement for checking debate, filibusters were difficult to terminate, much to the dismay of majoritarians. Finally, after weeks of squabbling in early 1975, Senate liberals succeeded in modifying rule 22 to provide for ending debate by a three-fifths vote of the entire membership (60 votes if there are no vacancies). The new rule has not, of course, brought an end to filibustering or to the threats of launching them. All it has done is to make it somewhat more difficult for a minority to win its way by tying up the Senate and talking measures to death. Many liberals in and out of Congress will not be satisfied until Senate debate can be halted by a simple majority of those present and voting.[17]

---

[15]*New York Times,* March 27, 1978.

[16]In early 1979 the Senate voted to postpone, for four years, the rule limiting the outside earned income of members to 15 percent of their salary ($8,625). Hence, at least for the present, under provisions of the Federal Election Campaign Act senators will be able to earn up to $25,000 a year in honoraria, with no honorarium to exceed $2,000. Full disclosure of outside earnings is required.

[17]From 1917 to 1970 there were forty-five cloture votes taken in the Senate, of which only eight were successful. From 1970 to late 1977 there were eighty-seven cloture votes; thirty-four (or about one-third) were adopted. An interesting variant of the filibuster was exploited in 1977 when, following the Senate's adoption of a cloture motion on a natural gas pricing bill, opponents of deregulation introduced hundreds of amendments as a way of delaying Senate action on the bill. This post-cloture ploy was finally broken by the chair's ruling that the amendments were out of order. See a listing of all cloture votes since 1917 in the *Congressional Quarterly Weekly Report,* October 1, 1977, pp. 2064–66.

Other changes during the 1970s were directed toward strengthening the position of Congress vis-a-vis the chief executive. Beginning with the New Deal, Congress came to play a distinctly secondary role in national policy-making. The Great Depression and World War II magnified the importance of the presidency and helped to fix in the public mind the notion that the president was the nation's chief initiator. Congress settled into the unenviable position of "no-win" politics: when it supported the president it was faulted for being a "rubber stamp" and when it opposed him, faulted for being a "roadblock." Blame for the frequent deadlocks between president and Congress were usually lodged with Congress, misshapened, critics said, by parochialism, unrepresentativeness, and minority domination.

An opening to change was presented by President Nixon. His aggressive pursuit of an unpopular war in Southeast Asia and his actions to control federal spending through impounding (or refusing to spend) funds approved by Congress led to widespread demands for a restoration of legislative initiative. And weakened by the reverberations and poundings of Watergate, the president was in no position to head off a resurgent Congress.

In its quest for parity with the executive branch, Congress adopted a War Powers Act in 1973 to limit the president's power to send American troops abroad without congressional approval and an act in 1974 designed to recapture the power of the purse. Although the war powers legislation is still to be tested, it is likely to increase congressional influence in foreign policy, long the peculiar province of the president. The Congressional Budget and Impoundment Control Act of 1974 is of larger significance. One result of it has been to constrict presidential opportunities for the impoundment of funds. More important, the act requires Congress to examine the budget as a whole to weigh and choose among priorities as it decides on the overall spending of government for the fiscal year. What previously was left to chance—a budget constructed out of the uncoordinated and piecemeal decisions of tens of committees and subcommittees acting in virtual isolation—is now a matter of central concern and decision, based on complex and predictable procedures, firm timetables, expenditure ceilings, and revenue floors. The essence of the process is that Congress as a whole assumes responsibility for the mix of spending, revenue, and deficit levels.

Nothing in the new budgetary system can prevent lobbies and legislators from joining to advance parochial interests (seeking, for example, to allocate additional money for defense, or for veterans' benefits, or for farm price supports) at the expense of an overall plan on spending—the politics of boodle is never far removed from the politics of budget-making. Nor, by itself, can the budgetary process prevent "out-of-control" federal spending.

What it can do is to sensitize members to fiscal realities, provide for a centralized reckoning on the budget (which is remarkable itself in a heavily decentralized system) and lay the foundation for a more coherent examination of two of the most important questions legislatures decide: where to spend money and in what amounts. The broad significance of the act is that it represents an effort to move Congress closer to where the Constitution intended it to be: in charge of the shop of national priorities.

The Impact of Recent Reforms

Change in political institutions always leaves tracks. The problem for the analyst is that years may be required to distinguish which way they are headed, and sometimes the direction never becomes clear. The rash of changes in Congress is a case in point. We are still a long way from knowing exactly what kind of Congress these changes, taken together, have produced. Their lasting power, moreover, remains to be seen. But if allowance is made for generality, certain broad observations about the thrust of these reforms can be made.

The upheavals involving the seniority system, coupled with the revival of the caucus, have brought an end to government by standing committee chairmen—the dominant pattern from the presidency of Roosevelt to that of Johnson. A chairman who leans noticeably toward autocracy will encounter difficulty surviving in the new Congress. In essence, the committee chairmanship is a new office, sharply reduced in independent authority, and reduced as well in its attractiveness for the occupant.

The decline in the authority of committee chairmen has been accompanied by a diffusion of power among numerous members, improving their opportunities for influencing legislative decisions. The increase in the number, independence, and importance of subcommittees has been spectacular. Concretely, these changes have pushed up the value of subcommittee chairmanships. At the same time, the proliferation of leadership positions and the antimonopoly stipulations concerning their distribution have produced a dramatic change in the opportunity structure of Congress. It now takes new members less time to gather power in their own right; for those in the majority party, a subcommittee chairmanship (in many committees) is not much farther than around the corner. Overall, the fragmentation of power has contributed to a condition under which individual members have greater opportunities to do what they want to do, free to ride all manner of hobbyhorses, relatively insulated from leadership controls. Perhaps at no time in the history of Congress have the individual preferences of members counted for as much as they do now.

In spite of the rediscovery of the caucus as an instrument of party,

party management has become much more difficult in both houses. The eclipse of party machines, the decline of party loyalty in the electorate, the fierce independence and anti-party posturings of many candidates—all converge to drain vitality from the congressional parties. For most members, the element of party has rusted out in their electoral connection. Their incumbent status (with its awesome advantages) is likely to prove much more important to their reelection than their party affiliation or their record of support for party leaders, including the president. What counts, members know, is pleasing the voters by developing an "appropriate" image, addressing matters of high moment to them, responding to the claims of key interest groups, concentrating on local and state matters, and taking care of constituent problems with government.

Organizational change in Congress has also weakened the parties. The emergence of subcommittee government means that leaders have more bases to touch, more independent power centers with which to reckon, more interests to be accommodated, more "one-on-one" games to play. Finally, the pervasive openness of Congress undoubtedly diminishes the opportunities for party leaders to press hard on members, hoping to bring them into line. When exposed to too much light, party controls wither.

In certain respects, Congress has become a more independent institution, better able to fend for itself, better able to resist the pressures and blandishments of the president and the bureaucracy. Its growing independence results in part from the sharp growth in professional staff and from the creation of two new research arms, the Office of Technology Assessment and the Congressional Budget Office. In addition, it can call on the experts of the Congressional Research Service of the Library of Congress and on those of the General Accounting Office. Congress now has more experts responsible to it and to its members than could have been imagined just a few years ago, a resource that lessens its reliance on the experts of the executive branch.

But probably of greater significance is simply the spirit of independence within Congress. Most members manage to get elected on their own, forming their own electoral organizations, raising their own campaign money, and creating their own personal followings. Their success as solitary political entrepreneurs has habituated them to the need to guard their own careers. To enhance their independence, they have shaped a Congress in which old hands count for less and in which even the newest members must be taken seriously. For members who are more concerned with their reelection than with majority-building, this is the best of all worlds.

Their freedom, of course, creates problems in the system. The independence of Congress has added to the tensions between the branches.

Congressional responses to presidential initiatives have become more un-predictable. There are fewer incentives for members to go along with the leadership, and party has become a less reliable link for bridging the separation of powers. The result is that it has become measurably more difficult to put together the firm majorities necessary to make decisions and to adopt new policies. Immobilization occurs all too commonly.

Of related interest is the question of whether the independence that Congress has achieved from the chief executive has been matched by a comparable distancing between Congress and interest groups. The over-whelming impression among observers is that it has not. Probably at no time has Congress been whipsawed so frequently by single-interest, non-class, high-intensity groups, arrayed on such passionate issues as gun control, abortion, conservation, nuclear power, equality, school prayer, and a thin slice of domestically-volatile foreign policy questions. Emerging in one context after another, these issues crowd the congressional agenda and inflame the debate. The independence that Congress and its members have won from the chief executive and from the parties has been diminished by a new vulnerability to narrow pressure groups that regard anything less than complete accord with their positions as betrayal, or worse yet, as reason to carry on the fight where it hurts, among the voters in the next campaign. Weary of the "rectitude" issues and the "new politics" encirclement, it is no wonder that some members, not only elderly ones, slip out between the wagons, headed back home to stay.

Democratization of the congressional system was a major objective of the reform movement. Proceeding along two dimensions, it led to opening up congressional workings to public view and to a redistribution of power among members and units. As a result of various "sunshine" provisions adopted in the 1970s, secrecy has been virtually eliminated—in committees and caucuses and in voting. The broad consequence of openness has been to change the way members do business, putting them "on the record" much more often than in the past and presumably increasing their re-sponsiveness and accountability to the public. At the same time, openness has increased the risks for members, at least as many perceive it, and added to the explanations (concerning positions, votes, and even personal finances) which they must make to those who pay attention and ask questions. It appears probable that the new openness has made members more likely to succumb to conspicuous displays of public pressure. Similarly, it may contribute to the success of interest groups in wringing larger accommo-dations out of Congress.

The redistribution of power brought about by alterations in the position of committee chairmen and in committee-subcommittee relations has pushed Congress toward extreme decentralization, offset only to the extent that party leaders, skillfully drawing on limited resources, can convince members to fall into line. The changes made in the name of democratization have contributed significantly to the further devolution of power in Congress.

The lasting importance of the changes made in Congress over the last decade remains to be seen. The immediate consequences, however, stand out, and are familiar by now. What is not clear is whether these changes have led to significantly different policy outcomes. That is the main question, and it is also the one on which there is the least systematic evidence. Investigation of the consequences of congressional reform for the political system, particularly in terms of public policy, ought to carry high priority for students of politics.

CONSTANCY

During a period in which reform is steadily celebrated, it is easy to lose sight of institutional constancies, the orientations and ways of doing things that change only slightly or not at all. In the case of Congress, many of its modes of behavior are beyond the reach of reform or, for that matter, beyond the reach of the electorate. Indeed, there is scant exaggeration in the holding that the more Congress changes, the more its essential behavior remains the same. And what remains the same, moreover, appears to be considerably more important than what is changed.

Like other institutions, Congress is a prisoner of its traditional out-looks—even in the midst of reform. A fundamental truth of Congress is that, regardless of its internal power relationships, it is both organized and inclined to deal with problems in customary ways to serve customary purposes. This conservative bias can be brought into sharper focus by considering a series of concluding propositions on the behavioral constancy, or stability, of our national legislature. For anyone save those who began reading this book on this page, the ideas should look familiar.

In shaping public policy, Congress is inclined to reward organized interests over unorganized ones, segmental interests over national ones. It is an inescapable feature of representative government that some interests within society will gain advantages over others as a result of legislative decisions. Their preferments may come in the form of new public policies, or in the preservation of existing law, or in exemptions from the applications of law. Opportunities for conveying advantages to narrow interests are present at all stages of the legislative process, but nowhere as much as in committees and subcommittees. Here the bargains can be struck that advance district or state interests and solve the political problems of members. Parochialism and reciprocity dominate the decision-making process:

It has generally been regarded . . . that the members of the committees should almost be partisans for the legislation that goes through the committee and for the special interest groups that are affected by it. . . . I am not . . . confident that the House can effectively work its will against a committee that is loaded on one side because the committee has the upper hand. There is a tendency on the part of many Members who are not on a given committee to go along with the committee.[18]

Defenders of Congress argue that the national interest is, in the last analysis, the sum of the local interests. This argument, however, rests on a mythical conception of how a legislature with the work load of the American Congress operates. Decisions—except for the greatest ones—cannot really be made by the collectivity of both houses. Issues have to be parceled out instead for piecemeal action by committees and subcommittees, and these are unlikely to be fully representative. . . . The decisions of the specialists have to be accepted by their colleagues most of the time without more than a cursory examination; a fresh and exhaustive review of every question by every member is obviously impossible. And through logrolling, the advocates of various local interests form coalitions of mutual support. Specialization is properly advanced as one of the strengths of the houses of Congress, and they could not function without it. Yet if specialization is to prevail, then by definition the effective power of decision is delegated mainly to individuals and small groups who reflect the views of relatively narrow geographic segments of the population; *if the sum of those views turns out in some cases to be the equivalent of the national interest, that has to be coincidental.*[19]

The bias of Congress in favor of parochial or special interests culminates in clientelism—a scheme of policy-making that allows groups which are the targets or beneficiaries of certain public policies to play a dominant role in shaping these policies, typically working in harmony with key committee members and bureaucrats whose agencies will administer the programs. Clientelism is a "cozy" relationship, one that obliterates the distinction between insiders and outsiders, governors and governed. The flawed quality of this form of policy-making is depicted by Roger H. Davidson:

Public policy . . . is too important to be delegated to the primary beneficiaries or subjects of that policy. Ultimately, every member of the society pays for benefits distributed to certain segments of society, no matter how innocuous the distribution may appear when considered separately. If it is true that war is too important to be left to generals, it follows equally that it is unwise to leave agricultural policy to the farmers, banking regulation to the bankers, communications policy to broadcasters, or environmental protection to the

---

[18]*Hearings* before the Select Committee on Committees, House of Representatives, 93rd Cong., 1st sess., 1973, p. 38. The statement was made by Congressman Charles E. Wiggins (R., Calif.).

[19]James L. Sundquist, "Congress and the President: Enemies or Partners?," in *Congress Reconsidered,* eds. Lawrence C. Dodd and Bruce I. Oppenheimer (New York: Praeger Publishers, 1977), pp. 230–31 (emphasis added).

environmentalists. Yet this is what frequently passes for representative policy making. . . . Of all arenas in our political system, the national legislature ought to be least in the thrall of particularistic pressures.[20]

From one election to the next, from one session to the next, constituency problems and politics dominate the lives of members. The cardinal truth to be known about members of Congress is that nothing matters as much to them as their "electoral connection."[21] Concern for their constituencies sensitizes and controls members in numerous ways. It shapes their committee assignments and their interests in legislation, influences their voting behavior, channels their interactions with administrative agencies, stretches their relations with legislative party leaders, dominates their work load, preoccupies their staff aides, inspires their public pronouncements, constricts their independent judgments, dilutes their interest in national problems, and prompts them to develop distinctive "home styles"[22] and to spend immoderate amounts of time cultivating the voters. No other factor so fundamentally affects the character of Congress and the quality of lawmaking. Internal reforms, of course, scarcely touch the linkages between members and their constituents.

Not all members, naturally, are equally burdened by constituency pressures or feel the same compulsion to concentrate their energies on constituency matters. Senior members, for example, devote more time to their Washington careers than do newcomers, who steadily feel the urgency to keep in touch with supportive constituents.[23] Nonetheless, no members can take constituency matters lightly:

> In our all-consuming effort to get reelected, we kept telling the people we'd do more and more for them, and they've come to expect it.[24]

> I'm from an agriculture-producing area, and I'm concerned for farmers' welfare and will look out for them. If New England consumers are suffering, why the hell should I care?[25]

[20]Roger H. Davidson, "Breaking Up Those 'Cozy Triangles': An Impossible Dream?," in *Legislative Reform and Public Policy,* eds., Susan Welch and John G. Peters (New York: Praeger Publishers, 1977), p. 31. Also see a comprehensive study of the linkages between administrative agencies, interest groups, and congressmen by J. Leiper Freeman, *The Political Process: Executive Bureau-Legislative Committee Relations* (New York: Random House, 1965).

[21]See David R. Mayhew, *Congress: The Electoral Connection* (New Haven: Yale University Press, 1974).

[22]See Richard F. Fenno, Jr., *Home Style: House Members in Their Districts* (Boston: Little, Brown and Company, 1978). Copyright © 1978 by Little, Brown and Company, Inc. Reprinted by permission. A major argument of Fenno's book is that the constituent support of members depends more on their activities at home than on their activities in Washington. An effective "home style," Fenno contends, increases the member's leeway in casting legislative votes.

[23]*Ibid.,* pp. 206–209.

[24]*New York Times,* March 27, 1978.

[25]John W. Kingdon, *Congressmen's Voting Decisions* (New York: Harper & Row, Publishers, 1973), p. 37.

I've got many, many families in my district who make a living on tobacco. Now, I never argued that cigarettes are good for your health. . . . If you could show me some way my people are going to eat if I vote against cigarettes, I'll do it. (Interviewer: So you start with this constituency factor.) It starts there and it ends there. That's all there is to it. If you don't, you aren't going to be around here very long. . . .[26]

I'm beginning to be a little concerned about my political future. I can feel myself getting into what I guess is a natural and inevitable condition—the gradual erosion of my local orientation. I'm not as enthused about tending to my constituency relations as I used to be and I'm not paying them the attention I should be. There's a natural tension between being a good representative and taking an interest in government. I'm getting into some heady things in Washington, and I want to make an input into the government. It's making me a poorer representative than I was. I find myself avoiding the personal collisions that arise in the constituency—turning away from that one last handshake, not bothering to go to that one last meeting. I find myself forgetting people's names. And I find myself caring less about it than I used to. Right now, it's just a feeling I have. In eight years I have still to come home less than forty weekends a year. This is my thirty-sixth trip this year. . . .[27]

Ralph Krug [the congressman in the adjacent district] tells me I spoil my constituents. He says, "You've been elected twice; you know your district; once a month is enough to come home." But that's not my philosophy. Maybe it will be someday. . . . My lack of confidence is still a pressure which brings me home. This is my political base. Washington is not my political base. I feel I have to come home to get nourished, to see for myself what's going on. It's my security blanket—coming home.[28]

Constituency effectively limits the options of legislators. Some policy alternatives are simply ruled out because members anticipate a popular outcry or fear the retribution of organized interest groups. A vote for even a mild form of gun control seems too risky for most members of Congress, who see, or think they see, the National Rifle Association poised in the shadows. Legislation involving abortion sends members scurrying for cover. A proposal to raise the federal tax on gasoline, supported by the Carter administration as part of its energy program, was overwhelmingly defeated in 1977. "Of course there's no constituency for a gas tax," remarked the chairman of the House Ways and Means Committee. "If you go out and talk to anybody in the country, they're not gonna say, 'Lay it on me baby'."[29]

Except in unusual circumstances, congressional decision-making is incremental and slow, the product of the steady workings of compromise and accommodation. Nothing about the passage of a law is simple in an institution whose layout

[26]*Ibid.,* p. 36.
[27]Fenno, *Home Style,* p. 216.
[28]*Ibid.,* pp. 217–18.
[29]*Congressional Quarterly Weekly Report,* August 6, 1977, p. 1628.

resembles an obstacle course. In the case of most legislation, the prime problem of enactment is that of accommodating or reconciling divergent interests. To pass a wheat price-support bill requires the votes of urban members who see wheat prices through consumer eyes; their support may hinge on adding quid-pro-quo provisions, such as liberal food stamp allowances. To pass a coal slurry pipeline bill (to transport crushed coal in pipelines from coal-rich states to coal-poor states) requires sponsors to search for ways to accommodate those members sensitive to the interests adversely affected—the railroads, rail-dependent unions, and environmentalists.

Members support bills for different reasons. The keys to passing many bills are the trade-off and the "sweetener,"[30] concessions that make legislation more attractive to members on the sidelines or mildly in opposition. Years, even decades, may be required to adopt a policy that departs sharply from conventional "solutions" to problems.

Lawmaking is slow because the process of reconciliation is slow, inevitably so in an institution with limited hierarchy, decentralized power, and weak parties. The need to build majorities, piece by piece, concession by concession, usually means that the changes from existing law will be smaller rather than larger, patched together rather than integrated, incremental rather than grand. The search for consensus dominates the mood of most lawmaking—and gaining it takes time. There is a "dance of legislation,"[31] as Woodrow Wilson observed, but it is more two-step than hustle.

The slow pace of Congress is consistent with its purpose: it is, after all, primarily a deliberative assembly, not commonly expected to make quick decisions. Its slow movement is also consistent with its organizational preferences, which Nelson W. Polsby aptly describes:

> Instead of having a single head, Congress looks like the hydra of Greek mythology. Instead of neatly delegating work downward and responsibility upward, Congress is a complex, redundant, not always predictable, and purposely unwieldy network of crisscrossing and overlapping lines of authority and information.[32]

Hence it is no wonder that Congress creaks along. At the same time, of course, its slowness in decision-making enhances the prospects that numerous voices will be heard, that initial policy assumptions will be questioned again and again, and that, as Richard F. Fenno, Jr., points out, its eventual decisions will be regarded as fair.[33]

---

[30]A "sweetener" is a provision added to a bill that carries some special benefit for a distinctive group, thus increasing the likelihood that a few more votes can be pulled over to the affirmative side.

[31]Woodrow Wilson, *Congressional Government* (New York: Meridian Books, 1956), p. 195.

[32]Nelson W. Polsby, "Strengthening Congress in National Policy-Making," *Yale Review*, 59 (June 1970), 481.

[33]Richard F. Fenno, Jr., "Strengthening a Congressional Strength," in *Congress Reconsidered*, eds. Lawrence C. Dodd and Bruce I. Oppenheimer (New York: Praeger Publishers, 1977), p. 263.

Congress looks to the president for both its agenda and for political leadership. Internal reforms can enlarge the capacity of Congress to control its destiny. The increase in professional staff, the development of additional research arms, the greater utilization of outside experts drawn from the private sector, and the placing of new requirements on itself (such as the congressional budget)—each represents an effort by Congress to assume larger responsibilities for policy-making. And in degree Congress has succeeded in creating conditions that should make it easier to make up its mind on questions that come before it. Favorable conditions, of course, do not guarantee favorable outcomes. And what the reforms of Congress have not been able to do is to lessen its reliance on the president for the main items on its agenda and for the mobilization of support to secure their passage.

"Laws and customs," wrote Richard E. Neustadt in the 1950s, "now reflect acceptance of [the president] as the Great Initiator, an acceptance quite as widespread at the Capitol as at his end of Pennsylvania Avenue."[34] Almost a quarter of a century later the statement continues to ring true. The only difference time has introduced is that it has become even more difficult for the president to secure sustained support in a Congress less centrally controlled, composed of many younger members intent on "doing their own thing" in a system redesigned to promote such free-wheeling activity.

In all probability Congress needs the president more now than in the past—even if some members are reluctant to admit it. Congress's need for the president has increased because Congress has changed. It has become less manageable, less integrated, less willing to subordinate parochial quests to broad plans, and of course far more individualistic. Put another way, congressional decision-making has become more difficult as the parties have declined in both Congress and the country, as voters and candidates alike have become more independent, as citizens have made more and more demands for congressional solutions to their problems,[35] and as the congressional structure has been altered to spread the action around, taking power from the few and distributing it to the many. The broad result is that there are fewer straps that bind Congress together.

One's view of Congress depends on where he or she stands. Those who are generally comfortable with the new Congress may say that it is now more democratic, more responsive, and more accountable. Those who are less comfortable with it may say that one of the large prices of the changes has been a reduced capacity of Congress, as a collectivity, "to get its act together." And that is where the president comes in.

[34]Richard E. Neustadt, *Presidential Power: The Politics of Leadership* (New York: John Wiley & Sons, Inc., 1960), p. 6.
[35]One member who retired in 1978 pointed out that his annual mail from constituents used to fill only three file cabinets. At last count it took fourteen to hold it. *New York Times,* March 27, 1978.

The fragmentation of power within Congress, accompanied by inde-
cision and particularism, impels the president to become deeply involved in
the lawmaking process. Better than anyone else, the president can focus
attention on national problems and help to break the deadlocks that
impede their resolution. His resources, moreover, are needed by legislators
to do their jobs, to help them to do what they cannot do by themselves.
Remembering his large campaign pledges, what is more, the general public
(at least some segments of it) now expects him to be active in the legislative
struggle.

*Congress is often as sensitive to member problems as it is to public problems; it is
always open to ploys that will get members "off the hook."* From certain perspectives Congress is a club, carefully organized to advance and protect the
interests of its members. The evidence of club is everywhere. Indifferent
administration of ethics laws—a reluctance to investigate members sus-
pected of wrongdoing or to press hard on members found guilty of abusing
their office—is one sign of the presence of club. The press and television, of
course, frequently exaggerate the corruption theme. Nevertheless, the
problem is serious. The belief that members transact large amounts of
unsavory business, protected in their cocoon, is undoubtedly a major
reason for Congress's poor reputation among the public. The broad point
is that even an occasional "club approach" to ethical questions—which
usually means looking the other way—leaves the institution vulnerable to
immoderate criticism.

The qualities of club pervade most aspects of congressional life. A
personal attack by one member on another is rare. Or consider the committee system, which is steadily used to enhance the political well-being of
members. Even though it leads to extreme forms of "stacking" and unrepresentativeness, committee assignments are made largely on the basis of
members' preferences. Committee and subcommittee investigations present
unusual opportunities for members to garner personal publicity. Field
hearings by subcommittees can be used by members to return home on
public business (or ostensibly on public business), giving voters an opportunity to see their own representatives at work; it is hard to imagine a more
effective form of "subliminal" campaigning. Committee staff can be and are
diverted from committee work to office work—and from office work to
campaign work. Indeed, office staffs are constantly engaged in reelection
activities. "The Hill office is a vitally important political unit, part campaign
management firm and part political machine."[36]

When redistricting rolls around, Democratic and Republican congressmen from the same state regularly cooperate, pressuring their state
legislatures to make the seats of all incumbents less competitive. When the

---

[36]David R. Mayhew, *Congress: The Electoral Connection* (New Haven: Yale University Press,
1974), p. 84. This book was useful in developing the argument of this section.

Defense Department announces that it may close certain military bases or hospitals, the club meets to plan ways to resist the threatened loss of jobs.[37] When an appointment such as a federal judge is to be made in a state, senators mill together under the umbrella of "senatorial courtesy," protecting the right of the senator of the president's party in that state to choose the nominee. When a proposal to provide for public financing of congressional campaigns comes up, numerous members find reasons to oppose it: why should they help to finance their challengers? And when a reorganization plan threatens to upset traditional committee jurisdictions, and therefore power allocations, members of all stripes coalesce to defeat it.[38] Unmistakably, members take care of "No. 1."

Strong parties are a threat to business-as-usual politics. Weak parties are not. For members, few things are more important than their freedom to speak and to vote in ways that carry advantages for them. The desire to protect their options intrudes on the selection of leaders. "Party leaders are chosen not to be program salesmen or vote mobilizers, but to be brokers, favor-doers, agenda-setters, and protectors of established institutional routines."[39] The congressional party, in a word, is a servant of the club. So also, of course, are the seniority system, the franking system, and the incumbent-benefit system.[40]

The preoccupation of Congress with distributive policies (and its aversion to redistributive ones, such as tax reform or civil rights legislation) is further evidence of the club spirit. Supported by the norm of reciprocity, members regularly trade votes to pass out particularized benefits—dams, harbors, irrigation projects, military installations, public buildings, public works in general, specialized subsidies, selective tax cuts, and so forth. All members in the "logroll" have claims to benefits for their states or districts. The charm of distributive policies for insiders is that beneficiaries immediately recognize that they have been benefited, but the costs are not easily detected by the general run of voters.

[37]"Congress is of two minds on these things," comments an assistant secretary of defense. "In the general sense they recognize our problem . . . that we have too many bases, and they have urged us to make reductions. On the other hand, obviously they do not want to see reductions in their particular area that affect their constituents." *Congressional Quarterly Weekly Report*, May 6, 1978, p. 1112.

[38]See an interesting study by Roger H. Davidson and Walter J. Oleszek of the efforts by the "Bolling Committee" (the House Select Committee on Committees) to reorganize House committees in the 93rd Congress (1973–74). Most of the Bolling Committee's proposals for jurisdictional realignment were lost—mainly because they threatened the positions and power of too many members. *Congress Against Itself* (Bloomington: Indiana University Press, 1977).

[39]Mayhew, *Congress: The Electoral Connection,* p. 100.

[40]The argument concerning the legislature's hospitality to its members' interests can be stretched out of shape. Our contention is simply that Congress has a private as well as a public personality and that there are private sides to public matters. Obviously, the committee assignment process, the seniority system, the party system, and so forth, have public as well as private dimensions.

Congress is replete with opportunities for taking members "off the hook"—saving them embarrassment, blunting potential opposition to them, and affording them convenient explanations for their votes. For example, they can vote for a bill because they are confident that the other house will kill it or that the president will veto it. They can support a bill in committee and privately lobby the (House) Rules Committee to prevent it from going to the floor. They can explain that a closed rule prevented them from working to change a bill through amendments. They can "pass the buck" by drafting general legislation, leaving to the executive branch the task (not to mention the problems and risks) of shaping the details.[41] They can vote one way at one stage of the legislative process and another way at another stage, thus obscuring their position. They can miss a "no-win" vote, claiming any of a number of other legislative responsibilities kept them away.[42] Parliamentary practices and institutional forbearance provide all sorts of "outs" for a member apparently trapped between a rock and a hard place.[43]

Chronically out of favor with the public and steadily criticized by its own members, Congress is an institution in trouble. Few good words are said about Congress. Members of the attentive public seldom find reason to praise it. Editorials and TV commentary favorable to Congress are scarce—surfacing only slightly more often than snail darters outside the Tellico River. (In general, of course, preoccupied with the president the national media simply demeans Congress by ignoring it). Prominent spokesmen for business, labor, agriculture, or the professions are much more likely to side with critics than with defenders when their public pronouncements turn to Congress; the inadequacy of Congress is, in fact, a central theme in the "conventional wisdom" of organizational leaders of all kinds.

Disaffection with Congress is at least as common among the general run of voters as it is among the attentive public. As shown by national opinion surveys, typically only thirty to forty percent of the people express approval of the way Congress is doing its job; at times the proportion dips below twenty-five percent. In addition, it is rare when Congress leads the president in popular approval ratings. There is some evidence, interestingly, that the popular view of Congress is shaped by the popular view of

---

[41]See a brief, instructive discussion of the delegation of legislative powers by Louis Fisher, *The Constitution Between Friends: Congress, the President, and the Law* (New York: St. Martin's Press, 1978), pp. 22–23.

[42]In two respects, club practices have been diminished by recent reforms. Open meeting rules for committees and recorded teller votes both reduce secrecy and, presumably, increase the member's accountability to the voters. They make it somewhat more difficult for members to hide or to dodge.

[43]For further discussion of this theme, see John W. Kingdon, *Congressmen's Voting Decisions* (New York: Harper & Row, Publishers, 1973), pp. 50–53.

the president. When his popularity increases, Congress's popularity increases; when his popularity fades, Congress's popularity fades.[44] Whether the legislative branch ever appears in sharp focus for most voters is problematical. But what they do see, when occasionally they glance toward Washington, apparently disillusions them.[45]

Not all of the damage done to the reputation of Congress is done by outsiders. Members contribute their share, perhaps more than their share. Their errant behavior in office, of course, takes a toll on the legislature's public standing—the broad outlines of a major scandal can be understood by even the most indifferent citizen. But the deprecatory campaign remarks about Congress made by members may exact an even larger toll. "Members of Congress," Richard F. Fenno, Jr., discovered, "run *for* Congress by running *against* Congress."[46] The essence of this popular campaign strategy is to differentiate oneself from the others in Congress and from the institution as a whole. The remarks of two House members running for reelection nicely illustrate the point:

> I do not accept responsibility for any actions of Congress. I do not want to be tarred with the brush being applied to other members of Congress. I want to be judged by how well Sam Smalley has done, what Sam Smalley has said, and what service Sam Smalley has given to the people of the Third District of this state.

> I've been giving some thought to the campaign theme. What people want in their public officials today is independence. We can't be so vulgar as to use the word "independence" in our literature. But we have to differentiate me from the rest of those bandits down there in Congress. "They are awful, but our guy is wonderful"—that's the message we have to get across.[47]

The strategy of differentiation is effective. The voters may not love their Congress, but they love their congressmen—and they reelect them

---

[44]Charles O. Jones, "Will Reform Change Congress?", in *Congress Reconsidered*, eds. Lawrence C. Dodd and Bruce I. Oppenheimer (New York: Praeger Publishers, 1977), p. 252.

[45]A nationwide survey early in 1977, conducted by Louis Harris and Associates for the House Commission on Administrative Review, found that three out of four persons held a negative view of Congress. They cited the following major reasons: "Democratic Congress and Republican President couldn't get together, couldn't agree, party politics;" "Congress opposed the President, wouldn't cooperate, stood in the way;" "Can't see that anything's changed, no signs of improvement, haven't done anything," "They bicker, haggle, waste time, are too slow, too big, inefficient;" "Haven't done anything about inflation, prices, economy;" "Too much scandals, graft, kickbacks." Interestingly, not many people linked their disapproval of Congress to disappointments over specific public policy outcomes. *Final Report* of the Commission on Administrative Review, U.S. House of Representatives, 95th Cong., 1st sess., 1977, pp. 817–18.

[46]Richard F. Fenno, Jr., *Home Style: House Members in Their Districts* (Boston: Little, Brown and Company, 1978), p. 168.

[47]*Ibid.*, pp. 165–66.

in record numbers.[48] In national opinion surveys, individual congressmen are twice as likely as Congress as a whole to receive high performance ratings.[49] What is more, many voters believe that their own congressman is superior to most other congressmen; only a handful believes their representative is worse than others.[50] All this comes down to the fact that members are remarkably successful in building personal followings and in escaping the criticisms that voters visit on Congress as a whole.

The significance of this unique relationship between members and their constituencies should not be lost. To the extent that voters enforce any form of responsibility for congressional performance, it is personal and individual, centering in each constituency's assessment of its own representative. Hence no one, in effect, bears much if any responsibility for what Congress, as an institution, does or fails to do.[51] The absence of overall legislative responsibility ought to be a major worry for those politicians and citizens concerned about the vitality and durability of the American political system.

Congress reflects the political realities of American society. In large degree government mirrors society. As the nation's representative body, Congress is especially sensitive to popular currents of thought. No barriers insulate it from the people. The events that play upon the public play upon Capitol Hill. The moods that dominate the public shortly dominate Congress.

The sharp loss of public confidence and trust in government, shown again and again in national surveys, is perhaps the outstanding fact of contemporary politics. Congress has of course been affected by this development, the sources of which are easy enough to identify. The jarring events of the 1960s and 1970s—the assassination of President John F. Kennedy, the unpopular and ill-fated Vietnam War, the evils of Watergate, and the resignations of the vice-president and the president—sent shock waves through the public. Along with the rest of government, Congress suffered from these breakdowns in the system.

[48]Richard F. Fenno, Jr., "If, as Ralph Nader Says, Congress is 'The Broken Branch,' How Come We Love Our Congressmen So Much?", in *Congress in Change: Evolution and Reform,* ed. Norman J. Ornstein (New York: Praeger Publishers, 1975), pp. 277–87.

[49]A recent Harris survey found that forty percent of the people rated their congressmen as doing a "pretty good" or an "excellent" job; only twenty-two percent described Congress as a whole in these terms. *Final Report* of the Commission on Administrative Review, pp. 816–18.

[50]*Ibid.,* p. 820.

[51]Ralph K. Huitt makes the argument this way: "What cannot be gainsaid is that the Congress cannot be held politically responsible for its overall performance. Congress is two houses, separate and distinct, with differing modes of operation. Congress is two parties, unable to hold party lines, not organized to take party positions. Congress is [thirty-seven] standing committees, many more special committees, task forces, etc., each with a piece of the job. Congress is 535 individual members, each catering to his own district or state and depending on his own resources to retain his seat. Nowhere is there a handle with which to take hold of the whole Congress." "Congress: Retrospect and Prospect," *Journal of Politics,* 38 (August 1976), 225.

The inability of government to solve major public problems—energy, inflation, unemployment, race relations, urban decay, to mention leading examples—has also cut into the public's support for political leaders. Numerous voters wonder whether it makes a difference who runs things in Washington.

Yet even as the list of intractable problems has grown, the voters have looked increasingly to government for assistance in their own lives. Individuals want the government to do more and more for them, to do things that in the past they did for themselves. When government fails or falls short, when it is unable to meet current expectations and claims, popular disillusionment and cynicism grow.

The doubts of the public about the capacity of government to act wisely and to solve problems have been matched by similar doubts and strains among officeholders. "We've come to realize," a House member remarked, "there is a limit to our powers. We have a feeling that we're not as great as we thought we were." Another member observed in a related vein: "There is so little joy you find among the members."[52]

Congress is an extension of the people. That is both its strength and its weakness. The public's confusion and apprehension is reflected, often magnified, in Congress. When the public is uncertain and divided over the energy problem, or over any other large problem, Congress is uncertain and divided. Extraordinary political leadership may be required even to make marginal policy adjustments in a public atmosphere clouded by skepticism, discontent, and division.

Except in tangential ways, congressional reforms do not address these matters. It is hard to conceive of structural or procedural changes, in fact, that could bolster institutional self-confidence at a time when, among the voters, individual self-confidence and optimism about the future are so conspicuously low. Probably only a new combination of events and political leadership (especially presidential) can overcome the malaise and discontents infecting American society and its institutions. The largest reality of all is that there is not much that Congress can do on its own to change the public's suspicions about government or the nation's underlying mood of negativism.

This, then, is Congress—the people's body. In some ways, it is a new institution. In the ways that count the most, it is quite old: the more it changes, the more it looks the same. But new or old, Congress is unrivaled among national legislatures in independence and power. No citizen should take it lightly. What it does really matters.

Although legislative majority-building is extraordinarily difficult when important matters are at stake, Congress solves or ameliorates a surprising

[52]*New York Times*, March 27, 1978. The comments, respectively, are those of Charles W. Whalen, Jr. (R., Ohio) and David R. Obey (D., Wis.).

number of public problems. More effectively than any other institution of government, it works to nurture consensus—indeed, in a broad sense, that is its most important contribution to the polity. And if it is true that it does not represent all citizens equally, it is also true that it represents a great many citizens quite well, probably about as well as any legislature could. All this comes down to the fact that the complaints about Congress need to be viewed in the context of its accomplishments and with full recognition that impossible demands are steadily made upon it.

The flaws of Congress are the flaws of free legislatures generally. Its messiness is the messiness of free legislatures everywhere. Its politics is the politics of a free people.

Index

Aberbach, Joel D., 24
Agranoff, Robert, 40
Alexander, Herbert E., 41, 43
Appropriations and budgetary process, 12, 15, 24, 63-64, 103, 104, 109, 119-20, 123, 147, 148, 152, 156-57
Asher, Herbert B., 14

Baker v. Carr, 32
Barone, Michael, 31
Bauer, Raymond A., 134
Bibby, John F., 149
Bicameralism, 2, 15
Biemiller, Andrew, 126
Bolling, Richard, 147
Bolling Committee, 110-111, 167
Bone, Hugh A., 83
Born, Richard, 88
Brademas, John, 8
Breslin, Janet, 138
Broder, David, 15
Buckley v. Valeo, 42
Budget and Accounting Act of 1921, 109
Budget and Impoundment Control Act, 119, 156
Bullitt, Stimson, 37
Bullock, Charles S., 9, 53, 74
Bumpers, Dale, 93

Campaigns:
    candidate-centered, 36-37, 89, 158
    characteristics, 36-41
    against Congress, 169-70
    finance, 41-44, 129-31, 167

importance of issues, 37-38
inside electioneering, 44-46
management firms, 39-40
and presidential leadership, 108-9
strategy, 39-41
Cannon, Joseph G., 81, 84, 91, 144, 145, 146
Carpenter, Douglas, 50
Carroll, Holbert N., 62, 107
Carter, Jimmy, 54, 104, 109, 113, 114
Chi-hung, Chu, 74
Chiles, Lawton, 10, 71
Church, Frank, 112
Clapp, Charles L., 13, 38, 39, 73
Clem, Alan L., 38
Cloture rule, 17, 155
Clubb, Jerome M., 90
Colegrove v. Green, 31
Committees:
    assignment of members, 6, 8, 17, 64, 71, 73-75, 81, 121-22, 126, 145, 162, 166, 167
    and bureaucracy, 6, 7, 24, 118-120, 161, 162
    chairmen, 3, 4, 7, 8, 17, 43, 65, 71, 76-77, 78, 79, 82, 106, 146, 150-52, 154, 155, 157
    clientelism, 161-62
    conference, 68-69, 85
    elite, 73, 75, 149-50
    goals of members, 4, 6-7, 62, 74-75, 122, 166
    House Rules Committee, 8, 17, 145, 146, 152, 168
    independence, 2-6, 8, 62, 63, 146

Committees *(cont.)*
  and interest groups, 121-23, 125-26, 127, 128
  joint, 68, 85
  jurisdictions, 65, 66-67
  meetings, 21, 25, 150, 159, 168
  power of, 2-6, 8, 12, 62-65, 106, 111, 126, 150-52, 153, 160-61
  representativeness, 6-7
  select, 67-68, 85
  seniority, 4, 6, 76-79, 106, 145, 150, 157, 167
  specialization, 3-4, 12, 14, 62, 70, 161
  staffs, 7, 95, 96, 98, 99, 100, 147, 165
  standing, 3, 65, 66, 67, 121, 146, 147, 148
  subcommittees, 7, 69-73, 91, 150-52, 157, 158, 160-61, 166
  "sunshine" rules, 25, 159
Congress:
  behavioral stability, 160-72
  campaigns for, 36-41
  careers of members, 2, 4, 9-11, 13-14, 16, 18, 57-58, 70, 71, 122, 139-40, 153, 154-55, 158, 159, 166-70
  characteristics, 1-18, 116-17, 160-72
  constitutional position, 15, 19
  decentralization, 2-9, 16, 69-73, 84, 106, 116-18, 122, 123, 145-46, 148, 149, 152, 157-59
  democratization, 148-60, 166
  errand-running, 13, 20, 23, 24, 25-29, 97-98, 100, 136-40, 162-63
  ethics, 130, 153-55, 166, 169
  functions, 18-26, 109, 118, 139
  incumbents, 10-11, 13, 33, 35, 36, 37, 39, 40, 41, 43, 44-46, 51, 52, 53, 57, 59-60, 98, 139-40, 151, 166-67
  and localism, 11-14, 22, 23, 25-29, 109, 112-13, 122, 136-40, 158-59, 161, 162-63, 165, 166-68, 171
  nominations, 46-47
  norms, 6, 12, 13, 14-15, 160-61, 168
  occupations of members, 56-57
  pensions, 10
  personal staffs, 35, 95, 96-98, 110, 140, 141, 147, 153, 154, 165, 167
  power of, 1, 116-118, 156-57
  public reputation, 168-71
  reform, 7, 25, 58, 66, 67, 71-73, 111, 135, 143-60, 167, 169, 171
  retirements, 10, 11, 20, 57, 59, 152, 154-55
  salary and perquisites, 58-59
  and Supreme Court, 32, 42, 44
  volume of work, 3, 10, 20, 21, 23, 25-29, 65, 99, 162
  voting, 20-21, 35, 45-46, 89-95, 126, 140-41, 153, 159, 168

  (see also Committees, Elections, Political Parties)
Congressional Research Service, 158
Constituencies:
  district characteristics, 30-31
  perceptions of constituencies, 34-35
  role, orientations toward, 136-40, 162-63
  and voting behavior, 140-41
  (see also Congress, House of Representatives, Representation)
Conyers, John, 10
Cooper, Joseph, 3
Cover, Albert D., 51, 53, 60
Cranston, Alan, 70, 97
Cronin, Thomas E., 103, 110, 120
Crotty, William J., 41, 43
Cummings, Milton C., 50

Davidson, Roger H., 7, 22, 23, 149, 161, 162, 167
Deakin, James, 130
Deckard, Barbara, 13, 88
Democratic Study Group, 87-88, 151
Dennis, Jack, 44
de Sola Pool, Ithiel, 134
Dexter, Lewis A., 134, 140
Dodd, Laurence C., 3, 12, 51, 57, 78, 93, 117, 119, 161, 164, 169

Eisenhower, Dwight D., 54, 103, 104, 113
Elections:
  competitiveness, 10-11, 49-53, 77
  influence of president, 54-55, 115
  membership changes, 57-58
  midterm, 55
  split results, 50, 114
  turnout, 47-48
Ellwood, John W., 119
Employment Act of 1946, 109
Executive-Legislative Relations *(see* Congress, President)

Federal Election Campaign Act of 1974, 41, 42
Federal Regulation of Lobbying Act, 134-35
Fenno, Richard F., Jr., 14, 15, 17, 34, 35, 63, 64, 69, 70, 74, 75, 116, 117, 122, 125, 126, 162, 163, 164, 169, 170
Ferejohn, John A., 53
Filibuster, 17, 106, 146, 155
Fiorina, Morris P., 9, 53, 139
Fishel, Jeff, 39
Fisher, Louis, 168
Ford, Gerald R., 102, 103
Ford, William D., 132
Fox, Harrison W., 96
Franklin, Grace A., 118

Freeman, J. Leiper, 162
Froman, Lewis A., 16, 41

General Accounting Office, 158
Gerrymandering (*see* Representation)
Gertzog, Irwin N., 74
Goldwater, Barry, 55, 70, 100
Goodwin, George, 75
Goss, Carol F., 6

Hammond, Susan Webb, 96
Hayes, Michael T., 134
Heard, Alexander, 130
Heinz, H. John, 44, 138
Hess, Stephen, 110
Hinckley, Barbara, 75, 109
Hofstetter, C. Richard, 109
Hollings, Ernest, 93
Holtzman, Abraham, 110
House of Representatives:
  constituencies, 30-36
  contrast with Senate, 15-18
  debate, 17
  elections, 46-55
  legislative activity, 21
  members' role orientations, 22-23, 25-29
  norms, 14-15
  occupations of members, 56-57
  party voting, 90-91, 95
  revenue bills, 16
  Rules Committee, 8, 17, 78, 81, 84, 145, 146, 152, 168
  specialization of members, 17
  Steering and Policy Committee, 8, 81, 84, 147, 152
  (*see also* Committees, Congress, Constituencies)
Huckshorn, Robert J., 37, 38
Huitt, Ralph K., 3, 4, 83, 170
Huntington, Samuel P., 9
Hutcheson, Richard G., 54

Incumbency (*see* Congress)
Interest groups:
  access to Congress, 19, 20, 121-23, 125-33
  alliances between, 125, 127, 128-29, 132
  business, 92-93, 125, 129, 131, 132, 133, 154
  campaign contributions, 42-43, 129-31, 153
  citizens', 124
  civil rights, 121
  and committees, 6-7, 65-66, 121-23, 125-26, 127, 128
  defensive lobbying, 121
  direct lobbying, 127, 131, 135, 141
  diversity, 123-24
  effectiveness, 159, 160-62, 163, 164
  expenditures, 131
  farm, 6, 121, 129, 161
  grass-roots lobbying, 127, 131-33, 135
  impact on policy, 133-34
  inside lobbyists, 125
  inspired communications, 131-32
  intermediaries, 127, 128, 141
  labor, 6, 92, 94, 121, 126, 129, 132
  legislator-lobbyist relations, 133-134
  lobbyists, 123-25, 126, 128, 130, 153
  paths of influence, 127, 141
  and political parties, 91-95
  power of, 125
  professional, 124, 129
  regulation of, 134-35, 147
  single-interest, 159
  techniques of lobbies, 126-33
Isaacs, Stephen, 100

Jacobson, Gary C., 43
Javits, Jacob, 93
Jennings, M. Kent, 38, 41
Jewell, Malcolm E., 74
Johnson, Lyndon, 9, 94, 102, 106, 113
Jones, Charles O., 38, 39, 53, 80, 83, 111, 145, 169

Keefe, William J., 46, 102
Kennedy, Edward, 138
Kennedy, John F., 113, 146, 170
Kernell, Samuel, 9
Kessel, John H., 88, 108, 109
Kingdon, John W., 113, 115, 128, 129, 133, 141, 162, 168
Knoke, David, 49
Koenig, Louis, 113
Kofmehl, Kenneth, 88, 96
Kostrowski, Warren Lee, 53
Kozak, David C., 20

La Follette, Robert M., Jr., 147
Legislative Reorganization Act of 1946, 7, 147-48
Legislative Reorganization Act of 1970, 149-50, 153
Legislative veto (*see* Oversight of administration)
Leuthold, David A., 38
Levitin, Teresa E., 49
Lewis, Anne L., 64
Lippmann, Walter, 112
Lobbies (*see* Interest groups)
Logrolling, 5, 12, 13, 15, 112-113, 121, 123, 161, 168
Long, Russell B., 154
Longworth, Nicholas, 84

McCormack, John, 126
McGovern, George, 49, 55
McPherson, Harry, 107
Magraw v. Donovan, 32
Maguire, Andrew, 132
Mahon, George, 10
Malbin, Michael J., 98
Manley, John F., 69, 93
Mann, Thomas E., 36, 88
Mansfield, Mike, 106
Masters, Nicholas A., 64
Mathias, Charles, 93
Matthews, Donald R., 14, 133, 134
Matthews, Douglas, 31
Mayhew, David R., 4, 45, 46, 51, 53, 55, 60,
    162, 167
Miller, Arthur H., 44, 88
Miller, Clem, 62
Miller, Warren E., 49, 141
Mondale, Walter F., 111
Monroney, Mike, 147
Moorhead, William S., 133
Morrow, William L., 61
Moss, Frank E., 71
Murphy, James T., 13
Muskie, Edmund S., 100

Neustadt, Richard E., 112, 114, 165
Nie, Norman H., 49
Nixon, Richard M., 95, 102, 110, 113, 115,
    119, 156
Norms (*see* Congress)
Norris, George W., 145

Obey, David R., 70, 99, 171
Office of Technology Assessment, 158
Ogul, Morris S., 23, 102
Oleszek, Walter J., 69, 144, 167
O'Neill, Thomas P., 8, 85, 104
Oppenheimer, Bruce I., 3, 12, 51, 57, 78, 79,
    93, 117, 119, 161, 164, 169
Ornstein, Norman J., 9, 57, 72, 110, 151, 170
Oversight of administration:
    adequacy, 24-25
    legislative veto, 109
    purposes, 24, 118-19, 138, 139, 140
    techniques, 24

Packwood, Robert, 125
Park, Tongsun, 130
Patronage, 114
Patterson, Samuel C., 98, 99, 143
Peabody, Robert L., 23, 57, 84, 85, 86, 116,
    140
Perkins, Lynette Palmer, 75, 140
Peters, John G., 7, 143, 144, 162
Petrocik, John R., 49

Political parties:
    campaigns, 36-41
    caucus, 8, 25, 64, 72, 78, 79, 81-82, 84,
        145, 150, 151, 152, 157-58, 159
    and committee power, 82, 91
    and committee seniority, 76-77, 81
    conservative coalition, 11, 77, 93-95, 118,
        146
    Democratic Study Group, 87-88, 151
    divided government, 50, 114
    and elections, 48-50, 60
    floor leaders, 2-3, 5, 8, 9, 16, 83, 86, 87,
        109, 115, 116, 141, 158, 159, 162, 167
    and gerrymandering, 32-34
    informal party groups, 87-89
    nominations, 46-47, 114
    party voting, 89-95
    policy committees, 7, 8, 81, 84, 147, 152
    and public policy, 89-95
    regional strength, 57-58
    southern Democrats, 76-77, 92-95, 146,
        151
    southern Republicans, 53-54
    speaker, 8, 68, 81, 83, 84-86, 126, 144,
        145, 152
    and state delegations, 88-89
    weakness, 2-3, 5, 6, 11, 80, 89, 104, 105,
        106, 114-16, 158-59, 165, 167, 170
    whips, 86-87
Polsby, Nelson W., 2, 18, 62, 116, 117, 140,
    164
Powell, Adam, 126
President:
    agenda-setting, 15, 102, 104, 116
    budget-making, 109, 119, 156-57
    and bi-party coalitions, 104
    constitutional position, 101-3, 107-8
    executive-legislative conflict, 103-7
    and impoundment, 119, 156
    information superiority, 110-11
    media advantages, 111-12
    messages, 102, 112
    party leader, 105-6, 113-16
    pocket veto, 102
    political advantages, 108-18, 165, 166
    public expectations, 108-10, 112
    special sessions, 102
    staff, 110
    trading, 113
    veto, 102-3, 168
Pritchard, Joel, 13
Proxmire, William, 44

Ranney, Austin, 149
Rayburn, Sam, 8, 84, 85
Representation:
    apportionment, 31-33

gerrymandering, 32-34, 53
representative-constituency relationships,
    4, 6, 11-14, 15, 17, 18, 20-23, 24, 25-29,
    30-31, 34-35, 36-39, 44-46, 51-53, 80,
    92-93, 97, 98, 100, 105, 112-13, 127,
    131-33, 136-42, 153, 162-163, 164,
    166, 167, 168, 169-70
and responsible government, 20, 22, 24
role, orientations toward, 22-23
Revolution of 1910-11, 81, 84, 144, 145, 146
Rieselbach, Leroy N., 149
Ripley, Randall, 2, 3, 87, 118
Robinson, James A., 106
Robinson, Michael J., 112
Rockman, Bert A., 24
Rohde, David W., 9, 57, 72, 110
Roosevelt, Franklin D., 103, 110, 113, 146
Rose, Charles, 139
Rutkus, Denis S., 112

Schattschneider, E. E., 18
Schick, Allen, 20, 96, 117, 118
Schneier, Edward V., 90
Scully, Michael Andrew, 98
Senate:
    appointments, 15, 167
    committee reorganization, 71
    contrast with House, 15-18
    debate, 16-17, 18, 146, 155
    direct election, 146
    elections, 51-52, 54-55
    independence of members, 2-3, 116
    norms, 14-15
    occupations of members, 56-57
    party voting, 92-94
    treaties, 15
Seniority (*see* Committees)
Shrum, Robert, 59
Smith, Howard W., 145

Speaker of the House, 8, 68, 81, 83, 84-86,
    126, 144, 145, 152
Spencer, Robert C., 37, 38
Staffs (*see* Committees, Congress)
Steiger, William, 111
Stevens, Arthur G., 88
Stevenson, Adlai E. III, 151
Stewart, John G., 83, 115
Stokes, Donald E., 140
Sundquist, James L., 12, 117, 122, 161

Tacheron, Donald G., 62
Thompson, Frank, 132
Thurber, James A., 119
Tidmarch, Charles M., 50
Traugott, Santa A., 90
Truman, David B., 3, 9
Truman, Harry S., 102, 146
Tufte, Edward R., 40, 53, 55, 91
Turner, Julius, 90

Udall, Morris K., 10, 23, 62
Ujifusa, Grant, 31
U.S. v. Harriss et al., 135

Verba, Sidney, 49

War Powers Act, 104, 119, 156
Waxman, Henry A., 132
Welch, Susan, 7, 143, 144, 162
Wesberry v. Sanders, 32
Westefield, Louis P., 70
Whalen, Charles W., 171
Wiggins, Charles E., 161
Wilson, Woodrow, 25, 107, 164
Wissel, Peter, 9
Witmer, T. Richard, 10
Wright, Jim, 82, 86

Zeigler, L. Harmon, 38, 41

DATE DUE
